The Servants

of Power

The
Servants
of Power

A HISTORY OF THE USE OF SOCIAL SCIENCE

IN AMERICAN INDUSTRY

by Loren Baritz

Wesleyan University Press

MIDDLETOWN, CONNECTICUT

To the memory of my father

JOSEPH H. BARITZ

Contents

Preface

INTELLECTUALS in the United States have long bemoaned the assumed fact that they are unloved and unappreciated by their society. Those men who live the life of the mind and who are critical of life in America have usually been able to cope with social alienation; many of them have understood that social hostility is merely payment in kind for their services. But another group of intellectuals has not enjoyed quite as clear a definition of their place in society or its attitude toward them. These are the men who have accepted at least what they believe to be the main contours of American society, the essential direction of that civilization. These more acceptable intellectuals still worry that other Americans do not distinguish between intellectuals—that is, between those who approve and those who do not. The "approving" intellectuals, with whatever justice, feel that American society simply mistakes the "critical" few for the whole intellectual body, and indiscriminately scorns all intellectuals. Some approvers are thus put in the position of being forced to criticize a society they do not want to attack—to criticize it for failing to see that at least one group of intellectuals does not deserve the hostility earned by the salmon, those who swim against the current.

Frequently an intellectual has been described as one whose most essential job depends on resistance to his society. Thus, the argument goes, any intellectual who accepts and approves of his society prostitutes his skills and is a traitor to his heritage. One question this work attempts to answer is whether or not such a conception is right: whether, by definition, a man of ideas must maintain the posture of the critic, and whether that intellectual who sincerely believes in and approves of the larger movements of his society can reconcile the demands of his mind and those of his society. Is even the suggestion of a potential antagonism between mind and society justifiable?

In order to understand the relationship of the intellectual to American society, it was necessary to make certain terms more precise. "American society" was the least difficult to refine. Because of the dominance of business in the United States during at least the twentieth century, and because the bulk of the approving intellectuals have believed that businessmen, because of their power, were most responsible for the confusion about the differences between intellectuals, it was decided to look at the relationship between intellectuals and business. But "business" is also a sloppy term; and, though it is not entirely satisfactory, "industry" was put in its place.

"Intellectual," because of its wonderful vagueness, proved to be another unworkable concept. Clearly the "intellectual" cannot be defined in terms of his occupation. It is the quality of mind that counts, and this is an individual possession. Some writers, for instance, may be classified as intellectuals, some may not; so also some professors, some journalists, some lawyers, some theologians, and not others. Despite this, it was necessary for research purposes to close one eye and assume that social scientists were intellectuals. Since social scientists are professionally concerned with many problems similar to those of the managers of industry, and since these managers, over the past half-century, have made increasing use of the services of social scientists, it was finally decided that an investigation of the social role of the intellectual and of the social use of specialized knowledge would be made most concrete by focusing on the industrial use of social scientists and their sciences. It is hoped that the precision gained from this reduction of terms and concepts will compensate for the obvious loss of sweep.

"Social science" as used here also requires some definition. This study deals with the industrial use of those disciplines which are primarily and directly concerned with human thought and conduct in the widest sense and which do not emphasize particular aspects of human experience. Thus by "social science" is meant only psychology, sociology, occasionally anthropology, and the new field of human relations. Other social sciences, for example economics and political science, become relevant at a very few points and are dealt with when necessary.

Professor Merle E. Curti of the University of Wisconsin supervised the early stages of research and pointed out the need for studying the social use of knowledge. Professors Michael Cherniavsky of Wesleyan University, Richard S. Kirkendall of the University of Missouri, and George P. Rawick of the University of Chicago criticized and improved the entire manuscript. My wife, Phyllis Baritz, was so outraged by many of my blunders and opaque expressions that she decided to help; her research and editorial skills were fully exploited, thereby demonstrating the major thesis of this work. Each of these people would be horrified at the thought of being held responsible for what I have said or have failed to say, and this responsibility is mine.

My thanks go to Mrs. Sidney S. Wasserman and Mrs. James Pratt for typing various drafts of the manuscript, and to the Procter and Gamble Company and the Western Electric Company for making the time of several of their executives available to me. The library staffs of the Harvard Graduate School of Business Administration, the Industrial Relations Library of the Massachusetts Institute of

Technology, and the University of Wisconsin all helped with the problems of hunting fugitive materials. A grant from the Social Science Research Council provided the funds for conducting this research, and the Faculty Committee on Research of Wesleyan University granted funds for preparing the manuscript.

Middletown, Connecticut
June, 1960

IT IS NOT *a question of what ought to be done, but of what is the course laid out by business principles; the discretion rests with the business men, not with the moralists, and the business men's discretion is bounded by the exigencies of business enterprise. Even the business men cannot allow themselves to play fast and loose with business principles in respon?e to a call from humanitarian motives. The question, therefore, remains, on the whole, a question of what the bus?ness men may be expected to do for cultural growth on the motive of profits.*

—THORSTEIN VEBLEN,
The Theory of Business Enterp?ise (1904)

CHAPTER 1

The Need
for Knowledge

INCREASINGLY, the men who manage and direct industry find themselves incapable of effectively controlling their organizations. Progressively, twentieth-century industry has become intertwined with every facet of the wider society, and this growing interrelatedness has confused the position of the modern manager. Of course industrialists have always had to seek for answers to new questions. But the twentieth-century manager, although he shares with his predecessors a concern with engineering and manufacturing, recognizes that he also has a different set of problems. He realizes that patterns of human thought and conduct control the effectiveness of his firm, and this knowledge requires unprecedented changes in both personal and institutional behavior.

Earlier businessmen had similar problems—of which they were, however, largely ignorant. In the nineteenth century they were mainly occupied, in America, with building the basic industry of the nation and with grappling for financial control; the stubborn idiosyncrasies of the human machine were either unrecognized or ignored.

The typical attitude of the nineteenth-century manager can be summed up by an example—flagrant, to be sure, but illustrative. The most Christian men to whom God gave fortunes, President George F. Baer of the Reading Railroad stated in 1902, knew best what was good for workers.

This assertion of the divine right of property presumably meant that God intended the poor working stiff to heed the voice of wealth, and that all laborers were identical in their need of the counsel of God's elect: the good, wise, and loyal—that is, the rich. With this ideology, several managements elaborated an ostensibly shockproof system of paternalism designed to regulate the actions of all the workers in their vineyards. With such an obstruction to thought to overcome, a formal understanding of workers as men was but slowly appreciated as a genuine need.

Conditions outside the factory, beyond the shadow of the test tube and the accountant's desk, helped to contribute to the growing confusion about the role of the modern manager. Occupations shifted in response to the changing nature of the American economy. The growth of organized labor, the disappearance of insecure immigrants, and the increasingly active role of the government in the economy all created problems with which the manager was somewhat unprepared to deal.

Thus, in the twentieth century's machine civilization, it became more essential than ever for managers to assess the nature of their positions in relation to the changing tang and character of American society. Since the heyday of the *fin de siècle* financiers, industry and society have become so interdependent, so interrelated, that the elaborate structure defies easy understanding. But an understanding of the new role of the manager in relation to both his factory and his society has become the *sine qua non* of managerial effectiveness.

The sobering realization that social knowledge was as essential as technical skill for the purposes of twentieth-century industry penetrated slowly but deeply into the minds of thoughtful managers. Some admitted that knowledge of man and of human relations, even in business terms, was of importance. However, the question of how to cope with employees as men remained unanswered by the usual kind of executive decisions. As this condition showed signs of becoming expensive and therefore intolerable, many managers concluded that the increasing complexity of modern life was forcing upon them new responsibilities, new demands. These they slowly assumed, among other reasons, out of a desire to maintain their competitive positions.

Among the developments that forced the manager to think in terms larger than those to which he had been accustomed was bureaucratization. As the brute size of the individual company grew, it became apparent that some kind of organizational change was required. The imposition of a rational design upon the unplanned industrial organization of the late nineteenth century resulted in stunning stresses upon the position of the manager, whether he owned the business or not. The captain of industry needed help.

As the industrial organization was wedged into a carefully designed plan, as managers began to think about lines of authority and communication as well as the problems of meeting a payroll and cutting costs, the bureaucratic pattern emerged. Levels of authority were carefully defined; job roles and positions were analyzed and assigned their predetermined places in the pyramid; relations among and between managers and workers were institutionalized as far as the nature of man would allow. Individualism obviously could not be planned or predicted or controlled and was, for the bureaucratic mentality, outlawed. Alfred Krupp, the German steel manufacturer, early gave this position its classic formulation: "What I shall attempt to bring about [in the Krupp Works] is, that nothing shall be dependent on the life or existence of any particular person; that nothing of importance shall happen or be caused to happen without the foreknowledge and approval of the management; that the past and the determinable future of the establishment can be learned in the files of

the management without asking a question of any mortal."[1]
The goal was to create an organization so perfect that, in
the language of classic liberalism, it would be run by law,
not by men.

No longer did one individual control the organization
by himself. In the bureaucratic plan, a collective will
and brain were created and imposed upon a growing number of industrial organizations, as well as upon most modern large-scale operations, including government and the
military. Individual will and caprice now usually gave
way to committees, conferences, group leadership, and
teamwork. The manager, therefore, lost the power to
control through the exercise of his personal will. He could
no longer sit in the dignity of his oak-paneled office and
send orders down the line, confident of obedience; now,
more often than not, he had to go through channels, elicit
cooperation, and know how to "get along."

The many specialists trained to aid the industrial bu-
reaucrat in handling problems of human relations could
complicate the manager's job. Centrifugal tendencies
sometimes developed as more and more specialists were
absorbed into the firm. To reverse this process and keep
the organization moving toward its predefined goals increasingly required the industrial manager to view the
organization as a whole and to concern himself less and
less with details that could be delegated down the hierarchy. But this need for the overview only occasionally
was met through the use of specialists; indeed, such use
often raised new and unsuspected problems. For example,
in 1949, the president of International Harvester stated that
the single most important job of the operating president
was to understand enough of the work and skills of his
specialists so that he could assign the right expert to a
problem when it arose.[2] To "understand enough" had
become the pressing need of the modern manager in his

efforts to pull together the complex pieces of his firm and guide them to approved goals.

While bureaucratization made it possible for industry to function with greater precision and predictability, it confused the power structure, not only within industry but between industry and other bureaucratized institutions of the whole society. As the layers of different status and function were rationalized in the industrial organization, the need for experts was intensified. And, on top of the whole, the finite executive sat in growing bewilderment, wondering just how he was to keep his fingers on the right places at the right moments.

From the human point of view there have been few changes more basic than the growth in the sheer size of industry.[3] The number of employees responsible to single managements today has become immense. How to control such masses has been one of the most nettlesome questions that managers have had to confront. The implications of such a question have been crucial to managerial authority.

Another development that helps to confuse the position of the men who manage American industry has been the much discussed separation of financial ownership from management. This problem extends farther back into time than does the simple recognition of its existence. But by Woodrow Wilson's presidency a few industrial managers saw the problem and understood its long-range significance. "I do not own my own plant," complained one executive during the First World War. "I am only the poor devil that has to run it. . . . What I own is a drop in the bucket. I cannot do the things that I want to do as I might jeopardize interests far greater than my own, and that is the position that the manager is in today."[4] Because of the uncertainties of his relations with the owners of the productive means, the manager again lost a part of the earlier delimitation of his job. It is true that managers have come to wield increasingly significant power in American society, but their status and functions have undergone such basic changes and their role has become so fluid that the understanding of their organizational activities needs fundamental reinterpretation.

One exciting analysis of the separation of ownership from management was offered by James Burnham, whose argument, however, was made of crumbly stuff that does not long withstand criticism. He argued that this separation constituted a revolution in the power relationships of American society: as ownership and management became distinct, the managers of industry assumed more and more power. Capitalists, as a class, have lost to the managers *de facto* power over the instruments of production. This phenomenon would extend throughout society, the thesis went, and force vital reorganizations of most of our basic institutions. Capitalism would cease to be.[5]

The separation of ownership from management has certainly made the position of managers more difficult, though the thesis that Burnham presented is exaggerated. Is this separation really a revolution in the sense that power has been transferred from one class to another? A different argument suggests that because managers are now salaried employees, they are not impelled by the profit motive of their predecessors; and, because it is no longer possible to identify capital, a class struggle between labor and capital becomes inconceivable. But this thesis is concluded with the almost incidental remark that the assumptions of most managers should be remembered.[6] Indeed, these assumptions are important, for it is on this point that the revolutionary aspects of the separation of ownership from management are shown to be misleading. It has been proved that the manager thinks of the corporation, whether he owns it or not, as *his* corporation. So complete is the identification of the manager with the interests of the owner that the profit motive operates as always.[7] Because of their own loyalties, the managers, including propertyless managers, cannot be distinguished from the earlier owner-managers.

However, the fact that the manager must recognize and accommodate to the stake that others have in his activities forces on him at least part of the new and unsettled character of his position. This, coupled with the bureaucratization and specialization of industry, has made the manager desperate in his need of assistance, not to build his product but to manage the organization of his firm.

Over a certain range of his problems the industrial executive has established a measure of firm control. The business applications of the scientific discoveries that have been so abundant in the last fifty years have been relatively easy for the industrialist to cope with. As products have been developed, refined, or manufactured, the men of industry have called in technical specialists who could offer quick and tangible assistance. In 1955, for example, industry spent four billion dollars on physical research; the same amount was planned for 1956; about 175,000 men and women, of whom more than 105,000 were engineers, helped managers develop new products and processes.[8] Now there is a critical shortage of these technically trained people, and industry wants and will take as many as it can get in the foreseeable future. But what is the competence of scientists and engineers to deal with problems of human relations? As managers realized that these technical experts were not competent to deal with human problems, the decision was forced: management had to look elsewhere.

Because the victory of the North in the Civil War provided an atmosphere congenial to the growth of an industrial economy, the kinds of jobs once familiar to Americans began to grow more scarce than newer forms of work. The more developed this economy became, the greater was the

emphasis on planning and administration rather than on
production. These newer jobs concerned the manipulation of people and symbols as opposed to material objects,
and managers were increasingly faced with problems about
people instead of things. The techniques of mass production have made less necessary certain skills that were
essential to the preindustrial artisan, but at the same time
they have demanded new skills. The basic idea that Henry
Ford implemented in his factory was not simply the
mechanical organization of the conveyor belt system, but
a conception of a predefined social organization in relation
to such technological innovation. Thus the new skills
required of the manager in charge of mass production are
not only technical in nature, but social too.

The very efficiency and dispatch with which industry
has resolved its technical difficulties have raised a host of
human and social problems. For instance, the deluge of
inventions has probably created difficulties in every sphere
of human activity. The fact that the number of patents
has increased markedly in virtually every decade since the
Civil War should not be, by itself, an occasion for rejoicing
or national self-congratulation. One of Herbert Hoover's
research committees reported that the application of inventions and scientific discoveries to social needs would lead
to moral, educational, and legal problems; unemployment
and leisure would certainly become more troublesome
because of applied science. The committee members
warned that many more unforeseen problems would arise
if the trend continued, as they were convinced it would,[9]
and as it has. Such problems are of direct concern to the
managers of American industry, even if they have not the
knowledge or experience demanded for the solutions.

The pressures contributing to the confusion about the
position of American managers have not come only from
the internal developments of industry. Other social forces
which impinge upon the thinking and function of manage-

ment have emerged. Not the least of these is the growth of organized labor.

In the United States, the ranks of organized labor did not exceed 3,000,000 until the drastic manpower shortage of the First World War. Quickly thereafter union membership almost doubled, but it declined in every single year of the 1920's until, by 1932, unions could claim no more than their prewar numbers. The emergence of the depression-born CIO, and the tight labor market that appeared when war again broke out in 1939, made it possible for labor organizers to report a post-World War II membership of about 15,000,000.

Labor did not grow in a social vacuum. From the myopic security of the 1920's, through the rather clear-sighted panic of depression, to the patriotic daze of over-work and mission during war, Americans witnessed a society changing at an incredibly fast rate. Responding to such flux, the American worker grew into a social type different in kind from his nineteenth-century predecessor. The changes in his psychology have forced repercussions throughout the length and breadth of the industrial world.

A union card has supposedly come to signify more to the worker than merely combination with others for economic power. Membership in a legitimate union has presumably been a vehicle by which workers can get a toehold on the ladder of social as well as economic mobility. One labor leader argued that the rise of organized labor resulted in a psychological change in the worker who belonged. Developing from a "helpless and unoriented" person, the individual worker had gained from union membership "certainty as to his rights and confidence in his ability to fulfill them."[10] A pair of anthropologists, with less of an axe to grind, agreed that unions have accomplished much more than forcing managements to make economic concessions, important as this function has been. In organization, they suggested, workers have sought and found security and status and have made management "recognize their worth as men."[11]

The availability of labor has always been a determining factor in industrial relations. During periods when there have been more workers than jobs, management has controlled the situation: personnel and industrial relations programs have tended to respond accordingly, including only those policies which employers were disposed to include. Not until labor sold its effort in a seller's market could it occasionally back its rhetoric with adequate force.

The immense immigration into the United States in the decades after the Civil War provided a full and cheap labor supply, and thereby hindered organization. The change in the source of immigration, from the industrialized north and west of Europe to the agrarian south and east, meant that the newer immigrants faced a more trying personal adjustment in the industrial cities of the New World, where their labor was most needed. At the beginning of the twentieth century, when labor was relatively abundant, management, just then emerging as a distinct function, gave little thought to industrial relations. The generally adopted labor policy was the maintenance of the open shop, toward which management bent vigorous efforts. Determined to counteract the trifling gains that labor had won during the first decade of the twentieth century, employers, led by the National Association of Manufacturers, waged a generally successful war on the closed shop. With the formation of many powerful local employers' associations and of the Anti-Boycott Association, labor was faced with a dismal prospect. Employers' associations broke strikes repeatedly and successfully prevented progressive labor legislation in most states. A labor policy somewhat more inclusive than simple anti-unionism would not emerge until management recognized the ultimate futility of such negativism, until labor itself grew out of its early frailty and sense of institutional insecurity.

The First World War put a halt to immigration, and restrictive legislation in the 1920's kept it at a trickle. From 1915 to 1918, about 5,000,000 men were taken from industry and put into the armed forces. With this reduction in the work force, the labor market became tight, and organized labor made progress. Second-generation immigrants who were starting to look for industrial jobs were more acclimatized to life in America than their parents had been, and they demanded different industrial treatment. The dictatorial foreman with whom their parents had had to contend lost ground to a whole new system of personnel techniques and devices.

On a different level, a gradual shift in the ideology of the worker has made itself felt in management counsels. Though it is exceedingly difficult to generalize about "the American worker," a few widely apparent tendencies may be indicated. Democratic ideals have been propounded so long in this country that their acceptance has probably become wider and deeper than once was the case. The democratized family of the last fifty years has also probably had an influence, perhaps tending to increase resistance to management policies that frustrate aspirations toward self-expression and self-determination. Though the reasons are not clear, it has become ever more difficult for the American worker to think of himself as no more than a simple cog in a complex machine.[12] Several important managements have taken serious note of this; American Telephone & Telegraph, for example, has told its management candidates that employees no longer passively accept management decrees, but want to understand the thinking that goes into decisions. Because of wide social changes, workers insist on satisfying whole clusters of psychological needs.[13]

As the psychology of at least some American workers shifted along these lines, their objective economic position also improved: real wages have gone up in the course of the twentieth century. With a higher standard of living, with extensive mobility, much (though not all) of the compulsion that formerly characterized the lives of many workers has disappeared, and management is itself now under a compulsion to respond accordingly. The industrialist who wants either to hire the worker or to sell him a product is forced to the conclusion that at least some and perhaps most workers do not have to respond if they do not want to.

Though legislation and judicial interpretations for most of the first half of the twentieth century consistently ignored or resisted the growing power of organized labor, a significant shift did finally occur. The change in temper from the hostile interpretations of the Sherman Act to the permissiveness of the Wagner Act provided the legal framework within which the position of the individual laborer could develop. The early opposition of management to the Wagner Act indicated a lack of perception; for, by and large, Gompersism has always been relatively acceptable to management. The struggle against the Wagner Act was a struggle against a myth, against an image of militant labor that had barely existed in the United States and was clearly not again to appear in the foreseeable future.

As his position became more confused through increasing bureaucratization, specialization, and separation of ownership from management, the manager was faced with the emergence of organized unions, maturation of the aspirations of individual workers, and legislation which at last came to grips with the fact of the existence and, finally, power of unions. A creeping consciousness of the implications of these developments compelled some thoughtful managements to include the human machine in their calculations. Thus the managers of American industry, through the pressure of conditions within industry and the wider society, have been forced to direct their attention to problems of industrial relations and personnel.

Modern industrial managers have had the need to utilize the findings of subjects as esoteric as psychology, sociology, and anthropology. In short, the twentieth-century industrialist has realized, to a greater extent than did his predecessors, that he must understand the living world contained by his factory. The day is gone when businessmen could believe that their power of personality and knowledge of technique and finance would prove adequate weapons in their competitive struggle. As managers realized that men, even more than nuts and bolts, played a determining role in the financial condition of their firms, the search for an understanding of men began.

During World War I the idea began to percolate that the behavior of men influenced the productive process and therefore profits. Managers came to see that many of their problems remained even after their best talent had worked over product design and plant layout. Excellence in engineering, sales, and production techniques did not automatically insure either a smooth-working or even a profit-making organization. Regardless of the skill that went into the solution of technical difficulties, the "labor problem" might remain and cloud the exciting vision of a continuously improved financial report. Thus it became vital to begin managing men and women as well as machine and process. With a greater grasp of the practical importance of their employees' behavior, managers in succeeding decades widened their scope until they became concerned with the social background and the personality of the worker. At last no problem of human behavior failed to arouse the interest of sophisticated industrialists.

There were several reasons for this growing concern with human behavior. Analysts like Peter Drucker could point out that the essential nature of the modern corporation was social, that an understanding of it must be in human terms.[14] But executives largely did not act upon such analyses because, though they might agree with

Drucker, his conclusions did not show an imperative need
for action. Until management became convinced of a
pressing and internal demand, it would not act. Managers,
pressed by the need to run their enterprises efficiently
and profitably, simply had to see what was in it for them.
The idea that more attention should be paid to the psychology of employees began to be accepted by American management when it was shown that such attention would pay.

Ever since the First World War, a growing number of
executives have admitted the importance of understanding
their employees. Some went so far as to say that this was
their most important problem. In time, many industries
spent large sums on complicated research into the problems
of human relations in industry. But despite various state-
ments of noble and generous sentiments, despite sundry
professions of unselfish beneficence, virtually all industrial
spokesmen, sooner or later, tacked on the idea that, inci-
dentally, such concern with human behavior was good
business. In simple terms, managers said that an understanding of employee behavior would permit management
to strengthen its control, thereby increasing profits. Henry
Ford II, for one, put this notion in concrete terms when he
said that the technological progress of his company was
assured; but Ford felt that his company could greatly
improve its relative position in the automobile industry if,
somehow, the Ford employees could be induced to be more
cooperative—that is, to raise their production.[15] Though
reformers convinced themselves that industry, in its concern with people, was finally humanizing itself, the reasons
for and results of this concern were quite different. Companies began social science research not a minute before
they were convinced that this was an effective and relatively inexpensive way to raise production and increase
profits.

Another thread running through managerial thinking
since the depression experience also had important impli-

cations: the more thoroughly management understood its workers, the less chance would there be to make those drastic errors which had nurtured unionism. If the social scientists were right, an understanding of human behavior would show how to control men.

The managerial conviction that people count gave rise to problems with which managers needed help. There were experts in the universities who specialized in an understanding of human behavior. Psychologists, and later sociologists and anthropologists, presumably knew what they were doing. If management could make use of the knowledge and techniques of these specialists, a new world of management control would open.

That many managements came to believe in the importance of understanding their workers proved, however, to be an insufficient basis for accepting the services of social scientists. In the United States men of affairs and men of reflection have usually distrusted each other. Some managers convinced themselves that most professors were radical and wanted to subvert the economic system and the thinking of their employees. Others openly expressed fear of the probings of the social scientist, hesitating to authorize studies which might highlight their own shortcomings.[16]

The nature of the social sciences further compounded the skepticism of managers. Unlike the exact sciences, social science often could not prove its results. Continual bickering between "schools" of social science conveyed the impression that the experts themselves could not agree on what they were doing. Furthermore, and most important of all, social scientists always operate within an ethical system (the validity or even applicability of which is debatable) which influences and may determine their results. And because much of the subject matter of the social sciences is verbal, the results seem intangible. The unintelligible jargon characteristic of social science also con-

fused managers (along with most other uninitiates) and led
them to believe that the work of social scientists would be
as opaque as their language. To managers interested in
earthly results for salaries paid, the efforts of social scientists often seemed simply irrelevant. Sometimes the concerns of the social scientist and the manager ostensibly had
little or nothing in common. "It's too big a jump . . . ,"
admitted one social scientist, "from findings having to do
with the rat cage or the Hottentot society or the 'free competitive market' to the factories and union halls or the
picket line."[17] Executives concerned with meeting a payroll, with getting a fair day's work for a fair day's wage,
looked askance at social scientists concerned with the effect
of toilet training on the mature personality. The social
scientists frequently appeared unwilling or unable to
disabuse management of its mythology.

But the single most important obstacle in the way of
an easy interchange between managers and social scientists came from the managers themselves. The deep
conviction that success proves worth and ability—the sur-
vival of the fittest—led many managers to believe that they
were themselves most competent to deal with any problems
of their organizations. The ability of the manager was
demonstrated by the fact that he was a manager. With the
acceptance of this cherished but blinding myth that had
served Andrew Carnegie so well, twentieth-century managers had to struggle with their souls and self-images
before they could admit an inadequacy sufficiently great
to justify a plea for help. Such an admission was neither
easily nor, in the early years of the twentieth century,
frequently made.

The only qualification required for controlling the
human variable, according to this stripe of the managerial
mentality, was *just plain horse sense.* This ingredient,
mixed lightly with equal sprinkles of "common sense" and
"experience," sufficiently equipped the managers, accord-

ing to managers, to cope with their problems. Hence there was no need to pay the fees of "super-psychologists" or "mental alchemists," for the good reason that managers themselves were masters of the field.[18]

Against this managerial self-confidence the experts have struggled. Time and again social scientists have admonished managers—those who would listen—that problems of human behavior would fester without the tender ministration of experts. The experience and intuition which the manager could claim were but clumsy sledges, tools unsuited for the control or repair of the delicate and fragile stuff out of which the human mind is made.[19]

With time, a splinter of American management finally became persuaded of the special expertness of social scientists; but even this group raised a dampening caveat: social scientists might be first-rate scientists but their ignorance of industry was quite appalling. Industrial problems were said to be unique; thus, when confronted with the heat and grease of the modern factory, social science experts became stumbling amateurs, outsiders who were worse than useless.[20] Occasionally an effort was made to show that because social scientists were outsiders they could see the larger meanings and relationships, which managers, seduced by detail, too frequently ignored.[21] This reasoning hardly convinced the social scientists themselves. The justice of the managers' claims was admitted when a psychologist warned his colleagues to shun industrial problems unless they were willing to put on overalls and meet the manager on his home ground.[22] Once there, the social scientist would have to tread lightly, for "shrewd business men" did in fact know a good deal about human behavior. The social scientist would have to learn as well as teach, and he had so much to learn.[23] Most professors, however, refused to learn, preferring the chalk-marked sports jacket to overalls, the security of the classroom to the strangeness of the factory. Hence, toward the end of this fifty-year colloquy about the industrial innocence of social scientists, some managers had still to be persuaded. Have the scholars who write about industrial workers "talked, really talked, to any lately?" asked the president of Westinghouse Electric in 1951.[24]

Have social scientists put aside their rat cages and artifacts of primitive cultures long enough to "really talk" to living men in the noisy world of mass production? What did management want of such esoteric intellectuals? What, indeed, have social scientists done to the pressurized processes of the modern factory? And what did the exposure to and absorption into the American industrial plant do to the malleable social scientists themselves?

CHAPTER 2

The Birth of
Industrial Psychology

THE ERA OF progressivism in American life was dedicated to the proposition that politics was the key to a golden future. Often the diagnosis of the nation's malaise concluded that large-scale business was somehow subverting or corrupting the promise of American life. The power of the trusts, according to the muckrakers, was changing American individualism and independence to collective subservience, public responsibility to irresponsibility, and worse. Lincoln Steffens and others talked of treason as they suggested that the growth of the economy was changing the political process, and that politics was the method by which to limit the power of the economic leviathan.

Politics too was changing, and those who had most faith in it did most to help it change. The growing intricacy of public problems convinced some—LaFollette is a good example—that classic oratory and public appeal were inadequate skills and attributes in the contemporary political scene. Experts, this group said, were needed to help the politician find the answers to increasingly difficult public problems. With the spread of the "Wisconsin Idea," including McCarthy's legislative reference library, and the growing acceptance of governmental commissions with their use of trained personnel, the public was exposed to the notion that the men from Academia might have something to contribute. And the public made a sometime college professor President of the United States.

The progressivist furor occurred when the nation, for the most part, was relatively well off. The standard of living and real wages were beginning to climb, and, though the bankers might create "artificial" depressions, America was on the road to world power, had won an empire from Spain, had recovered from the depression of the 1890's, and seemed intent on solidifying hard-won economic gains.

But there were a few blemishes on the otherwise satisfactory scene. American labor was becoming increasingly angry. De Leon and Debs were ruining the digestion of that fraction of the nation that had been gay during the nineties. Since the efforts of union organizers and even Socialists seemed to be resulting in slight but potentially damaging success, the "progressive" manager needed some kind of protection. In this climate of labor problems and growing faith in experts, managers clutched at virtually anything that promised even a small measure of defense. Included among the least promising of such schemes were psychology and its expert practitioners.

Before the last decades of the nineteenth century, psychology had been largely devoted to a search for universal and immutable laws of human behavior, for regularities in conduct and thought which would explain any individual's behavior under any specific set of circumstances. Most early psychologists had accepted the notion that the human mind was composed of a series of "faculties" including, for example, will, emotion, imagination, and reason. "Very interesting," the directors of industrial personnel work might say, "but what possible practical use can we make of all that? Managers are concerned with men as individuals and not Man in the abstract." The exceptional individual was, however, of little interest to the faculty psychologists. To them, the formulation of laws of human nature indiscriminately binding all men was the important task. Individual man was submerged in intricate and a priori systems of introspection and, during the seminal last half of the nineteenth century, in massive quantitative averages.

Only when Wilhelm Wundt, a German psychologist, opened his Leipzig laboratory in 1879, did the scientific method intrude itself into this resistant psychology. Before Wundt, most psychologists depended upon introspection to gain insight into the nature of man. By understanding themselves, they thought that they would come to an understanding of others, since, as they believed, God's image could not significantly vary. Though Wundt did not entirely abandon introspection, he began to explore a new dimension when he measured, with whatever precision his early contrivances allowed, the responses of his subjects to controlled stimuli. From statistical tables and quantitative averages he constructed a "psychological man," as the economists had earlier conceived of their "economic man."

At the very moment that Wundt was adding up his long columns, a fresh and imaginative breath was exposing the aridity of all static views of the world. Darwin's *The Origin of Species*, published twenty years earlier, had given the death blow to the old idea of the immutability of creation. What this meant for psychology was not seen until a cousin of Darwin's, Sir Francis Galton, grasped the psychological implications of evolution. In 1879, the same year that Wundt opened his workshop, Galton brought out an appeal for a study of individual differences. Four years later he published the first serious attempt to arrive at a psychology of the individual.

The importance of Wundt's method and the ramifications of Galton's conclusions indelibly impressed a young mind that both men had trained. James McKeen Cattell took his doctorate at Leipzig where he had assisted Wundt. Later, working with Galton, he became convinced of the importance of the Darwinian approach, which asked, for instance, why some minds adapted to their environment and others did not. Moving to the University of Pennsylvania, where he was America's first professor of psychology, Cattell began to investigate the differences among men. Using Wundt's measuring techniques, he looked not for the similarities between person and person but for the extent of difference. To Wundt, who described Cattell's work as *"Ganz Amerikanisch,"* this was simple heresy. But in 1896 Cattell published his study of the abilities and capacities of students at Columbia University, where he was now teaching, and the psychological individual was finally recognized.

If Galton and Cattell were right, if the differences among men were actually significant, to isolate the source of such difference was of instant importance. The debate about the origin of human variability became fierce. Whether individual differences were inherent or acquired was a pregnant question even for industrial managers. If differences were acquired, managers could influence their workers' conduct through training programs. If nurture was less important than nature, training might be wasted. In such a case, managers would be wise to discover means of screening the work force in order to avoid hiring workers who were inherently unsuited to the work required. Thus the study of individual differences helped make psychology meaningful to managers. And psychological testing, the technique that psychologists employed to discover the extent and nature of these differences, was eventually to become standard industrial equipment.

The discovery of the individual did not, however, disrupt all previous psychological theory. The search for universal mainsprings of human conduct continued, but with a new twist. For a number of decades, the academic view of man had followed the lead of Adam Smith. All men, insisted the classical economists, were motivated by conscious and rational decision. Against such a view, three powerful minds began to work. Marx, Darwin, and Freud all emphasized the nonrational character of man and society, and an onslaught of this magnitude could not be ignored. Taking their cue from Freud, psychologists and economists now began to use instincts as explanations of behavior and thought.[1]

A Harvard professor of psychology articulated the instinct theory in its most persuasive form in America. In 1908, William McDougall published *An Introduction to Social Psychology*, in which he argued that instincts were processes which led the individual to perceive certain objects in a certain way. This perception, in turn, would always elicit particular actions or at least an impulse to such actions.[2] In his hands, instincts became dynamic and formed the basis not only of individual conduct but of social life. For more than ten years McDougall's argument "swept everything before it." Almost every year, for the next twenty, his book was reprinted, and over 100,000 copies were eventually sold.[3]

Now, even if man were nonrational, psychologists could continue their thrilling hunt for the key that would unlock the mysteries of human behavior. The agreement about the controlling role of instincts seemed, for the moment, to be a large step in the right direction. The psychologist's job, at this juncture, was merely to relate specific behavior to the appropriate impelling instinct. Since instincts imprison all men to a greater or lesser degree, and since behavioral manifestations of any given instinct are closely limited, psychologists, after the threat of Galton and Cattell, again had a net sufficiently wide to contain all struggling mankind. Psychology seemed on the verge of breathtaking success.

Despite the immeasurable energy, thought, and time psychologists lavished on this attempt to cross the threshold into the wonderful world of certain knowledge, they did not succeed. For the sandy foundation of the whole instinct theory was the recognition of specific instincts, the search for which proved to be fatal. William James had said that there were twenty-eight instincts; McDougall listed first eleven and later fourteen; Ordway Tead discovered ten while Carleton Parker insisted on sixteen; others built lists ranging from Freud's two instincts up. The process was virtually endless and, as it proved, thankless. Slowly emerging from such confusion was a clear conviction of the inadequacy of the instinct theory. Throughout the 1920's one psychologist after another abandoned this approach until, by the end of that decade, social psychology was shorn of instincts and left without any theoretical base.

But before the instinct theory was dismissed as an oversimplified view of man, psychologists found themselves in possession of a salable piece of presumed knowledge. If human conduct was determined by a particular constellation of instincts, people could be induced to buy a given product if it was scientifically presented. If advertising copy appealed to the right instincts, the urge to buy would surely be excited.

Indeed, the very first application of professional psychology to the world of business and industry was in advertising. At the turn of the century, a few advertising agencies and the advertising trade press said that their fundamental business was influencing the mind. As early as 1895 *Printers' Ink*, one of the leading advertising trade journals, reported that when copy writers in particular and ad men in general became "a little more enlightened," they would study psychology.[4] Presumably, those whose business was the understanding of the human mind could give significant aid to those who wanted to influence it. Thus the advertising agencies welcomed the work of psychologists; the impetus for a psychology of advertising came, not from the psychologists, but from the advertisers.

Though he was not the first to study advertising, Walter Dill Scott, a psychologist at Northwestern University, did the earliest applicable work on a psychology of advertising. During 1902, two years after he had earned his doctorate at Leipzig, Scott published in serial form the articles that made up his first book on the subject, *Theory of Advertising*. *Printers' Ink* was glad to have Scott's ideas, though it insisted that he had said nothing new. "Advertisers," the journal maintained, "have reached all of the Professor's basic laws by the very serviceable kind of psychology called 'horse sense,' and his principles, while reduced to scientific fact, are all drawn from actual advertisements. . . . He is following the advertiser, not leading him." "Every one of the conclusions" at which Scott arrived had earlier been discussed in the pages of the trade press.[5]

In 1908 Scott published a second work, *The Psychology of Advertising*, in which he admitted that the initiative for a psychology of advertising had been taken by the advertisers. Indeed, the encouragement given by these businessmen stimulated several other professional psychologists to begin similar work. Among the mainsprings of conduct that Scott thought advertisers could profitably release were, for instance, the clothing, hoarding, hunting, and constructing instincts. The basic appeals were bodily and social gratification, acquisition, curiosity, and man's "higher nature." Since Scott feared that such a list might be too abstract for easy implementation, he offered a few more concrete tips; he warned ad men, for example, to avoid mentioning the fact that meat is animal flesh because the sensibilities of the reader would be deeply offended.[6] Though other psychologists soon began to experiment with advertising in a more scientific fashion,[7] the kind of impressionistic prescription upon which Scott relied persisted.

A significant aspect of the Academia in which these early psychologists lived was their need to conceal their interest in anything as unedifying as advertising. This type of vulgar concern simply did not do for either a gentleman or a scholar. Scott himself reported that if his

associates or the administration at Northwestern had discovered his interest in advertising, he would have lost
caste. Thus his early work was pursued in secret. Fellow
psychologists, including Wundt and E. B. Titchener, increased the measure of scorn heaped upon such "impure"
projects, "since," they reasoned, "any such activity could
only humiliate their associates and lower the dignity of
their chosen profession." (Later Titchener himself accepted a position as one of the directors of a business
formed to apply psychology.) One result of this early
disdain was that, when applied psychology later became
respectable, few of the researchers knew the work of their
predecessors.[8]

While psychologists were developing their merchan-
dise, individual differences and instincts, another group of
specialists was preparing the industrial groundwork for
them, leavening managerial hostility toward research with
equal parts of wonder and willingness. Scientific management, in a very real sense, softened enough of the severity
of the industrial atmosphere so that the more esoteric psychologists could take their first few faltering steps.

Scientific management had roots extending at least to
the early 1870's if not to Wedgwood's Etruria and Watt's
foundry in England of the late eighteenth century. But
not until Frederick Taylor began to publicize his notions
during the 1890's did any kind of enthusiastic movement
begin. Using the American Society of Mechanical Engineers as his sounding board, Taylor began to outline his
blueprint of increased industrial efficiency. Gathering
around him a small coterie of talented men, he persuaded
a few firms to implement his plans. Two Philadelphia
companies, Tabor and Link-Belt, became the outstanding
show places of Taylor's ideas in action. By 1907 Taylor
and his disciples, along with Harrington Emerson's "efficiency experts," counted among their clients well over a
dozen companies, including steel mills, railroads, found-

ries, bleacheries, and printers.[9] Many Americans became increasingly interested in the movement until the 1920's, when popular discussion declined.[10]

The substance of scientific management's argument was that the production process should be functionalized and standardized. The best (most efficient) way of performing a job was determined by subdividing it into the smallest possible units of time and motion, then recombining them into "methods of least waste." Labor skills, in other words, would be transferred to management for analysis, then handed back piecemeal to workers—with the result that they could no longer be masters of a craft. Instructing laborers in the scientific methods of performing their jobs was said by scientific managers to be the heart of their system. Such teaching would stress the "right methods of doing work" and the "right habits of doing the right methods." The worker would acquire judgment "without . . . being obliged himself to experience all the elements of the judgment." Though some of the leaders of scientific management were aware of the work psychologists were doing on individual differences, most still wrote of the "one best way" of performing a task. The engineering mind that believed that analysis and measurement would suggest a single best way was typical of the whole movement. The grand benefits of the system were purported to include increased production at lowered costs, higher wages, less waste, elimination of unskilled workers, a reduction in the cost of living, and the promotion of industrial peace.[11]

Before World War I, organized labor was unconvinced of the blessings that were supposed to flow from Taylor's touted package, though several unions were later temporarily to accept the system. Whatever the intrinsic merits of scientific management, labor feared that the system, in the hands of unscientific and committed industrial managers, would simply mean more work for the same or even less pay.[12] Labor, in short, was convinced that the scientific managers and efficiency experts ignored the human element; later, even a few of these experts admitted the justice of labor's fears.[13] Many psychologists, looking back over this prewar period, also criticized the scientific managers for this ostensible neglect of human behavior.[14] Here, apparently, was an area in which psychologists might profitably work, where there would be no competition from the usual engineering mentality of scientific management.

The engineers, of course, did have assumptions about human nature which influenced their work. And most of these assumptions were related to the thinking of the classical economists: man was rational and always sought to serve his self-interest. Thus the surest way to heighten man's motivation was to relate his effort to a financial reward, and pay on a piecework basis became one of the main props of the scientific-management movement. Several times, in 1895 and 1903, Taylor tried to show that financial incentives were only a partial answer to the problems of more efficient production, but his audiences were too wage-conscious. Though Taylor's complete system of management reorganization spread very slowly, many managements did accept the notion that men would work harder if their pay depended upon their output.[15] Taylor and a few of his followers went even further by saying that the human element was of major importance, and if psychologists could help in this area, their work would be welcomed.[16] Despite such efforts to broaden and humanize scientific management, the concrete industrial application of the system almost always meant the use of time-and-motion studies to devise wage-incentive systems. Indeed, by 1940 over 90 per cent of American industry had adopted the wage-incentive aspects of Taylor's blueprint of industrial utopia.[17]

Scientific management did not encroach upon the territory that the psychologists had carved out for themselves.

Even though the engineers occasionally talked about the necessity of understanding human behavior, even though some of them recognized individual differences and admitted that a mechanical approach to the human variable was foredoomed, the implementation of their ideas in America's well-regulated industrial plant did not include these few insights. However, scientific management had accustomed industrialists to the idea that a study of the production process would pay. Taylor and his followers had demonstrated to management that it could "expect a definite return from an investigation and analysis of human behavior." Because of this demonstration, a few bold managers allowed the early industrial psychologists to "conduct investigations designed to increase human effectiveness in industry."[18] For this the industrial psychologists would be eternally in debt to Taylor's movement.

Scientific management not only conditioned the industrial climate for the psychologists; it determined to a large degree the direction, scope, and nature of psychological research. The engineers raised most of the problems with which the later psychologists grappled. And, most important, scientific management gave to industrial psychology its purpose, its ethic. The financial condition of the firm was the ubiquitous criterion of the success of scientific managers, and to an improvement of this condition they gave their attention. Increased efficiency was the goal. The aim was to help industry achieve the ends it defined for itself in the most efficient way. A similar acceptance of the industrialist's ethic became characteristic of industrial psychology as it criticized scientific management for failing to make industry efficient enough.

In these prewar years, the idea that people mattered slowly began to filter into the industrial mentality. But this did not lead managers, as it had led advertisers, to look kindly upon supposedly eccentric social scientists. Sensing the steady toughening of their institutional muscle, most

managers made almost a religion of their own ability to
solve not merely all the problems of their businesses but all
problems of any kind; while the few exceptions to this lock
step made small difference in the total picture. Occasionally managers conferred in a formal way with psychologists; occasionally an article by some psychologist in a
trade journal aroused some interest among executives.[19]
But businessmen, witnessing the mighty result of their planning and vision, hardly could admit the need for advice on
problems that were only slowly coming to be recognized
as problems. Certainly human behavior was important,
but the captains of industry would take care of it.

An example of the managers' assurance of their own
competence to deal with workers as men was the profit-
sharing scheme developed by Ford before World War I.
John R. Lee, the executive in Ford's employ who was instrumental in developing the famous five-dollar day, said
that not until 1912 did the Ford company begin "to realize
something of the value of men." This realization was literally forced on the company as the labor market tightened
in response to the expansion of all of Detroit's industry.
The tremendous turnover that ensued was intolerable. In
1913 Ford required between 13,000 and 14,000 employees
to run his plants, but in that same year over 50,000 workers
had quit. "Some sort of plan that would hold the workers
was badly wanted." Hence the Ford company was reor-
ganized. Though foremen could still transfer employees,
they lost the right to fire and the right to invent wage-
incentive systems. The workday was reduced from ten to
nine hours as time studies were made, pay rates reclassi-
fied, and an automatic promotion plan adopted. The company realized a number of benefits from these changes and
was encouraged to proceed "to a further consideration of
the human element."

In January, 1914, Ford startled the industrial world
with the announcement that he was ready to raise the pay

of his men from $2.30 to the unheard-of sum of $5.00 a day.
Explaining the idea to newspapermen, Ford said that "this
is neither charity nor wages, but profit sharing and efficiency engineering." The plan was to work as a spur to
greater production and firmer loyalty to the company,
though Henry Ford insisted that one of its most important
functions was to motivate his workers to "proper living."
Afraid that such easy money might seduce his employees
into evil ways, Ford established, under Lee's direction, a
"Sociological Department" which was staffed with thirty,
soon one hundred, "investigators" (later called "advisers").
These, supplied with car, chauffeur, and interpreter, were
empowered to go into the workers' homes to make sure that
no one was drinking too much, that everyone's sex life was
without blemish, that leisure time was profitably spent,
that no boarders were taken in, that houses were clean
and neat, and so on. An employee who did not measure up
to the standards established by Ford lost his claim to the
five-dollar day, but after a period of probation he could
again qualify if he had behaved himself. No outside advice
was sought in the creation of this department; company
employees conceived and executed the plan.

The most recent historian of Ford shows that turnover
had been satisfactorily reduced before the five-dollar day
was instituted; Ford, however, did succeed in further reducing turnover from 1913 to 1915. Absenteeism, measured by the now archaic standards of that day, dropped
from 10 per cent to 0.5 per cent. Small wonder that Henry
Ford could jubilantly exclaim that the decision to pay $5.00
for an eight-hour day was "one of the finest cost-cutting
moves we ever made," while his Sociological Department
told the *Ford Times* of 1916 that, "looked at from a cold-
blooded point of view of business investment," the concern
with human behavior was "the very best investment it
[Ford Motor Company] has ever made." In reviewing
Ford's labor policies, one historian concluded that "the

Ford Company, which in 1911 had no labor policy at all, possessed three years later the most advanced labor policy in the world, and was regarded by wage earners from Sydney to Bangkok, from New York to Copenhagen, as a source of hope and inspiration."[20]

Ford's error lay in resting on his laurels. The five-dollar day was significant in 1914; but the cost of living steadily increased through the war years until, by 1918, it was 78 per cent above the depressed 1914 level. In a vain hope of reducing war turnover, Ford began to lecture his workers about loyalty, gratitude, and patriotism. But by January, 1919, he was finally forced to unbend, and an increase to a six-dollar day was authorized. The business recession of 1920 dampened the ardor of those at Ford who had struck gold through "understanding" human behavior. As the company retrenched, the 247 advisers in the Education Department—as it was now called—were reduced to a skeleton crew. Finally, in 1920, the Ford profit-sharing scheme was reshaped into a bonus and investment plan—based on skill and seniority, not on proper living.[21]

Ford's historian concludes that "the enlightened new labor rules, the five-dollar minium, and the struggle of the Sociological Department to raise living standards, constituted, despite inescapable shortcomings, a lustrous chapter in the history of the company and a memorable page in the record of American industry."[22] For several decades to come, paternalists would point to the five-dollar day and Sociological Department of Ford as a thrilling example of how employers could convert willful workers into "good men." Because he had the touch of Midas even in his labor policies, because these policies worked just the way Ford intended, the "memorable page" that he contributed was read by those in search of methods to ease labor tension.

Ford had made his point. If management would devote time and effort, and a very little money, to a consideration of the human element of its business, production and profits would rise as surely as if better machinery were introduced. The lesson was not wasted. From 1913 to 1920, in increasing crescendo, management voices were raised to proclaim that the human element was important, that intelligent management should realize that it had a monetary investment in men as well as in truck horses, "that a careful study of this 'human factor' pays in dollars and cents," that "it is admittedly good business to consider the psychological side."[23] One manufacturer said that since good machinery was available to all, the difference between success and failure in industry was the human element; "my success would be enormous," he continued, if only a way could be found to select workers who were half as good as his machines.[24]

This was the immediate background for the rise of industrial psychology. Managers were accepting the notion that human behavior colored the competitive positions of their companies. To train workers, or control them by methods like those Ford had devised, might prove prohibitively expensive. A few managers had put their fingers on the lines most promising: to select workers half as good as their machines was the most intriguing problem. By 1910, psychologists, armed with their knowledge of individual differences, were becoming aware of their industrial usefulness. Some of the odium earlier attached to an applied psychology was slowly diminishing because of the success of psychology in medicine, education, and law, and because of the more general use of experts in the public life of the progressive period. With the more direct encouragement of scientific management and psychology in advertising, a few psychologists were preparing to talk to industry.

The first systematic outline of an industrial psychology was formulated by Hugo Münsterberg. Born in Danzig in 1863, Münsterberg took his doctorate in psychology at the University of Leipzig when he was twenty-two years old and two years later earned an M.D. at Heidelberg. After spending some time in the early 1890's as an assistant professor at Harvard, he returned to Europe; but continued invitations from Harvard's president Charles W. Eliot and William James induced him to return to that university in 1897.

In 1910 Münsterberg began actively to think about the psychological problems of industry. In that year he circularized several hundred executives, asking what psychological traits they believed to be necessary in their employees. To Münsterberg, the specific content of the responses was less significant than the genuine interest the executives showed in his questions. Encouraged to explore further, he accepted a lectureship at the University of Berlin as an exchange professor during the academic year 1910-1911, during which he sketched the possibilities of a psychology of industry. The lectures were published in 1912 as *Psychologie und Wirtschaftsleben* and translated into English the following year under the title *Psychology and Industrial Efficiency*.

Early in his statement, Münsterberg warned his colleagues that their former disdain of applied psychology was no longer justified because, if psychologists were to delay implementation of their knowledge until their experiments and theories were perfect, the time for application would never come. At the start of the twentieth century a certain hesitancy had been justified, but by 1912 any reluctance to apply psychological knowledge was, he said, an "inexcusable lack of initiative."

He described a psychology of industry as "a new science which is to intermediate between the modern laboratory psychology and the problems of economics: the psychological experiment," he continued, "is systematically to be placed at the service of commerce and industry." He acknowledged the debt such a "new science" owed to scientific management, but Taylor's plans were inadequate because of "helpless psychological dilettantism." The "vague longing for psychological analysis" characteristic of scientific managers remained unfulfilled. It was therefore the "duty" of psychologists to come to their rescue. Professional psychologists must do the actual work, but "the representatives of practical life are much better able to indicate the points at which the psychological levers ought to be applied."

Keeping in mind the managers' desire to select workers half as good as their machines, Münsterberg said that psychology could detect for industry "those personalities which by their mental qualities are especially fit for a particular kind of economic work." He was quick to insist that, though managers should decide where and how to apply the "psychological levers," the results of industrial psychology would benefit labor as well as management, for wages would rise and the workday would shorten. Unable to resist a panacean flourish, he claimed that industrial psychology would cause "overflowing joy and perfect inner harmony" to radiate through the whole society.[25]

In 1915 Münsterberg clarified his thinking about the social consequences of industrial psychology. Industrial conflict was none of the psychologist's business. Whenever the values of labor and management collided, then the psychologist should withdraw. Psychologists should perfect their techniques, should achieve complete scientific detachment, and should leave the solution of social problems to others. The psychologist should limit his activities to predicting what effects would issue from specific stimuli. "But," he added, the psychologist "has no right to decide which effect is good and which effect is bad."[26]

With Münsterberg's publications, industrial psychology was formally launched. Many of his successors granted his importance, though several thought his work was unscientific, a result of chance.[27] But, by formalizing the case for a psychology of industry, he sparked a movement of increasing significance.

Perhaps more important than Münsterberg's writings was his actual work in industry. Drawing on the findings of Alfred Binet regarding the techniques of psychological testing, he developed selection tests for traveling salesmen of the American Tobacco Company and for conductors of the Boston Elevated Company. A series of tests that he devised for the selection of ship captains was adapted by the Dallas street railway system for its motormen.[28] Other psychologists soon picked up his lead by constructing selection tests for telephone operators, telegraphers, salesmen, typists, and stenographers.[29]

By 1915 Walter Dill Scott also had started to work on selection techniques. American Tobacco, at the suggestion of a consulting engineer, turned from Münsterberg to Scott and his assistants at Northwestern for help in reducing its turnover. After a long selection process, Scott picked ten out of twenty-four candidates, and nine of these, according to a company spokesman, were "among our best bonus earners." By the end of the year Scott's efforts had persuaded the National Lead Company, Western Electric, Loose-Wiles Biscuit Company, and the George Batten advertising agency to install a form of psychological testing. All of these firms—along with Metropolitan Life, whose tests were developed by Edward L. Thorndike—reported their satisfaction.[30]

The first instance of a company using such tests for the selection of factory workers also occurred in 1915. In the Clothcraft Shops of the Joseph and Feiss Company, Cleveland, Scott developed tests of intelligence, dexterity, and general ability. The tests were helpful, said Clothcraft's manager, because they indicated what an individual could not do, though they did not show what he could do. Because the test results were continually checked against job performance, the cooperation of the workers was essential. Mary Gilson, Clothcraft's employment manager, remembered how she had to run frantically around the plant on the days when Scott appeared. In search of specimens to be sent to the ominous-sounding "tower room" for testing, she had to assure the workers of the tests' harmlessness. "I was not popular on the factory floor on those days," she recalled, for "the girls thought it was a lot of nonsense to have to run a needle up a metal alley or do some other 'high jinks.' " The employees' wages, she concluded, "did not suffer for the time they were guinea pigging up in the tower, but they thought it was a lot of flubdubbery in spite of all the explaining we did." Regardless of consistently low correlations between the test results and job performance, Clothcraft decided that Scott's tests did aid in the over-all selection program.[31]

By 1915, just two years after Münsterberg's original formulation, industrial psychology was already being taken seriously. It was being clothed with a respectability —indeed, in some quarters, with an urgency—that two or three years earlier would have seemed incredible. Deriving mostly from the work of Münsterberg and Scott, curiosity about the potentialities of the field was becoming apparent in the academy as well as in industry.

At the Carnegie Institute of Technology, in the same year, the first psychological consulting service for industry was established. Under the direction of Walter V. Bingham, a Division of Applied Psychology, soon called the Division of Cooperative Research, was started. Bingham had taken his Ph.D. in psychology at the University of Chicago in 1908, after which he taught at several universities before moving to Carnegie. He believed that industrial psychology at Carnegie was rooted in the growing awareness of managers that poor selection and the resultant high turnover were expensive.

In the first year of the Division's operation, a Bureau of Salesmanship Research was started when Edward A. Woods, a district representative of a life insurance company, told Bingham and the president of Carnegie, A. A.

Hamerschlag, that the courses in salesmanship being offered in the United States were inadequate. Because the criteria of a "good" salesman were vague, they decided to begin research on the ingredients of success in selling. The program was to be supported by annual contributions of $500, later $1000, each from about thirty companies. The initial budget was underwritten personally by Woods; H. J. Heinz, the food processor; and Norval A. Hawkins, Ford's sales manager. These men, with Hamerschlag's assistance, induced a number of other companies to participate, including American Multigraph, Armstrong Cork, Burroughs Adding Machine, Carnegie Steel, Packard, and Westinghouse. In 1916 Bingham persuaded Northwestern University to lend Walter Dill Scott to Carnegie to direct the research. Scott there became America's first professor of applied psychology. After the war Clarence S. Yoakum directed the organization under a new name, the Bureau of Personnel Research.

Again as a result of the initiative of businessmen, the work at Carnegie began to proliferate; Edgar A. Kaufmann, a major executive of Pittsburgh's largest department store, persuaded six of his competitors that they all had similar problems which the Carnegie group could help solve. Hence in 1917 a Research Bureau for Retail Training was opened at Carnegie; to this the seven stores agreed to furnish $32,000 for a five-year period, the expense to be apportioned among the stores in relation to the number of employees each kept. For this sum, the bureau devised training and merchandising manuals, employment tests, "and specific procedures for correcting defects of sales personality and supervision." "That the stores have found their investment a profitable one," Bingham reasoned, "is shown by their request for a renewal of the contract for another five-year period."[32]

Within the first fifteen years of the twentieth century, while progressives discovered that they could neither crush nor control America's corporations, industrial psychology grew into an undersized but overconfident movement. Filling the gap left by the scientific managers, industrial psychologists seemed to a small but influential group of managers to hold some promise for the future. During the period of increasing union militancy, of Socialists and Wobblies, of violent strikes and violent strikebreaking, a few managers turned to psychology in an effort to solve their labor problems.

CHAPTER 3

War

IN THE SPRING OF 1917, when Woodrow Wilson asked his nation to go to war, the German navy was destroying allied shipping faster than it could be replaced. The French had failed in several important campaigns, and Britain had lost more than she gained in Flanders; within a year, Russia was to sign a separate peace, withdraw from the war, and release German troops from the eastern front. The United States was hardly in a position to make a telling contribution to the increasingly dismal military situation; on hand were supplies for an army of only 500,000 men. A sufficiently large army could be raised, but how to equip it? American industry was faced with demands for production greater than any it had ever known. In a war of lumbering machines, the factories of America were prepared to supply small arms and munitions; but tanks, big guns, and airplanes were desperately needed. The resiliency of the American industrial plant was to be tried beyond its capacity.

Despite the fact that a complete inventory of the nation's industrial resources had been taken before the United States entered the war, industrial mobilization quickly became chaotic. As 1917 wore on, it became increasingly clear that some kind of central authority was needed to standardize supplies, coordinate the productive plant, and oversee labor relations; for such purposes the War Industries Board was created late in July. Charges of disorganization and inefficiency persisted and, in January, 1918, forced Wilson into action. Bernard Baruch, made chairman of the WIB, became virtual dictator of America's industrial system, and the agency began to function.

For American labor, the war years provided an expansive impulse when, because of a sellers' market, strikes began to succeed as almost 2,500,000 workers joined the labor movement. Most of this increase went to the AFL, which, unlike the Socialists and the Wobblies, favored the American war effort. The insistence of federal agencies that suppliers accept collective bargaining undoubtedly encouraged this drift into unionism, but such an insistence was a mixed blessing. Unwilling to forfeit contracts, many managements encouraged the formation of company unions, a number of which remained as a war legacy to plague the more independent labor movement. Such agencies as the National War Labor Board, however, did help labor in general; for, after the government backed out of industrial relations, the number of workers involved in strikes rose in one year from over 1,000,000 to over 4,000,000.

With the decision of the Congress to accept Wilson's declaration of war, the most pressing personnel problems of the nation moved from industry to the infantry. It was far less difficult to draft men than to make soldiers of them. Of the 24,000,000 men registered by the nation's draft boards, almost 3,000,000 were inducted into the armed forces. To equip these men was a gigantic problem for both the military and industry. To train them was equally difficult; for this job the military, always willing to gamble during war, looked to the personnel experts, including psychologists, who before the war had begun to demonstrate their usefulness to management.

As America turned to the consuming business of making war, industrial psychologists had moved beyond the tentative suggestions of Münsterberg. In 1917, for instance, the first general textbook in applied psychology was published,[1] and the *Journal of Applied Psychology* was started. That the majority of managers were still hostile to psychology, however, continued to trouble the profession. Despite the achievements of Münsterberg and Scott, most managers had still to be convinced of the utility of social science in general and psychology in particular. One executive, late in 1917, voiced this typical attitude: "Of the social scientist I know nothing by experience and only very little by hearsay"; social scientists might be of some help to management, he was willing to admit, but only if they accepted "the standpoint of the managers." Even if the social scientist could analyze certain long-term business trends, this executive seriously questioned "how much help he will be day by day."[2]

The involvement of America in World War I gave psychologists an opportunity to show what they could do. The personnel techniques that some had already implemented in industry could now be tested on a scale vaster than anything industry could provide. But, most important, their achievements would be publicized, which would help to overcome the suspicion of industrial managers when peace came. With the unlimited canvas allowed by the army, the techniques and tools necessary for a psychology of industry were developed and refined at a highly accelerated rate. Not least important, the teams of psychologists working in the army "learned for the first time how to pool their efforts and how to cooperate with physicians, psychiatrists, line officers, and practical men of affairs."[3] The war, in short, shattered the cocoon in which psychologists had lived and introduced them to problems intimately familiar to America's managers. As a result of their war work, the world was taught to take a lingering look at the results and promises of applied psychology.

In 1916, under the auspices of the National Academy of Sciences and the Engineering Foundation, the National Research Council had been organized; its function was to inventory and mobilize the scientific resources of the nation. A Committee for Psychology, established the following year, largely concerned itself with discovering ways of using psychology in the training and selection problems of the armed forces. This committee, working from the office of the Surgeon General, was given the job of measuring the intelligence of military personnel. Robert M. Yerkes, a Harvard Ph.D. in psychology who had taught at both Harvard and the University of Minnesota, chaired the committee with Bingham as its secretary. Yerkes, Bingham, and five other psychologists reviewed the hundreds of already developed intelligence tests and agreed that the manuscript test submitted by A. S. Otis of Stanford University was the most useful. From this basis, the committee drew up a series of tests, resembling the Otis test, to which they could all give their support.

Before subjecting the entire army to their tests, the committee agreed to a trial in only four cantonments. The trial presumably was successful, and the committee was ordered to test the whole army—excepting, for some reason, field and general officers. The army intelligence tests were eventually given to nearly 1,727,000 men, of whom 41,000 were officers. To administer a program of such size it was necessary to train army personnel in psychological testing; at Fort Oglethorpe, Georgia, a special school in testing was established where 100 officers and over 300 enlisted men were instructed in "military psychology." As the testing program widened to thirty-five army camps, more than 500 additional clerks were assigned to the staff.

At Columbia University a statistical study of the test

answers was made. When it was discovered that 30 per cent of the recruits were illiterate, special tests not requiring reading or writing skills were developed. In some 83,000 borderline cases individual tests were given. As a result of the testing program, almost 8,000 men were discharged and 10,000 others were assigned to labor or other service duties. Still another 10,000 were sent to development battalions for observation and preliminary training. In only nine months of 1918, almost 46,000 men were found whose mental age was less than ten years. The psychologists concluded that none of these men would be worth the cost of equipment and training.

The chief advantage of testing, according to the committee, was the speed with which "officer material" could be located and men of "mental inferiority" could be eliminated. Though the psychologists admitted that the army, by itself, through a process of trial and error and experience, eventually would have placed its men just as the psychologists had advised, the time wasted would have been enormous. "Speed counts in a war that costs fifty million dollars per day," the psychologists pointed out. And speed was their contribution to the army selection and training programs.

Knowing that intelligence is only one of many criteria useful for the classification of personnel, psychologists began to refine techniques other than testing for military application. Associated with the office of the Adjutant General, a Committee on Classification of Personnel was formed. Directed by Walter Dill Scott, it was composed of psychologists who were members of the National Research Council's Committee on Psychology or of committees of the American Psychological Association. Bingham, who in 1919 was made a lieutenant colonel; John B. Watson, the founder of behaviorist psychology; and others devoted themselves to the work of the Committee on Classification. The assignment of military personnel to specialized tasks was the problem, and methods of rating officers for appointment and promotion also were devised. Eventually, almost half of the men in the army were rated according to their abilities, education, and experience, and were placed in appropriate jobs. To support this work, the War Department spent almost one million dollars, and the techniques developed reportedly influenced every aspect of military personnel.[4]

Walter Dill Scott, later awarded the Distinguished Service Medal for his war work, was the guiding force in the creation of the various rating methods. In a few cases rating techniques had been used before 1914. One company, for instance, had used a rating scale as early as 1907 and may have been the first to do so in a systematic way. In 1912 the Larkin Company rated its supervisors and had sufficient faith in its system to award a bonus to the highest man. In the same year the faculty of the Pratt Institute used a systematic scale to rate its students.[5] From 1914 to 1916 Scott turned his attention to rating. His goal was to find an expression of the comparative worth of men that would be "objective," preferably a numerical statement. To convert qualitative personality characteristics into a quantitative expression was the target. In a number of industrial companies, Scott had begun to implement his ideas about rating; in every case the combined judgment of "interviewers" about the relative usefulness of the candidates provided the foundation for his system. "This judgment," Scott explained in 1916, "is based on personal appearance, tact, industry, promise of usefulness to the company, etc. Whatever the qualities are that are judged the 'Interviewers' must summarize their judgment in a single figure. . . . The judgments of all the 'Interviewers' are then combined into a single figure expressive of the personality of the applicant."[6]

Despite the insuperable shortcoming of Scott's method —the faith that personal opinions would become scientific if a sufficient number were gathered—his scale served as the basis of the military work and, later, of many of the scales adopted by industry, including Sperry Gyroscope and Standard Oil of New Jersey.[7] Though he was finally to abandon the early crude attempt to get a single numerical statement of relative worth, Scott persisted along the same general lines. However, regardless of all of his later refinements, several professional psychologists still questioned the reliability and validity of a rating scale built on the assumptions and prejudices of the men doing the rating.[8]

Encouraged by a growing national awareness, industrial psychologists began to speak with more confidence. Springing from the recognition of the problems of wartime industrial disorganization, the literature of industrial psychology swelled rapidly.[9] An increasing number of psychologists were turning their skills to "practical" problems. Indeed, by 1920 more than half of the psychologists in the United States were engaged in research in applied psychology of one kind or another. About twenty-five of almost four hundred members of the American Psychological Association reported that they were conducting research in the problems of industry.[10]

The work the psychologists had done for the army was widely discussed, and popular interest grew steadily to a peak reached in 1924.[11] The results of the intelligence-testing program shocked the nation, but psychology was draped in respectability and ostensibly had demonstrated its usefulness. The reaction of industrial managers to the promise of psychology was immediate. Shortly after the armistice was signed, for instance, both the National Research Council and the office of the Surgeon General were "besieged" with requests for information about testing.[12] The personnel work that the psychologists had performed was called a "war gift to industry," and the question

of how the techniques developed for the army could
be smoothly transplanted into industry was raised with
increasing frequency. "Might it not be possible," asked
an industrial journal in 1919, "to work out some oral trade
tests for different jobs so that by a few questions your
employment man can better judge the applicant?"[13]

The lure of the miraculous had taken hold. More and
more managers trudged to the door of psychology with
their overstuffed bags of problems, hoping to leave unbur-
dened. For example, after listening to Yerkes describe the
work of the war psychologists, an engineer with the New
Jersey Zinc Company in 1919 wanted to know "whether
these tests showed whether a man were moral or honest
and whether he was likely to go to sleep on the job."
Yerkes was compelled to answer that the tests measured
"mental alertness" and nothing else.[14] The faith that many
managers now had in psychology would not down until
psychology was shown to be something less than a panacea.
The price paid by management for this discovery was high,
and inevitably disillusionment blurred its sanguine image
of the future.

Out of the tight personnel situation of the war came
a number of ideas which made a great deal of sense to some
managements. The revelations of the army testing program
dramatized the importance of individual differences. But
it was not enough to determine the precise abilities of any
given job applicant; just as important was the need to
understand the requirements of the job. Job analysis was
therefore pursued with greater energy than had been the
case even in the days of scientific management. Now it was
hoped that, through job analysis and man analysis, it would
be possible to place square pegs in square holes. The
importance of morale was also coming to be appreciated,
as a growing number of managers realized that problems
of attitude might nullify all the skill and care devoted

to selection and job placement. Here were large areas demanding that management cooperate with specialists in human behavior.

The war, in brief, focused the attention of management on personnel problems in general. Throughout the emergency, popular interest in personnel problems increased until the presumed security of the 1920's convinced managers that the situation was under control.[15] Though some companies had adopted centralized personnel practices long before 1917, the war forced a general reorganization of industrial personnel practices. The antecedent elements of personnel management can be found in the scientific management fad, the evolution of cost accounting, industrial welfare work, increasing use of staff departments, and the growing specialization of the foreman's role.[16] A centralized personnel office was the necessary first step in the implementation of the growing managerial concern with human behavior. This is not, however, to suggest that the movement toward centralized personnel was wholesale, since even during the war years not more than 10 per cent of the plants successful enough to support the added overhead of centralized personnel actually did so.[17] Despite the disinterest of most companies, the idea that personnel was a distinct aspect of management's responsibilities began to spread. Scientific managers had earlier made functional analyses of the production process; now personnel experts began to functionalize personnel.

As the attention of the American people turned from the problems of war to the problems of peace, as the President and the Congress began to pull in different directions with sufficient stubbornness to keep the country out of the League of Nations, the United States contained a tense industrial plant that was eager to go. Problems of readjustment to the ways of peace began slightly to cloud the face of America's industry, but the future seemed secure. Emerging from this war as a creditor nation in the affairs of the world, the United States enjoyed economic prospects that excited the imaginations of even the most dour.

There were good reasons why the postwar economy should have seriously suffered. By the time the armistice was signed, about one-fourth of the civilian work force was employed in war industries. The day after the signing of the armistice, Washington began to cancel war contracts; within one month, over two billion dollars in orders had been canceled. Somehow four million soldiers would have to be absorbed into the peacetime economy. Disregarding the advice of the Committee on Classification and Secretary of War Baker that soldiers should be released from the army in the order of their adaptability to the industrial needs of the nation at peace, the Chief of Staff ordered the usual demobilization process to proceed by military unit, regardless of the likelihood of civilian employment. Despite these pressures, the boom was on. The resumption of private construction and, most important, the continuation of the brisk export trade, encouraged by the needs of European relief, helped bolster the economy. Rising slightly in 1919, the gross national product of goods and services, even in terms of 1914 prices, did not seriously dip until, on the threshold of depression, the "roaring twenties" were born with a whimper.

In such an atmosphere the army psychologists were turned loose. Their problem was simple: how to work on industrial problems. Many decided that they should form their own companies and work only as consultants for other businesses. The managerial mood seemed right, as one industrial psychologist reported that if William James were alive he "would undoubtedly be one of the most sought-after business consultants,"[18] thereby displaying his ignorance of James' abhorrence of the "bitch-goddess success."

The first psychological consulting organization to be established was the Scott Company; in 1919, under the presidency of Walter Dill Scott, the Scott Company Laboratory was opened in Philadelphia. This firm was a direct outgrowth of the Committee on Classification of Personnel; all of the nine active members of the company had been associated with the Committee during the war. The Scott Company lasted only a few years because of the growing conviction of the officers that each industrial or business firm should have its own trained personnel man as a permanent staff member. They came to believe that a consulting arrangement between psychologists and industrialists was merely delaying the day when industry would itself undertake the kind of research and application that the future of their profession demanded.[19]

In 1921, two years before the Scott Company disbanded, James McKeen Cattell, pioneer in the study of individual differences, founded the Psychological Corporation. The starting capital of $10,000 was entirely subscribed by professional psychologists, and the roster of directors included many of the most prominent psychologists in the country: Bingham, Cattell, G. Stanley Hall, H. L. Hollingworth, McDougall, Scott, Lewis M. Terman, Titchener, Watson, and Yerkes among others. Intended as a holding company for psychologists, facilitating communication among them and with the general public, the corporation originally was not itself to undertake research, but was merely to inform the interested public about the facilities of existing laboratories and the competence of available psychologists. To convince more industrialists of the utility of psychology was one of the main purposes of the firm. Cattell believed that the cooperation of labor was also essential, and he began an exploratory correspondence with Samuel Gompers, each man convincing the other of the compatibility of their interests.

According to one of its later officers, the importance of the Psychological Corporation was "that by obtaining its charter as a *business corporation* its founders established *psychological work* as a legitimate means of producing profits through private business enterprise." In this company, psychologists invested their money as well as their arguments, in the conviction that they could provide management with added tools to accomplish its goals. In 1921, however, there was some difficulty in selling the services of this company to industry. Industrial psychology had made a start; a few managements were even eager to apply the findings of psychologists; but the day was still distant when American management, as a body, would be sufficiently interested in psychology to put the Psychological Corporation in the black. With time, after more managements became convinced that psychologists could help make money, the Psychological Corporation was to grow to quite respectable dimensions. Eventually 125 people would be employed on its general staff and about 250 psychologists would contribute their part-time services, as the gross annual receipts exceeded a million dollars.[20]

By the time the Psychological Corporation was started, a large number of other agencies, both private and public, had begun work in some area of personnel research. The lack of coordination and communication worried both the Engineering Foundation and the National Research Council. These two groups asked the Bureau of Labor Statistics to conduct a survey of all the existing personnel research agencies. When it was discovered through this survey that hundreds of different groups had started personnel research, the two sponsoring organizations called a conference in November, 1920, to create some coordinating body; the Personnel Research Federation was the result. Organized in March, 1921, the Federation was supported by contributions from the member businesses and industries. One year later Bingham was elected chairman. Through its official organ, the *Journal of Personnel Research*, later called the *Personnel Journal*, information regarding personnel research was circulated. The scant 11 members that began the Federation increased, in only seven years, to 213.

Eventually, personnel of the Federation conducted research in its own name.[21]

The United States did not, of course, monopolize industrial psychology. As this discipline grew from the base supplied by scientific management in this country, as scientific management became a major export item in American trade, industrial psychology began to appear in Europe. There were, however, several basic differences in the way European and American psychologists defined their professional roles. Going beyond the usual American concern with selection techniques, European psychologists believed that human relations enveloped virtually all business activity. Most of them were convinced that their research areas should not in any way be restricted, and that any tools, including even the methods and frames of reference of scientific management, should be used where applicable. And, of great importance, European industrial psychologists went much further than Americans in interesting labor in the applications of industrial psychology.[22] The greater maturity of European unionism perhaps explains why psychologists and managements alike believed that it was important to convince labor of the utility of the new personnel devices. Such compulsion, as will be shown, was conspicuously absent in the United States.

One of the main characteristics of industrial psychology in England was its highly organized development. Growing out of the work of the wartime Industrial Fatigue Research Board, the National Institute of Industrial Psychology was established in 1921. Under the direction of Charles S. Myers, the NIIP focused its research energies on studying methods of work and of training, effects of rest periods and of working conditions on productivity, and causes and cures of monotony and fatigue, as well as selection devices. Realizing that the success of industrial psychology depended in large measure on the attitudes of businessmen, the NIIP embarked on an extensive program of education. Popular lectures on the use of industrial psychology were broadcast by the British Broadcasting Company, and the subject was offered in the London School of Economics. Members of the NIIP staff addressed trade unions and Rotary Clubs. Such large-scale methods made possible more rapid acceptance of the discipline in England than in the United States. For instance, at a time when only a few American universities offered courses in industrial psychology, such courses were given in the universities of Birmingham, Edinburgh, Cambridge, Liverpool, Manchester, and London. By the mid-1920's popular interest had been aroused not merely in the promise but in the achievements of industrial psychology. A few British firms, including Rowntree and Company, kept a professional psychologist on the permanent payroll.[23] One American psychologist unhappily compared the two countries: "Although English psychologists are in general far behind those in America, yet in the field of industrial psychology they are so far ahead of us that we find it almost painful."[24] American psychologists wanted some national organization similar to the British NIIP, associated perhaps with the Bureau of Standards.[25]

In Germany, as in the United States and England, psychology was given an industrial toehold through its war efforts. The German army, in 1916, made use of psychologists to help devise techniques for the selection of drivers. Within a few years the Saxon Railway Company in Dresden and the Greater Berlin Tramways started their own psychological laboratories to aid in the application of selection techniques. By 1922, twenty-two German firms had begun such laboratories, and almost twice that number were operating by the close of the next twelve months. Institutes devoted to the application of industrial psychology were started in almost all of Germany's large cities, including Berlin, Munich, Dresden, Mannheim, Halle, Hamburg, and Hanover. Some of these institutes were associated with

universities or technical schools, and some were supported
by the contributions of individual companies.[26]

According to one American psychologist, industrial psychology was "apparently more important and more sure of
itself in Germany than in either England or the United
States." Cattell agreed that more was being done in Germany, but he thought that this was only a temporary situation.[27] In most other countries, the depression which set
in during the summer of 1920 retarded the application of
psychology to industry. But during the incredible inflation
that Germany experienced just after the war, psychology
was established as a practical approach to increasing productivity, making more efficient use of severely limited manpower, and generally strengthening the weakened economy. The Fatherland, reported an American observer, was
sinking and industrial psychology was embraced as a possible key to industrial reconstruction. But because German
industrialists had such pressing needs, they overempha-
sized, as did American industrialists, the potentialities of
psychology, and thus forced psychologists to move faster
than the results of their research warranted. Serious errors
were made, in Germany as in the United States, in the pursuit of immediately practical results.

Especially in Germany did labor take an active interest
in the application of industrial psychology. Moving further
than American labor was to do for the next thirty years, German trade unions, by the middle of the 1920's, accepted
psychology as a promising tool for industrial relations, and
therefore influenced somewhat the scope and direction of
industrial psychology. Virtually no such influence was to
be felt in the United States. In the 1920's, for instance,
Berlin trade unions made an annual financial contribution
to the Psychotechnical Institute of the Charlottenburg
Hochschule. A number of trade unions even compelled
workers to pass a minimum standard devised by various
psychological institutes before they would be granted full

union status. Most impressive of all was the situation at the Essen plant of the Krupp Works, where over 250 men were organized to study systematically the accomplishments and potentialities of industrial psychology.[28]

A nervous economy of boom and bust was intolerable. By waving the supposedly magic wand of psychology, industrialists, government officials, and indeed psychologists themselves hoped that economic crisis could be averted. In vocational guidance in the Soviet Union, in selection techniques and methods of work in Italy's cotton and silk plants, in Milan's shoe factories, in the Italian Air Ministry and state railway system, in Spain, Belgium, France, Sweden, Switzerland, and Czechoslovakia, psychology was applied to industry. Spreading eastward to Japan, the enthusiasm for a psychology of industry mounted. Interested in finding methods of ensuring industrial peace, the government of Japan underwrote the establishment of "an association for harmonious cooperation" to aid the work of industrial psychologists.[29]

In contrast to the European acceptance of industrial psychology, the American experience was confused and disorganized. In the United States, except for the wartime emergency, there was no governmental sponsorship or subsidization. Industrial psychology had to make its own way. With little aid, industrial psychologists had to persuade management of their utility. A few hardy men persisted in their effort to market their knowledge. The most tangible instrument they had developed was the psychological test, and on the success of this tool industrial psychologists were to stake their future.

CHAPTER 4

In Search of
a Science

It is always misleading to characterize periods of history by a few dominant images, and the 1920's have an unusual abundance of such images: the decade roared, flapped, shimmied, jazzed, alienated a few of its intellectuals, asked for Joe through the peepholes of speakeasies, and watched Babe Ruth hit sixty home runs. But more: the decade saw an economy drift away from the notion that production would automatically guarantee consumption; it heard Henry Ford and others argue for a more intensive concentration on the problems of distribution and on methods of creating demand; it witnessed a tremendous spurt in advertising. The decade was certainly prosperous, but countercurrents were there for those with eyes to see. Some saw, most did not. Farm income and land values collapsed, not to recover for twenty years. Labor staggered under the appearance of ease as wages rose and the cost of living rose faster, as productivity increased while union membership declined. The economy of the decade was simultaneously pulling in several directions, and only from the vantage point of 1929 did the dominant strands become somewhat clear.

The industrial managers of the time had somehow to make sense of the contradictions and confusions of the business life of the nation. Never had they been so high in public esteem; never had their place in government been so secure. But the memory of earlier labor militancy remained as a drag on too easy optimism. The blood spilled in Gastonia, North Carolina, in the last year of the decade, proved that their fears had some substance.

What to do about labor? From among the many alternatives open to management, several significant decisions were made. Perhaps the most important was the agreement among the managerial *avant-garde* that workers were human beings who would respond with gratitude to personnel programs designed to consider their feelings, attitudes, and hopes. Early in the decade, for instance, a trade journal recognized this trend: "Now that human friction is recognized to be an exceedingly destructive element in plant efficiency, its causes and the means of elimination claim the attention of managers and workers."[1] Time and again, different executives stated that a consideration of the human element would pay in cash terms, that workers' attitudes were more important than economic laws, that a regard for the welfare of employees would increase efficiency, and that economic success, not morality and sentiment, prompted the view of workers as men. "Men," reported the president of a steel company, "are much more precious material than steel."[2]

This growing attitude, translated into personnel policy, took several shapes. Though it was certainly not the only tendency, paternalism did become the most characteristic form of personnel programs. Management would take care of its workers in the hope that they would reciprocate with appreciation, loyalty, and harder and more efficient work. Welfare plans were invented to cover virtually every aspect of the worker's life, from the moment when he was hired by a centralized and "scientific" employment department to his retirement years when he would benefit from a carefully constructed pension plan. Hundreds of such personnel programs emerged in this decade. And the ranks of organized labor declined steadily.[3]

Though fewer than fifty companies used scientific personnel methods in 1921,[4] most of the plans and policies they developed were to become rather standard in American industry. These few firms set the tone and pace of the coming movement. The many trade associations that emerged, under the mantle of Herbert Hoover in the Commerce Department, also contributed to the research and development of personnel policies.[5]

The distinction between the personnel movement of the 1920's and the earlier scientific-management movement lay in the former's emphasis on the human being. Many managers who had installed scientific-management schemes, including the "best possible working conditions" and perfectly "scientific" methods of pay, began to feel that their production costs were still too high. Workers were not working as hard as they could. The solution to the problems remaining after the scientific managers had done their work was to be found in an even greater emphasis on the worker as man, an increase in personnel work.

During the last five years of the decade, personnel and industrial-relations programs steadily grew, both in substance and in popularity.[6] It was reported at the time that, because the labor supply was becoming stabilized, a number of important companies were abandoning elaborate personnel programs;[7] but such plans did continue to spread, moving even into a large number of small plants.[8] Between 1925 and 1930, insurance plans (especially group insurance), medical services, and luncheon facilities were the programs most frequently installed.[9] The productivity of the average worker steadily increased; the membership of organized labor steadily decreased. Paternalism seemed to work.

But paternalism could succeed only if the workers re-

sponded in the appropriate fashion. It was a mistake, the
war psychologists had shown, to underestimate the extent
of individual differences. Perhaps some men would be
more easily persuaded by the paternalistic personnel policies of the decade than others. It was therefore clearly the
obligation of management to devote time and thought to
the problems of selection—those very problems with which
industrial psychologists had worked earlier.

Though the much publicized work of the army psychologists did a great deal to soften the hostility many managers
felt toward psychology, enough suspicion and skepticism
remained to worry the psychologists. Bending much of
their talent to the task of convincing American management that they had something useful to contribute, an increasing number of industrial psychologists slowly began
to be accepted by a few progressive companies. And they
continued their efforts to convert the larger group of managers who were not yet convinced of their worth.

The tack most psychologists took was self-criticism.
The values and goals of the managers were accepted as
given. Believing that managers would accept their discipline if enough practitioners behaved in a more "useful"
fashion, these psychologists tried to explain the facts of
business life to those of their colleagues who had lived too
long in isolated Academia. "If the psychologist is to help
[industry]," an industrial psychologist explained to his colleagues, "he must help make money." Psychological research must not be too expensive, another explained; such
research, he pointed out, should reduce costs, not increase
them. Professional jargon was also blamed for part of the
resistance shown by management.[10]

The impact of this attitude on the psychologists was
serious. Management was unconvinced of the practicality
of psychologists? Well then, psychologists would be practical. In 1925, for example, the chairman of the psychology

department of Washington University showed that he could do without professional jargon and could use the language of management:

Galileo failed because he was an investigator and not a salesman. Consequently, he could not get his goods marketed. . . . He failed . . . when he tried to sell his telescope . . . by letting a selected group of distinguished citizens look through it and see the satellites of Jupiter. Galileo thought that only facts and arguments were needed to sell goods of guaranteed quality, but he was so greatly mistaken that at the end he was compelled to deny publicly everything which he had said about the value of his wares. His competitors, Aristotle, Moses, and the church fathers, had monopolized the market, and their stockholders would not let him do business.[11]

The most practical device yet invented by psychologists was the war-proved psychological test. On the success of this tool, rather than on the persuasiveness of their arguments, psychologists placed their hopes for their industrial future. If they could make psychological tests work in industry, they believed that managerial acceptance would certainly follow. Hence an increasing amount of energy was spent in the effort to improve testing.

The first problem was to clarify, if possible, just what a psychological test was. In 1924 two industrial psychologists entered the discussion by saying that "the principle of the psychological test is . . . to use a sample of one's behavior to indicate his abilities or other tendencies, and hence to predict his probable future behavior." The following year, Max Freyd and a number of other psychologists argued that testing could succeed only if a statistical instead of a clinical approach was used. A typical formulation of statistical testing was given by Harry W. Hepner, an industrial psychologist who had been in charge of personnel research at the Goodyear Tire and Rubber Company, the Philadelphia Company, and Kaufmann's Department Store in Pittsburgh: "*A psychological test is any problem or series of questions which has been tried out on persons of known ability; and it has been shown that the scores made by these persons correlate with their records in some form of ability.*"[12] The main drift of the testing movement, to this day, has been based on such a formulation.

The next serious problem with which the testing psychologists had to come to grips was far more elusive: what personality characteristics were desirable for different occupations? It was common knowledge that the personality types of the successful salesman and the successful machine operator were different; but different in what ways? Was intelligence important for a given job? How much intelligence? In vain, men had long debated such questions. Late in the nineteenth century, for instance, E. L. Godkin, the journalist and publicist, articulated his conviction that men who rose from rags to riches, like Alger heroes, had superior intelligence. But businessmen also had argued that intelligence was not the issue; indeed, business had more intelligent men than it knew how to use. Regardless of how much intelligence a man had, many of the problems of business would be solved if he were willing to use it "faithfully and honestly."[13] By the 1920's the issue was clear: psychologists were faced with the gnarled problem of determining what kinds of personalities were best for specific jobs.

It will be recalled that this was precisely what Bingham and his staff at Carnegie Tech had attempted. They had sought for criteria of success for salesmen, though the project was abandoned. Some twenty years later a member of the original staff admitted that the attempt to use intelligence tests in the selection of salesmen "got us nowhere fast." No positive correlation between general intelligence and sales ability was found at Carnegie.[14] What, then, were the determining characteristics of successful salesmen? All that the Carnegie group had proved was that general intelligence or "mental alertness" was not crucial.

The experience of psychologists in the intelligence-testing program of the army seemed more promising. They believed that they had discovered an occupational hierarchy corresponding to intelligence. Military personnel who had been in a profession before the war had the highest intelligence scores; semiprofessional men and high-ranking business executives came next; skilled, semiskilled, and unskilled workers followed in that order. The rankings were even broken down into specific occupations, so that it was possible, for instance, to compare the intelligence of teamsters with that of carpenters.[15] What did all of this mean? There was considerable overlapping of intelligence scores from one occupation to another. To what degree were the men in the lower levels of intelligence successful in their own occupations? How was success itself to be defined? Perhaps the army tests did not measure intelligence at all; perhaps those tests accurately measured only the amount of schooling of the candidates, despite the efforts of Robert Yerkes and his committee to counteract this possibility. Such unanswered questions were eventually to be studied systematically, but before this happened several companies accepted the "intellectual hierarchy" discovered in the army program as a key to their selection problems.

One example of this will do. In the spring of 1919, Harold E. Burtt, a Harvard Ph.D. in psychology, then at Ohio State, became a consulting psychologist for the Canadian Consolidated Rubber Company; he was hired to develop tests for the employment office of Canadian Consolidated's tire factory. Administering intelligence tests similar to those given in the army program, he discovered an "occupational hierarchy" corresponding, he believed, to intelligence scores. The higher the positions held in the company by his subjects, the higher they scored on his

tests. Burtt concluded, with a Darwinian twist, that "there
are different kinds of industrial performance, each with its
minimum intelligence requirements and that a person
tends finally to reach the highest level for which his intelligence qualifies him."[16]

The results of the army tests as well as industrial intelligence testing did not altogether escape criticism. In
1921, at a symposium called to answer the question "What
is Intelligence?" it was found that the psychologists present
could not agree on what it was that intelligence tests tested.
In the same year Morris S. Viteles, then an associate professor of psychology at the University of Pennsylvania and
a consultant for the Milwaukee Railway and Light Company, forcefully argued that "the tests which are being
used successfully in industry are those which measure the
specific abilities of individuals for particular jobs, and not
tests for general intelligence."[17]

Still, in 1922, Robert Yerkes, who had headed the army
testing program, maintained that "a reasonably reliable
measure of intelligence was the best available single indication of a person's occupational usefulness."[18] It was undoubtedly hard for the men who had been involved in the
army program to abandon their dramatic conclusions. But
Walter V. Bingham, who had been the secretary of Yerkes'
committee, was willing; in a paper read to the American
Psychological Association in 1923, he reported the results
of intelligence tests that had been given to 102 businessmen at the Babson Statistical Conference in Wellesley Hills
during the previous summer. Believing that the group was
representative of successful American businessmen, he
found that at least average intelligence was necessary for
business success; but this was saying no more than that
"no significant relationship was found between intelligence
. . . and relative business success." Concluding that there
was a minimum intelligence level below which success
would be unlikely, Bingham insisted that this minimum

was much lower than ordinarily supposed; such nonintellectual personality traits as dependability, energy, and the ability to control people were the key factors in business success.[19] During the next few years, others came to similar conclusions.[20]

Despite the effort of Yerkes and Burtt to defend the military testing program, the tide of psychological opinion was against them. Discussing his work in the tire factory, Burtt in 1926 took the pragmatic position of denying the importance of defining intelligence at all; he did not care what the definition was so long as the test scores seemed to group themselves in "averages [which] are tantamount to the intellectual requirements of the occupation in question."[21]

By the middle of the 1920's a new element was introduced into the discussion. A. J. Snow, a Northwestern psychologist and director of psychological research for a taxi company, reported that it was possible for a worker in a given occupation to have too much intelligence. He agreed that too little intelligence would result in inferior work, which in turn would increase turnover. A worker with too much intelligence, however, "is likely to quit in favor of the first job which offers a better opportunity for the use of his capacity. He is also apt to resent the monotony occasioned by the fact that his duties demand only a small part of his mental endowment; he may even use this excess capacity in morbid imagination of his ill lot and eventually cause considerable dissatisfaction among other employees." Bingham and Freyd agreed with Snow that turnover was sometimes predictable from intelligence-test scores.[22] But the issue was still murky: how much intelligence was too much or too little for a given occupation?

Such fundamental disagreements and confusions among psychologists about the nature and usefulness of testing spread, in an even more intense fashion, to managers. The psychologists' war work had greatly impressed some managers and had led them to look forward to remarkable results from industrial testing. Several management spokesmen, in this period of overconfidence, expected that industrial implementation of the army tests would greatly reduce worker fatigue by matching the worker with the job for which he was best qualified—putting square pegs into square holes.[23] But psychologists were just beginning to do research on the nature of fatigue, and there was virtually no agreement among them. Misinterpretations multiplied. The most common error was the notion that a greatly simplified version of the army tests would expose to the employer the nature of the candidate's personality and talents. Speaking to the Chicago Chamber of Commerce, for example, Walter Dill Scott in 1919 conveyed the impression that the use of "simple oral, picture and performance tests" would permit the employer accurately to assess the level of the candidate's skills for any given job.[24]

But Scott was aware of the dangers of such managerial enthusiasm; also in 1919, he warned a convention of employment managers that, because of misunderstanding, testing was likely to turn into a fad.[25] He was right. Though no more than thirty-two companies used testing in a patient and experimental manner before 1921,[26] hundreds of others bought ready-made tests, applied them indiscriminately, and hoped for the imagined miracle. Both the Bell Telephone Company and Dallas Consolidated used tests to measure certain motor, personality, and intelligence traits, the significance of which were not known. Some skills, however, were clearly important for specific jobs: typists had to know how to type and stenographers to take dictation. Before the 1920's, psychologists had developed techniques for measuring certain motor skills such as finger dexterity. For such skills they could provide tests that would measure what they were supposed to measure.[27] But the problem remained: how to determine the relative importance of any trait or skill? Was finger dexterity more essential for a typist than, say, her loyalty to the company?

A calm appraisal of psychological testing was becoming increasingly difficult. Managers were thrilled with the prospect of an easy solution of their labor difficulties, and psychologists were quite as excited by the vision of managerial appreciation and acceptance. By 1922 one psychology professor affirmed that accurate tests had been devised for typists, stenographers, conductors, motormen, mechanics, clerical workers, minor executives, salesmen, "and many others."[28] The few companies that had attempted a scientific approach to testing fought a losing battle. One such company was Cheney Brothers, silk manufacturers in South Manchester, Connecticut, which began intelligence testing in 1916. This firm, with the advice of a staff psychologist, broadened its testing program in 1919 to include all of its 5000 employees. Cheney was careful enough, however, to realize that intelligence tests would "never . . . indicate the full measure of an individual's mental resources or possibilities in performance."[29] Many other firms had less restraint. In 1920, even an agency of the national government concluded that no employment manager should do without a testing program. One manufacturer employing 21,000 workers developed a program, using the army tests as a model, and no psychologist was consulted. When, several years later, a psychologist was finally employed, he had to convince the company that its test was useless. Proceeding more cautiously but still seduced by eagerness, Macy's department store in 1919, the Waverly Press in Baltimore in 1921, and the Atlantic Refining Company all began intelligence testing. In at least one case it was believed that a critical score was found for managers; thus it was supposedly easy for the employment department to see whether any job candidate had the necessary intelligence to become a successful executive. Atlantic Refining hoped that its test would help in selecting supervisors. Its authors labored to eliminate the "ludicrous features" of the usual intelligence test as, for example, "How many legs has a Zulu?" Regardless of the technical discrimination of such items, it was their conviction that one result was to prejudice the applicant against both the test and the company. The correlation between the results of Atlantic's test and salaries was .37, and after about one year the test was abandoned.[30]

The unrealistic expectations of psychological testing inevitably led to trouble.[31] Many managers, ignorant of the actual potentialities of testing and attracted by the promise of trouble-free labor relations, were easy prey for a swelling horde of quacks. The intense hope with which the army testing program had been greeted enriched the opportunities for character analysis, physiognomy, graphology, and other systems whose fantastic claims seemed no less real to managers than the claims of industrial psychologists.[32] The most popular of these was character analysis, whose practitioners had long busied themselves with the sufficiently wealthy and gullible.

In 1913, Dr. Katherine Blackford interpreted character analysis for the industrial situation. Previewing her system in an industrial trade journal, she argued that any individual's personality traits could be determined by analyzing his physical traits: blonds were more agressive than brunettes and would therefore make better salesmen or advertising men. By analyzing handwriting, language, walk, and so on, the employer who understood the Blackford system could match the qualities of the applicant with the demands of the job. The following year, in a more complete statement of her system, Dr. Blackford articulated the basic faith to which all future character analysts would subscribe: "*There is a constant correspondence between the mental and psychical characteristics of any individual and his physical characteristics.*" By the 1920's this "observational method of character analysis" was increasingly advertised, and its advocates insisted, of course, that industry could save thousands of dollars each year through its use.[33]

Professional psychologists were also guilty of clothing their own preconceptions in scientific language, even though demonstrated fact to the contrary was available. Despite his other services, Hugo Münsterberg was among those who gave industrial psychology a costly false start. He had argued, in 1915, that what he called "group psychology" should be used by the employer when a large number of applicants had to be hired and when individual testing would be too expensive or too slow. His point was that "when several hundred men are to be employed for work which needs particularly certain mental traits and it is known from group psychology that just these traits prevail in an especial group, for instance, among the Italians or the Russians or the Irish, it seems safe to prefer men of that stock." Münsterberg's lead was picked up by other psychologists. In December, 1919, for example, Eliott Frost told colleagues in the American Psychological Association that "the laborer's attitude toward industrial relations is determined by his nationality more than any other single factor." Jews were described as "radical" and "keen-witted"; Italians were "highly emotional" as well as "sullen and moody"; Germans and Swedes were "placid"; and Poles and Croats were best for the "dirty work in the plant."[34] Any attempt to implement such a point of view was, of course, bound to fail. This kind of misdirection had to be overcome by scientific experimentation and practical demonstrations, which took time. In the interim, a host of quacks and frauds had an opportunity to persuade some managers to allow them to exercise their so-called skills.

To Mary Gilson, who was in personnel work and interested in scientific management in the 1920's, it was "incredible that certain well-known men, holding important positions in business and industry, shrewd in their

competitive activities, could be so naïve in adopting char-
latanry in their attempts to judge human beings." She
remembered that the period immediately following the
news of the military testing program "was a time when
businessmen were paying large fees to self-styled 'psychologists' who advised them, in all seriousness, concerning
the choice of executives and workers on the basis of such
traits as 'convex' or 'concave' faces."[35] One of the large
automobile manufacturers, for example, hired a character
analyst to select two salesmen out of a group of fifty applicants; after carefully measuring the cranial and facial characteristics of the group, the "expert" made his recommendations, which the company accepted.[36]

An example of the appeals made by these quacks is
found in an advertisement that appeared in 1920 describing the qualifications of a man who was looking for a job
as an employment manager. He described himself as "a
college graduate, who has specialized in sociology, psychology, economics, and preventive hygiene, also has taken
courses abroad in sociology, with eight years human engineering experience, combined with a knowledge of
character analysis, psycho-analysis, placement psychology,
safety, sanitary engineering, general welfare and industrial
democracy."[37] Needless to say, a man with such talents
could make a tremendous contribution to any company.

Though most employers were quick to realize when they
were being taken, they did not distinguish between frauds
and bona fide psychologists. Because of the utter confusion among psychologists about the nature or possibilities of industrial testing, it was indeed often difficult to
tell the difference. As more and more quacks were discovered, the reputation of genuine psychologists suffered.

The reaction was inevitable. From around 1922 to 1925
scores of firms discovered that psychological tests were not
producing the promised or anticipated results. One psychologist estimated that approximately 90 per cent of the

companies that began to use testing after the First World War found that the tests simply did not work and abandoned them. Another, reviewing this period in 1947, concluded that "so many mistakes were made that tests were discredited nearly everywhere." Though some revival of business interest in psychological tests was reported in 1925, the general managerial reserve persisted throughout the rest of the decade. In 1928, for instance, one observer wrote that "there has been considerable skepticism . . . in certain quarters in regard to just how far psychological tests can be applied in industry under the acid test of paying for themselves in the balance sheet."[38]

To some industrial psychologists it became increasingly clear that their future in industry largely depended upon their ability to convey accurate information about tests to management and to each other. The dismal record of most industrial-testing programs was a result of mistaken expectations and bad tests. As scientists, this group believed that if tests were refined and perfected they would actually work, and then management would be forced to admit the utility of psychologists in industry.

The limitations of industrial tests were only quietly discussed in the 1920's. Henry C. Link was perhaps the first industrial psychologist to insist that the first duty of the employment psychologist was to "test *tests* rather than applicants." He pointed out that, even in 1919, there were thousands of tests available to industry, but too little research had been done on a majority of those tests to permit an accurate statement of what they could do. Link also insisted that no psychological test was a complete predictive instrument because no test could foretell the degree of success or failure of any given individual in a particular job. All that tests could do was to predict that the chances of success of any one individual were better or worse than the chances of another. A few other psychologists also contributed to the discussion of the limitations of testing.

Among the difficulties they pointed out were the facts that tests were not final; criteria of success were lacking; tests for complex jobs could not be designed; groups large enough for statistical significance were difficult to obtain; correlations were always low; ability to improve, volition, likes, and interest were factors seldom included in a testing program. In 1927 John B. Watson, the major figure in behaviorism and then a vice-president of the J. Walter Thompson advertising agency, wrote that industrial tests "may help us to separate the sheep from the goats, [but] they will not tell us much about the flock of sheep left from which to make our individual selections." One survey toward the end of the decade concluded that psychological tests in industry failed because they did not test the whole personality; indeed, the argument continued, those aspects of personality which the tests ignored were perhaps the crucial factors in the success of the worker.[39]

A significant start had, however, been made in the direction of testing the whole personality of the worker. Westinghouse Electric in 1919 authorized research on the measurement of individual interests and likes, with the hope that the results would help to reduce training costs. The psychologist retained, B. V. Moore, after a period of sound research, concluded that the idea of testing such personality traits was promising. Most of the later "interest inventories," so popular in the 1940's and 1950's, were based on the work done at Westinghouse.[40]

A very few other companies conducted scientific testing programs during this period. At Clothcraft, where Walter Dill Scott had introduced testing, careful studies were made of the correlation between test results and on-the-job performance. Because the tests tested language skills and not intelligence, and because language skills had virtually nothing to do with job success, the correlation was .002, "practically nothing." But Clothcraft never expected the miraculous; the tests, said the employment manager, were used "merely as an additional check to what we had discovered by cruder means."[41] At Winchester Repeating Arms under the guidance of Link, at Procter and Gamble under Herbert G. Kenagy, at General Electric under Johnson O'Connor, at Scovill Manufacturing supervised by Millicent Pond, at Western Electric's Hawthorne Works, Eastman Kodak, Dennison Manufacturing, and the Southern California Gas Company, psychological testing was begun in a prudent and experimental manner. Validated testing for accident-proneness was conducted by Morris S. Viteles for both the Milwaukee and Philadelphia transit systems, by Bingham and Charles S. Slocombe for the Boston Elevated, and by A. J. Snow for the Yellow Cab Company of Chicago.[42]

Such caution, however, was not typical. Swiftly receding from the crest reached shortly after the war, the testing fad had all but disappeared by the mid-1920's. When managers and psychologists were forced to admit that the psychological test was something less than the ultimate panacea, testing was immediately abandoned by most companies. In 1925 only 4.5 per cent of even the "best-known" companies used tests; in the next five years the number of companies rose to only 7 per cent.[43] Many firms that had started psychological testing programs discontinued them because they did not work or because the economic and labor relations picture became so favorable that their use seemed unnecessary. In the later years of the decade, only a very few firms continued their efforts to refine and implement psychological testing.

Despite the scant use of tests, the image of what a good test might accomplish remained in the background of managerial thinking. If only it were possible to find a test that would actually do what it was supposed to do, all the problems of labor relations and personnel would certainly vanish. The image of what might be done was clear, for an industrial psychologist had painted it in certain strokes:

"The ideal employment method is undoubtedly an immense machine which would receive applicants of all kinds at one end, automatically sort, interview, and record them, and finally turn them out at the other end nicely labeled with the job to which they are to go." Alas, "it will be many a day before this consummation is reached."[44] Management would have to wait a bit before its problems of human relations could be solved by its technological skill, since, after all, the "immense machine" was a complicated affair.

Unlike their European counterparts, most American industrial psychologists were unconcerned with labor's reaction to "scientific" personnel, testing, and the "immense machine." During the 1920's a majority of them concerned themselves only with the attitudes of management toward their tests and with ways and means by which their tests could be improved. Only a very small group of these specialists asked themselves questions about the social implications of what they were doing.

Among the group that was worried about the implications of a psychology of industry, the usual position taken was that if psychology hurt labor it was management's fault, or perhaps psychology had been mishandled. Two psychologists in 1924 put it this way: "It is the obligation of every employer who introduces tests, and of every psychologist who works with them, to use care and tact, to regard them himself, and to describe them to others, in terms of the larger social perspective." A few years later another industrial psychologist argued that if workers were antagonized by the use made of psychology, the tests and test scores were not handled fairly. Toward the end of the decade still another psychologist suggested that management sometimes made unfair use of tests; even so, he felt that most of labor's resistance was a result of ignorance. Most of these men made a point of mentioning that industrial psychology, of itself, was impartial.[45]

All industrial psychologists failed to make one point.

They failed to note that the decision about the use to which industrial psychology was put was always made by management and never by the psychologists. Management had always reserved the right to make use of information supplied by paid consultants and to do with it whatever seemed wise. Psychologists supplied tools and information, not policy. They were therefore not in a position to argue that industrial psychology was impartial, for once their work was sold they lost control over it.

The final factor necessary to an understanding of the growth of industrial psychology during the 1920's is the reaction of labor. Unfortunately, this reaction is obscure, and for good reason. In that decade the right to determine the ability of employees was clearly a prerogative of management. Most of organized labor, in the 1920's as for the preceding thirty years, continued to concentrate on Gompers' program of a "bigger slice of the pie." Steadily losing membership—because of the persistence of company unions which were formed during the war, increasing productivity, paternalistic beneficence, and the pressure of hostile public opinion—organized labor was officially apathetic to the activities of the industrial psychologists. And trade unions themselves did practically no research in any area of industrial relations.[46]

Unhampered by labor resistance, encouraged by a few forward-looking managements, and aided by a growing body of empirical data, industrial psychology at the end of the decade was ripe for significant strides. But before the 1920's roared to their miserable close, industrial psychology found itself with a new partner in industrial research. New movements in industrial social science were started, and an entirely new and persuasive argument against psychological tests was formulated. In a factory on the outskirts of Chicago, sociology was to enter industry.

Hawthorne

THE SINGLE most important social science research project ever conducted in industry was carried out in the oldest manufacturing plant of the Western Electric Company, the Hawthorne Works. Before the studies at Hawthorne were completed, personnel of the National Research Council, Massachusetts Institute of Technology, Harvard Business School, and Western Electric were involved in one phase or another of the research. Eventually the company spent well over a million dollars on the research program and devoted thousands of man-hours to its completion. The Hawthorne research eventually modified permanently the nature and direction of industrial personnel work and became standard material for students of industrial sociology and human relations; the mark of this research on many other areas of social science has likewise been deep. Indeed, the research done at Hawthorne has been called "the first major social science experiment."[1]

One of the participants in some phases of the Hawthorne research said in 1929 that the conclusions of the studies were so important that industrial reorganizations quite as fundamental as those of the industrial revolution would result, and that the implications of the research were so basic that all of society would be inescapably affected. Stuart Chase, too, believed that if American managers became aware of the results of Hawthorne, "American industry would be revolutionized."[2]

The Hawthorne Works of Western Electric is located on Chicago's west side. In the 1920's the neighborhood was, as it is today, a low-rent district with a large immigrant population. Cicero Avenue, which runs along one side of Hawthorne, is dotted for miles both north and south with factories. As is typical of many sections of Chicago, the neighborhood is predominantly industrial, though residences of a kind separate one plant from another. By almost any standards, the area is a dismal place in which to work and live; there are few trees, a few patches of soot-coated crab grass, and littered streets.

The research program was started in the mid-1920's when there were some 25,000 employees at Hawthorne, by far the largest operating branch of the Western system (altogether Western Electric employed some 45,000 workers, who were located in almost every part of the United States). Western Electric has been the manufacturing and supply branch of the American Telephone & Telegraph Company, manufacturing telephones and other kinds of communication apparatus, installing central telephone offices, and buying and selling other electrical supplies.

The research at Hawthorne developed because of the failure of a series of experiments. In fact, at almost every stage of the research program, the researchers and company officials were forced to admit failure. But, because the management insisted on finding answers to the research questions, the studies developed from one phase to another, the experiment mushroomed from the original simple design into perhaps the most complicated industrial research ever conducted.

Before the experiments began, and even for a while afterward, psychologists assumed that the physical conditions of work were significantly related to the happiness and productivity of the individual worker. Especially did they point to lighting as a determining factor in accuracy, safety, and efficiency. Adequate lighting, they agreed, could make the difference between a successful and an unsuccessful factory.[3]

Late in 1924 the National Research Council, under a special grant, decided to determine the precise relationship of illumination to individual efficiency. The Council appointed a committee at M.I.T., under the direction of Professor D. C. Jackson, chairman of the department of electrical engineering, to conduct the research. To locate an appropriate industrial plant for the research was the task of a subcommittee appointed for the purpose (a member of this group was C. G. Stoll, who later became the president of Western Electric). After considering a textile mill in Pennsylvania and a jewelry plant in northern Massachusetts, the subcommittee accepted the suggestion that Hawthorne was the best possible site.[4]

At Hawthorne, the so-called illumination experiments progressed from one phase to another as the researchers were forced to conclude that they were not getting answers to their questions. The experiments on lighting lasted until the spring of 1927, when the research veered off in an entirely new and uncharted direction.

The first phase of the illumination experiments was quite simple. A test group of employees was put to work in a room where the lighting was experimentally altered, and notations of respondent production changes were made. In order to have a control over the experiment, a similar group whose lighting facilities remained unchanged was also observed. After experimenting with the lighting in the test group, the researchers concluded that illumination was only one factor, and that other factors not being measured also influenced productivity. They decided to eliminate or at least to control these other factors.

In the second illumination experiment, the researchers were startled by the results. The representative of the National Research Council at Hawthorne reported that as the lighting in this more carefully designed experiment was increased, production in the test group increased. This was expected. But production similarly increased in the control group, whose lighting had remained the same. "Consequently," he concluded, "we were again unable to determine what definite part of the improvement in performance should be ascribed to improved illumination."

This led to the final stage of the illumination experiments. The lighting intensity in the test room was decreased. Production went up. In the control group, too, production increased. The researchers finally reduced the level of illumination to about the intensity of moonlight, at which point the workers finally had to admit that they could no longer see what they were doing. Up to that point, production in both the test group and the control group had slowly but steadily increased.

The researchers and the company officials were compelled to admit that the illumination experiments failed to answer the question about the relationship of lighting to efficiency. They noted that lighting was only one apparently minor factor among many which affected productivity. So many uncontrolled factors operated on the employees that an attempt to measure only one could not succeed.[5] Vannevar Bush, then a professor of electrical power transmission at M.I.T., who was involved in the illumination experiments, recalled that the changes in output could not be explained by the researchers. The fact that productivity increased in ostensible defiance of the researchers' efforts seemed at the time to be so striking that Bush and the others had several conferences about it with the management of Western Electric.[6]

Any management would be fascinated by such persistent production increases, and that of Western Electric was no exception. It decided to search further for the reasons behind the increased productivity. This meant that the many factors influencing the efficiency of the workers would have to be isolated and measured. Not until the illumination experiments failed to answer the original question was it clear that these early studies were built on an overly simple view of human behavior. The company was now determined to pursue further the reasons for which workers were willing to work harder. From the failure of the illumination experiments and the determination of the company to continue its search for its employees' motivations, industrial sociology, as a distinct discipline, was born.

Even before the illumination studies began, Gestalt psychologists and others had pointed out that a human being always reacts to much more than the experimental stimulus or situation designed by the researcher. It took the people involved in the illumination experiments two and a half years to realize the validity of this, and then a new research program was instituted.

In April, 1927, the substance of the Hawthorne experiments began. At this time the plant employed about 29,000 workers. Because of the results, or lack of them, of the illumination studies, the management of the company believed that the "human reactions of people engaged in productive work have a much more important effect on their morale and efficiency than had previously been realized."[7] In cruder terms, the management wanted to find out how their 29,000 employees could be better motivated to increase their output. But the management did not know what it was getting itself into; nor did the social scientists. Western Electric stumbled into the Hawthorne studies.

The superintendent of inspection, G. A. Pennock, was perhaps the most influential company official to insist that the research be continued. The company decided that the best way to approach the problems uncovered in the illumination experiments was to isolate and observe a small group of workers, recording on as broad a front as possible the variations in output resulting from experimental changes in the working conditions. Seven months after this test group was started, Pennock, himself an M.I.T. graduate, called on the president of M.I.T., explained the Hawthorne researches, and asked him to suggest a man who could lend a professional hand. Pennock was sent to see Clair E. Turner, then an instructor in biology and public health at M.I.T. Turner was interested from the standpoint of a hygienist in the work that Western was conducting, and he insisted to Pennock that "a broad observational approach would be essential because many possibly causative factors would be changing in addition to the one factor . . . which had been purposely introduced." Pennock invited Turner to "undertake at once an evaluation of the statistical significance of the data coming out of the test room." Turner accepted, and in April, 1928, he became a consultant to Western, made periodic visits to Hawthorne, and observed the subsequent operations of the test room. He prepared some of the detailed reports of the experiment, and with his suggestions and assistance the design of the later stages of the test room was completed.[8]

On April 25, 1927, the relay assembly test room was opened in a corner of the regular relay assembly department. In this room were placed six experienced women operators whose job was to put together a little gadget called a relay, which was made up of between thirty and forty pieces.

The researchers expected that definite answers to the questions raised by the illumination experiment could be found here in a relatively short period of time. "At the beginning of the inquiry," two of the investigators reported, "the general interest was primarily in the relation between conditions of work and the incidence of fatigue and monotony among employees. . . . It was anticipated," they continued, "that exact knowledge could be obtained about this relation by establishing an experimental situation in which the effect of variables like temperature, humidity, and

duction of rest pauses and a shorter workday reduced the effects of cumulative fatigue. The third interpretation was that the rest pauses and other variations of hours and working conditions provided a relief, not from fatigue, but from monotony. Another suggestion was that the different wage system introduced in the third period, which allowed greater individual control of the amount of money received by each worker, caused greater effort on the part of the girls. And the last interpretation pointed out that the testroom changes in supervision better motivated the girls to their greater efforts.

At an early stage of the experiment the most persuasive of these interpretations probably was that the change in the methods of pay caused the increase in productivity. In order to test this hypothesis, two other experiments were conducted. First, a group of workers, mica-splitters, who were paid on an individual piecework basis, were selected and placed in a test room similar to the relay assembly test room, and no change in the method of payment was made. All of the results of the mica-splitting experiment corroborated those of the relay assembly test room: production increased regardless of the experimental changes imposed. A second experiment in the relay assembly test room also showed that production increased regardless of the method of payment.

After demonstrating that a better wage incentive did not explain production increases, the researchers were still in need of an answer. They were by now convinced that a higher wage incentive was, like lighting, only one factor in worker motivation, and that this single factor "was so dependent on its relation to other factors that it was impossible to consider it as a thing in itself having an independent effect on the individual." But the investigators began to get a glimmer of what eventually seemed to be the most adequate theory. The effect of the wage incentive on productivity, they suggested, could be determined "only in connection with the interpersonal relations at work and the personal situations outside of work."[11] ℛ

Even before the Hawthorne experiments were started, there had been much interest in the effect on production of rest pauses—which were also considered as an explanation of the results. Managers had believed that productivity might decrease if workers were given time off during the regular working day. Though some psychologists admitted that they did not know whether rest pauses would alleviate fatigue, more believed they knew enough to make recommendations to management. Psychologist Rex Hersey suggested that workers engaged in repetitive jobs would steal rest periods if they were not authorized by the management. It was his feeling that less time would be lost if definite and scheduled periods of rest were ordered, rather than left to the discretion of the workers. Elton Mayo, before the Hawthorne research began, also believed that he had discovered the real meaning of rest pauses. In the Continental Mills, a textile firm in Philadelphia, Mayo had introduced rest pauses in a department that had a high turnover and low production. Mayo believed that, as a result of these breaks, the workers had fewer "pessimistic reveries" and that morale improved; and a bonus for production was earned for the first time by workers in that department. Continental's president, Colonel Millard D. Brown, told a Rotarian audience that Mayo reduced turnover from an annual 250 per cent to 5 per cent. He ascribed this result to the rest periods, because of which the men became less fatigued, thought happier thoughts, and were generally better disposed to his company.[12]

The researchers at Hawthorne concluded that the rest pauses they had installed in several of the experimental periods of the relay assembly test room more effectively organized the personal time of the workers. They also concluded that rest pauses did shorten the working time of the employees because the rests were actually used for rest "and not merely as a disguised form of personal time out."[13] *Rp582*

Throughout the course of the experiments, the management of Western Electric watched for ways by which the rise in the productivity of the test room could be spread to the rest of the plant. Rest periods were tangible devices that could easily be instituted in any number of departments, and the management authorized their increased use in the hope that, even though the test-room studies never spelled out exactly the effects of rests on output, production might increase. The management was gratified to learn that production did rise as rest periods were installed in department after department. By the spring of 1930, about 5000 Western workers had been granted rests and the management had become convinced of the utility of such a departure.[14]

Though Elton Mayo had not been significantly involved in the test-room experiments, he felt strongly about the conclusions. The work on rest periods at Hawthorne seemed to him extremely useful; in fact, he wrote Pennock that "all the work on rest-periods prior to the Hawthorne inquiry . . . must be discarded as probably worthless."[15] But, it must be repeated, even the Hawthorne research failed to disclose the precise relationship between rest periods and output.

The explanation of increased productivity in the test room as a result of diminished fatigue was also part of an earlier tradition. Usually, the early industrial psychologists conceived of fatigue in purely physiological terms. But soon B. Muscio, one of the leading British investigators of industrial fatigue, admitted the failure of all of his research. In 1921 he concluded that fatigue was so complicated that no psychologist had yet made even faint progress, that all the tests of fatigue then in use were worthless, and that no test of fatigue would be possible even in the future. Seven years later the study of fatigue was reported to be "at a standstill." By the early 1930's, however, some American industrial psychologists, while admitting the essential validity of Muscio's position, insisted on retaining the concept of fatigue as well as a number of the typical tests. Even if fatigue was merely "a subjective state of mind," said one of these men, it "means a great deal to the person who is experiencing it." Fatigue could be understood only if its three major manifestations were kept in mind: a physiological state, a subjective feeling of tiredness, a decline in output. Eventually, psychologists and managers alike were forced to the pragmatic position of defining fatigue as that phenomenon, whatever it was, that reduced productivity.[16]

The Hawthorne experiments proved that relief from fatigue was too simple an explanation for the increases in production. The researchers concluded that all of the girls in the test room were working at all times well within their physical capacities. "There is no evidence," the official report of the studies continued, "in support of the hypothesis that the increased output rate of all these operators . . . was due to relief from fatigue." This hypothesis was therefore abandoned. The relief-from-monotony theory was similarly dismissed.[17]

What then had the investigators at Hawthorne found to be controlling the production increases? They learned that the six girls had responded to changes unimposed by the experimenters. The researchers found, as in the original illumination experiments, that they had still not succeeded in designing the experiment so as to eliminate extraneous influences on productivity. The six girls had become a group. This might not seem particularly significant, but the implications of becoming a group are crucial. Mayo described the girls this way:

At first shy and uneasy, silent and perhaps somewhat suspicious of the company's intention, later their attitude is marked by confidence and candor. Before every change of program, the group is consulted. Their comments are listened to and discussed; sometimes their objections are allowed to negative a suggestion. The group unquestionably develops a sense of participation in the critical determinations and becomes something of a social unit.[18]

Members of management and the researchers agreed with Mayo that the fact that the girls in the test room became a group was the most significant single fact about the experiment.[19]

In short, through the implementation of the research plan, the investigators unwittingly had changed every important characteristic of the social environment within which the girls worked. The research design, of course, allowed only for experimental changes, but the changes that resulted from merely placing the six girls in the same room were so important that the researchers were forced to rethink their positions. The girls became a conscious group. The researchers, however, were not entirely clear as to just what this meant. The Hawthorne experiments therefore had to take a new direction—to find out what a group was, what the implications of group activity were, what pressures and sanctions a group imposed upon its membership, and so on.

Before this next experiment was started, Elton Mayo was introduced to the Hawthorne studies and engaged as another consultant. Mayo, an Australian, took his M.A. degree at the University of Adelaide in 1899. Over twenty years later he came to the United States as a research associate in industry at the University of Pennsylvania. Moving in 1926 to the Harvard Business School as an associate professor of industrial research, he was promoted to a full professorship three years later. During the rest of his active academic life he remained at the Business School, where he eventually became head of the department of human relations in business.

Mayo was a warm and enthusiastic individual who dedicated his long and productive life to a search for ways in which human relations could be improved, especially in industry. His early approach to human relations was psychological, and he conceived of group, social, and indeed world problems in individual terms. The Hawthorne studies converted him into a social analyst, one who deeply believed in the primacy of the group as the major influence on individual behavior. His many experiments, of which Hawthorne was the most telling, were a dramatic step-by-step education for him. As his interests and convictions responded to the results of his industrial studies, he became the most prominent of industrial social scientists. He probably did more than any other individual to instigate the "human relations approach" to industrial problems. And it all started, or matured, during the course of the studies at Hawthorne.

During the winter of 1927-1928, Mayo spoke to a group of personnel men at the Harvard Club in New York City, where T. K. Stevenson, Western Electric's comptroller of manufacturing, told him about the test-room studies. Stevenson, in March, 1928, sent Mayo the available results of the studies and invited him to come to Hawthorne, at Western's expense, to observe the test room and to make suggestions; Mayo was assured that the Hawthorne studies were sufficiently broad in scope to hold his interest. A few days later Mayo accepted the invitation, and on April 24, 1928, with two assistants, he made his first trip to the Hawthorne Works.[20]

When Mayo first saw the Hawthorne plant, the relay-assembly test room was in its tenth period. At this time Mayo's interest was focused on the effects of rest periods on production, and the few specific suggestions that he made illustrated his belief that fatigue was essentially physiological and that blood-pressure readings were indicative of the effects of rest periods. This first visit was mainly conversational, but he firmly established a personal relationship with some of the Western officials who were interested in the experiments.[21]

Mayo was impressed with the fact that the Western Electric Company had authorized such basic and unguided experiments. Despite the rapport already existing between the management and university people, Mayo labored hard to improve the relationship and to break down the remaining barriers that separated managers from academicians. One of his closest colleagues recalled that, instead of taking the Hawthorne executives to their country clubs for lunch, Mayo took them for a bowl of onion soup at one of the several lunchrooms on Cicero Avenue. Apparently the folksiness of this gesture and of Mayo's whole approach was successful, for the relationship between Mayo and his Harvard colleagues and the Western Electric executives began well and apparently continued amicable for as long as they were in contact.

Fritz J. Roethlisberger, one of the authors of the standard account of the Hawthorne studies and a friend and associate of Mayo's, was significantly involved in the progress of the research after the completion of the test-room studies. He described these experiments as a "latching on" process. Mayo would bring to the factory different academicians who would then attach themselves to one phase or another of the studies depending upon their own interests.[22]

The experiment designed to illuminate the nature and significance of group life was greatly influenced by such a process. For Mayo introduced the anthropologist W. Lloyd Warner to the Hawthorne studies. Just before his first visit to the plant, one of the officials of the company wrote to Mayo that he believed that Warner's coming would be of great benefit. Warner was instrumental in designing the experiments aimed at explaining the impact of the group on the individual, though again the company officials did most of the work of designing the various phases of the experiments.[23] Roethlisberger believed that it was novel to apply the methods of anthropology in a modern society,[24] though others, especially the Lynds in their "Middletown" studies of Muncie, Indiana, had already used the anthropological approach. The next phase of the Hawthorne studies did rely on techniques and concepts developed by anthropologists.

In November, 1931, the bank wiring room phase of the Hawthorne experiments was started. Aside from Warner, others involved in the design of this research included Roethlisberger and four men of the Hawthorne Works: William J. Dickson, G. A. Pennock, M. L. Putnam, and Harold A. Wright. This experiment was designed to obtain "exact information about social groups within the company," as well as to determine the extent to which anthropological methods would be applicable to a modern factory. For six and one-half months, before the depression ended the experiment, the researchers observed a group of fourteen male operators. These men were neither placed in a separate test room nor subjected to experimental changes in the conditions of work, and the pay system remained unchanged. The researchers wanted the workers to be as little affected, in all particulars, by the experiment as possible. The memory of the fatal pitfall of the relay assembly test room, where the group under observation radically changed because it was under observation, was still quite fresh.

A major discovery that the investigators made in the bank wiring room was that the workers were intimately involved in a most intricate social organization of their own. Within the whole group there were several subgroups, cliques, and isolated individuals. Each worker's personal relations in this informal though rigorous social organization determined, to a large degree, his status in the group, the expectations of the other members, and the

kinds of satisfactions and expectations he ~~
In fact, the researchers learned, the pre~
that each individual had with the other ~
determined much of his behavior in the~

The standards of behavior, sentimen~,
and traditions to which the men in the bank w~
responded served two distinct functions: their socia~
ganization prevented deviant behavior of the group members, and it protected the entire group from outside inter-
ference or control. By ridicule and sarcasm the members
of the group kept their internal organization functioning
smoothly. Adjusting the reports of their daily production,
the wiremen controlled the amount of their work and thus
prevented management from imposing production quotas
or other demands upon them. The group itself decided
how much work was to be done, and regardless of the
efforts of management, the sanctions of the informal organization were more effective than those of the formal
organization. In other words, the small group, not management, determined the level of production.[25]

The major conclusions drawn from the bank wiring
room now seem so simple and obvious that one wonders
why they were not expected by the researchers rather than
reported by them with such breathless excitement.[26] But
hindsight may be misleading. In any case, the conclusions
of this phase of the experiments were of the utmost importance, for out of the bank wiring room came the subsequent widespread interest among both managers and
academicians in the human relations of industry.

The first conclusion of the researchers, and one which
deeply troubled the management of Western Electric, was
that every member of the group was "restricting"—that is,
regulating—his output. Not a single wireman was working
either as hard as he could or as hard as management had
ordered him to work. Despite the fact that the workers
received a bonus for production above a certain level, the

group pressures to conform to lowered productivity were too strong to resist. Regulation of output took two forms: the group's concept of a "fair day's work" was considerably lower than management's expectations, and regardless of the amount of production of any individual, the workers' reports of production did not vary from day to day or from week to week. "The departmental output curves were devoid of individuality," Roethlisberger and Dickson reported, "and approximated a horizontal line in shape." This meant that the workers distorted their output reports in two ways: first, they simply did not report accurately the amount of work they completed each day, and second, they reported inaccurately the time they actually worked, frequently claiming to have been prevented from working by conditions over which they had no control. For such "daywork allowance claims" the workers were paid their average rate. By increasing or decreasing such claims the wiremen could further adjust their production reports; for, if unavoidable delays prevented them from working, so their reports went, they could not be expected to produce.

The last conclusion of this experiment was that the performance of the men on the job bore no relation to their capacity to perform. Group standards seemed to determine the individual's productivity. Thus, ability and performance were not related. This conclusion was a direct criticism of the work of the industrial psychologists who had labored so hard during the 1920's to demonstrate their usefulness to management. Now, the Hawthorne investigators insisted, "tests of dexterity and intelligence showed no relation between capacity to perform and actual performance."[27] The relation of the individual to "the team" was the single most important factor determining individual productivity. Mayo, too, said that the work of the industrial psychologists had missed the main point in the motivation of workers. "The belief," he said, "that the behavior of an individual within the factory can be predicted before employment upon the basis of a laborious and minute examination by tests of his mechanical and other capacities is mainly, if not wholly mistaken."[28]

If the Hawthorne researchers were right, if performance and ability were unrelated, the industrial psychologists of the 1920's who had searched for the perfect psychological test had been wrong. The discovery that men with great potential and adequate training were among the lowest producers in the bank wiring room had many significant overtones. From Hawthorne on, the problems of selection, training, efficiency, and control would never seem as simple as they had appeared to the testing psychologists of the 1920's. But with the close of observations in the bank wiring room, the Hawthorne research was far from complete; indeed, the most significant phase was yet to come.

CHAPTER 6

Hawthorne
and Managerial Sociology

FROM AN academic point of view, the results of the bank wiring room phase of the Hawthorne experiments shed considerable light on the behavior of people in groups, and to this extent the experiment was highly successful. Management, however, was left with a number of troublesome problems. The informal social organization of the bank wiremen was sufficiently potent to regulate the behavior of the group; how to get the informal organization to accept the goals of management, the goals of the formal organization? If the informal groups proved too resistant to change, could not some way be found to address workers as individuals instead of as members of a group? Management, in short, had now the problem of doing something about the situation uncovered in the bank wiring room. Either the thinking of the group would have to be changed or the power of the group would have to be canceled.

Even before the bank wiring room experiment, there had been some discussion of informal groups within industry. Some men had known the major fact eventually to be discovered at Hawthorne: that group pressures control the behavior of group members. As early as 1918, for instance, an engineer with an Ohio utility company reported that his use of a "team system" resulted in increased production. Two years later, a different observer said that by transferring low producers to different groups, the manager could raise the production of all groups within the factory. Soon it was shown that in every industry, in every company and factory, there emerged spontaneously "natural groupings of workers" that were functional to the specific jobs. The formation of these groups could not be prevented by management, but management could learn—indeed, had better learn—how to handle them. By the late 1920's, even psychologists were writing about the importance of a "we feeling" in the modern factory.[1]

Ordway Tead, a personnel expert, recognized the "great potentialities" of controlling the kind of informal organization that had been discovered in the bank wiring room. "The conscious use of small groups," he wrote, "to forward the constructive thinking of the members of a corporation about its policies and methods is a possibility but newly recognized in the executive world."[2] The obvious trouble with the men in the bank wiring room, from management's viewpoint, was that the logic and traditions and sentiments of the men were opposed to the logic and traditions and sentiments of management. The workers insisted that production be at a much lower level than management desired and demanded. It would be extremely valuable to management if social scientists could show it how to make such ubiquitous informal groupings of workers think, as Tead put it, along "constructive" lines.

The phenomenon of regulation of output, or, as management and management-oriented social scientists termed it, "restriction" of output, was also recognized before the conclusions of the bank wiring room experiment were publicized. Many of the scientific managers were convinced that their systems of factory rationalization would eliminate such regulation. In 1911, for instance, Frederick Taylor wrote that "the workmen together had carefully planned just how fast each job should be done, and they had set a pace for each machine throughout the shop,

which was limited to about one third of a good day's work."
Taylor believed that this situation was characteristic of
virtually every factory in the country, and he saw it as his
task to devise methods whereby the control and determination of rates of production would be taken from the hands
of the workers and put into the hands of management.
Lillian Gilbreth, too, was convinced that scientific management could end "soldiering" in the shop.[3]

Some American workers, however, had ideas and convictions different from the ideas of scientific managers.
Indeed, it was probably the work of the scientific managers,
more than any other single factor, that increased the determination on the part of many American workers to
regulate their output. With the increasing appearance of
time-study men, workers began to believe that the retiming
of a job almost always meant a cut in pay. One worker put
it simply when he said that he "never knew a rate to be
raised after a time study."[4]

Men not committed to scientific management also had
recognized that workers regulated their production. In
1919, for example, it was said that "the rank and file believe restriction of production to be a practicable way of
attacking the problem of unemployment."[5] One executive,
who had labored in steel mills and coal mines for months
in an attempt to understand American workers, recalled in
1921 his experience when put on a job shoveling bricks out
of a ruined blast furnace:

When I started in I figured I'd keep going as long as I could
and loaf after I was played out. I couldn't get on with the pro-
gramme. First the little Italian boy tapped me on the shoulder
and advised "Lotsa time! Take easy!" I slowed down a notch
or two. A little later the Russian ... cautioned: "You keel yourself. Twelve hours long time." Finally, after everyone had
remonstrated, I got down to a proper gait—so you'd have to
sight by a post to see if I was moving. But at that I guess they
knew better than I—I'm certainly tired enough as it is.[6]

But he also indicated that workers regulated output not solely to conserve their physical energies. Working slower than management wanted meant to the worker that his job would last longer. In the hard times of the early 1920's, this was probably a compelling thought to large numbers of men.

As national unions lost strength in the 1920's, some workers found that regulation of their production was an effective means of protecting themselves against the logic of management. By regulating the amount of their work, employees had a powerful defensive weapon against a management using speed-ups, stretch-outs, and other "business interest" methods. At the beginning of the more severe depression of the 1930's, regulation of output constituted a major problem for management, for, as this depression deepened and workers saw increasing numbers of their fellows being laid off, the conviction became stronger that stringing out their own jobs by finishing them more slowly would keep them on the payroll that much longer.[7]

Perhaps the best expression of the sentiments that impelled the worker to regulate his production, despite incentive plans and production bonuses, is found in a poem hung on the bulletin board of an industrial shop in which its author labored. He called his poem "Harmony?" and this is how it went:

> I am working with the feeling
> That the company is stealing
> Fifty pennies from my pocket every day;
> But for every single pennie
> They will lose ten times as many
> By the speed that I'm producing, I dare say.
> For it makes me so disgusted
> That my speed shall be adjusted
> So that nevermore my brow will drip with sweat;
> When they're in an awful hurry
> Someone else can rush and worry
> Till an increase in my wages do I get.

No malicious thoughts I harbor
For the butcher or the barber
Who get eighty cents an hour from the start.
Nearly three years I've been working
Like a fool, but now I'm shirking—
When I get what's fair, I'll always do my part.
Someone else can run their races
Till I'm on an equal basis
With the ones who learned the trade by mining coal.
Though I can do the work, it's funny
New men can get the money
And I cannot get the same to save my soul.[8]

Regulation of output is a device used by executives and managers quite as much as by organized and unorganized labor. Entire companies, of course, control the output of their factories. As an economics professor pointed out in the early 1930's, "the same conditions that lead business men to curtail production when prices are falling, and to cut wages when labor efficiency is increasing, cause workers to limit output and reduce efficiency when wages are increasing. . . . If the workers' reasoning is wrong," he concluded, "then business economics as it is taught by employers and the business practices of modern industry generally must be equally wrong."[9]

The researchers at Hawthorne concluded that the regulation of output discovered in the bank wiring room was an example of "irrational" behavior on the part of the workers, and they believed that the workers' fear of a rate cut or of a layoff was not rational because in the recent past of the Western Electric Company such things had simply not happened. What, however, was to prevent the Western management from cutting rates and laying off workers? In fact, the bank wiring room experiment itself had to be discontinued because the depression so reduced the orders for the work of the wiremen that several were laid off.[10]

Elton Mayo felt that "restriction" indicated a sense of exasperation and "personal futility" on the part of the workers. The supposedly conflicting loyalties of the individual laborer could be eliminated only through "improved understanding."[11] But regulation of output meant something much more simple and compelling; it meant that workers did not trust management.[12] It was a defensive device that laborers employed when faced with the vastly superior power of management and management-oriented public opinion; it was a device calculated not to earn more money for the laborer but to protect his right of self-determination.

Why did the girls in the relay assembly test room increase their production while the men in the bank wiring room limited theirs? The relay assemblers were oriented toward the assumptions of management because, during the course of their experiment, the researchers took the girls into their confidence, asked for suggestions and criticisms. In a very real sense, the girls had an active voice in decisions impinging upon their conduct, and this genuine participation in policy gave them a stake in the outcome of the experiment. It was important to them to have the experiment "turn out right." Faulty social science turned out to be profitable management practice. The bank wiremen, on the other hand, were left alone by the researchers. Because the relay assembly experience had demonstrated the danger to science of allowing the subjects to become involved in and committed to the experiment, the men in the bank wiring room were allowed to maintain the informal organization they had developed before the study began. Because the Hawthorne researchers themselves accepted and approved of management policy, they were unable adequately to explain why the informal organization, the logic and sentiments, of the bank wiremen were opposed to the logic and sentiments of management, so they ended by describing the workers' behavior as "irrational."

While the bank wiring room research was under way, the Hawthorne investigators spent much of their time and focused their attention on yet a different matter. Before the bank wiring study was completed, they began to interview selected groups of Western Electric employees. This interviewing program originally was designed as a method of determining ways of improving supervision in the company. An Industrial Research Division at Western Electric was formed early in 1929; its job was to continue the interviewing program and the test-room research, and to conduct supervisory training.

At first, the interviewers gathered workers' responses to a series of management programs, then constructed a catalogue of complaints, which the company hoped would be useful in the formulation of policy. But, to their surprise, the interviewers could not keep the workers on the preselected subjects. Employees wanted to talk about what was important to themselves, not about what the interviewers thought was important. The researchers then decided that the interviewing program should be greatly modified—that the interviews should become nondirective, that whatever the workers wanted to talk about would be allowed. After this change, several workers commented about "improved" working conditions, which in fact had not been changed; one worker even said that he thought wages were better since the beginning of the interviewing, though the wage scale had not been changed in any way. One of the company researchers said that nondirective interviewing provided several advantages: a feeling of confidence on the part of the employees was stimulated, an "emotional release" was experienced by many employees, and others gained a "feeling of recognition."[13]

Fritz Roethlisberger, who spent the sumer of 1931 at Hawthorne beginning the interviewing of supervisors, concluded that working conditions, wages, and hours were not "things in themselves." "They must be interpreted," he said, "as carriers of social value," and he elaborated this point:

To understand the meaning of any employee's complaints or grievances, it is necessary to take account of his position or status in the company. This position is determined by the social organization of the company: that system of practices and beliefs by means of which the human values of the organization are expressed, and the symbols around which they are organized—efficiency, service, etc. In these terms it is then possible to understand the effect upon the individual of . . . the events, objects, and features of his environment, such as hours of work, wages, etc.[14]

Before the interviewing program was closed, over 40,000 complaints were voiced, though, the official report added, "there was not one single unfavorable comment expressed about the company in general." Perhaps even more surprising was the fact that in the 20,000 interviews no employee mentioned unions.[15] A University of Wisconsin sociologist, C. W. M. Hart, found several possible explanations for this strange silence. The first, which Hart seems not to believe, was that because there was no union at Hawthorne at the time the interviews were conducted, the workers conceivably were as uninterested in unions as the researchers indicated. His second and most plausible suggestion was that unionists in the factory simply avoided the interviews. Hart's last explanation was that all the researchers, at this time, were gentle Harvard men, who, "while completely competent to . . . listen intelligently to the workers' preoccupations on the job, . . . [have] not been so enthusiastic about following the worker *off* the job into the sleazy union halls and crowded noisy taverns where his union preoccupations find freer expression."[16]

To the researchers the single most impressive fact that emerged from the interviewing program was that many favorable comments were made by the employees about the interviewing process itself. Being interviewed, being allowed to blow off steam, seemed to do the workers some real good. As nondirected interviews were substituted for the original question-and-answer approach, a definite emotional catharsis was achieved. After an interview, workers seemed to be happier. Any management is deeply interested in ways to make its workers "happy," so long as the costs in terms of power and cash are not thought to be prohibitive. The fact that a sympathetic listener seemed to make workers happy had profound meaning to both the researchers and the management of the Hawthorne Works, as well as to the Western Electric system as a whole.

In 1936 this fact was made the basis of an active program. The researchers, Mayo, Roethlisberger, Putnam, Pennock, and Dickson, called the program "personnel counseling." Mayo was instrumental in convincing the management of Western to begin a permanent counseling program.

Counseling, as the management of Western Electric conceived of it, was a method of helping people think in such a way that they would be happier with their jobs. American Telephone & Telegraph thought of counseling as a process through which employees made their ideas clearer to themselves by trying to make them clear to someone else. Both companies continuously pointed out that the counseling process was entirely voluntary: "People," said Dickson, "cannot be 'counseled' against their wishes." From 1936 to 1955, about 22 per cent of the interviews conducted, nearly 120,000, were initiated by the employees; however, over 73 per cent, nearly 400,000, were initiated by the counselors with the consent of the worker involved, and 3 per cent were initiated by the worker's supervisor. It seemed as if management had at last found a way to "encourage" employees to think "constructively."

At Western Electric, counselors were appointed from the departments in which they would serve, and no educational or professional experience was required, though the Division of Counseling gave them in-plant training.

Most important of all, they had to be "well-liked" by the people in their departments. A dominant theme throughout Western's discussion of counseling was that a well-trained counselor would be a likely candidate for promotion to a supervisory position, and it was thus hoped that counseling would both provide a recruitment pool for managerial positions and perform a service for workers.

The functions of the counselor were rather clear. A former counselor said that she and her colleagues were instructed to deal "with attitudes toward problems, not the problems themselves." Regardless of all the technical gobbledygook that has been written about the functions of the counselor, it all simmered down to the plain injunction that he was to listen to any problem of any employee, good worker or not; that he was not to give advice or argue; that he should make no promises about remedial action. The counselor was not to be limited by a problem- or efficiency-oriented approach; he was just to listen to the employee talk. Among his duties, according to an official publication of the Western Electric Company, was one of particular interest: he was to watch constantly for signs of unrest and to try to assuage the tension by discussion before the unrest became active.[17] He was to try to dilute or redirect dissatisfaction by helping the employees to think along "constructive" lines. Management hoped that through this process of adjusting people to situations rather than situations to people, grievances, tensions, absenteeism, turnover, low production, and militant unionism would be avoided. In counseling, management hoped that it had found a counterweight to the kind of informal organization discovered in the bank wiring room.

Though Western instructed its counselors not to try to adjust people to what it thought were really bad situations,[18] a former counselor argued that the counseling process, in practice, functioned in precisely that way. Mrs. Jeanne L. Wilensky, who was a counselor at Hawthorne from 1947 to 1950, said that "one would have to be extremely naïve . . . to claim . . . that counseling does not drain off grievances that might otherwise find expression in other channels." "Other channels" could be union channels.

The Hawthorne Works had successfully resisted the organizing efforts of all "outside"—that is, national—unions. For several years, in the 1940's, both the International Brotherhood of Electrical Workers and the United Electrical Workers, among others, tried in vain to organize the plant. The independent Communications Equipment Workers was formed and began functioning at Hawthorne in 1937. Apparently many workers were dissatisfied with this "inside" union but were not able to switch their affiliation to a stronger and national organization.[19] The research director of the Communications Workers of America put the whole matter briefly when she pointed out that the entire telephone industry was anti-union and relied on personnel procedures to frustrate legitimate union purposes. Both American Telephone & Telegraph and Western Electric were shown in a congressional investigation to have been anti-union.[20]

Starting with a single counselor appointed in 1936, the organization grew rapidly. At the end of the first year, five counselors were active, and by 1938 the number doubled; by 1941, twenty-nine counselors serviced about 10,000 workers. In a single year, 1949, including the pay for time lost by the workers who were being counseled, the program cost Western Electric $326,000. By 1954, about sixty-four men and women were devoting full time to counseling duties in the Western system. Despite this, only five of the twelve Western Electric plants had counseling services, and even at Hawthorne the coverage was far from complete, for about one-third of the workers never made use of the counseling system.[21]

In 1956, for reasons not disclosed by the company, the entire counseling program was put under review with an eye to its possible discontinuance. One suggestion was that, thereafter, counseling should be handled by supervisors. Even though the Western management, before the research began, and the Hawthorne researchers believed that the supervisor was the key man in determining the conduct of workers, the supervisor simply neither had the time nor could get the practice to function adequately as a counselor. For all practical purposes such a transfer would mean the virtual end of counseling in the organization which gave it birth.[22]

Through these stages the research at the Hawthorne Works progressed. Beginning with the illumination experiments in 1924 and continuing through the relay assembly test room, the bank wiring room, interviewing, and counseling, the total program developed from an attempt to pinpoint the effect of specific conditions of work on the productivity of the worker, to the broad attempt to understand and influence the motives and behavior of people at work.

The precise impact of the Hawthorne studies, even on the Western Electric Company, is difficult to assess. Rest pauses were instituted as a result of this research, and counseling was introduced to American industry and other institutions because of the work done at Hawthorne. But, as one Western Electric official observed, the Hawthorne research was not reported to management in the form of specific recommendations, but was descriptive, emphasized a point of view, and was not directed at any single managerial problem. An executive of the Illinois Bell Telephone Company suggested that the impact of the research could best be found in a changed emphasis in the management-training program of his company, while an officer of American Telephone & Telegraph believed that the effect of Hawthorne and other social-science research would be more important in a few years than it had yet become.[23]

In an attempt to widen the effects of the research, two

of the Hawthorne men who were involved in the research were moved to the New York headquarters of Western Electric and American Telephone & Telegraph. Both, however, were given vague staff jobs with little authority and little definition of their duties. Putnam at American Telephone & Telegraph and Wright at Western Electric were unable to implement the Hawthorne results to any great extent, and eventually both men left the company. It was Roethlisberger's opinion that the main reason for this failure was the low prestige in the Bell System of Western Electric; if the Hawthorne results had come from the Bell Laboratories, he suggested, it would have been a different story. The point remains that, even now, the implementation of the Hawthorne research is more widespread in some other companies than it is in either the Bell System or Western Electric.[24]

To Elton Mayo, the most significant discovery that emerged from Hawthorne was that workers and management both were largely devoid of what he called "social skills." He believed that the work industrial psychologists had done before Hawthorne was excellent in its way but was dangerously narrow. Because psychological-aptitude and other kinds of tests focused on technical skills, the attention of researchers and managers alike was diverted from the real need of human society, industrial and otherwise—the ability to cooperate. Because Mayo did not conceive of ways in which labor could contribute to cooperation except by adjusting to the given situation, he always insisted that the obligation for cooperation was management's. The final conclusions of the official report of the Hawthorne research emphasized this point of view: "(1) Management should introduce in its organization an explicit skill of diagnosing human situations. . . . (2) By means of this skill management should commit itself to the *continuous* process of studying human situations—both individual and group—and should run its human affairs in terms of what it is continually learning about its own organization."[25] *R - 60Y*   *Mayo p ǰ 20*

Before Mayo had become involved in the research, he had approached the problems of industry and society in individual terms, psychological terms. This is best illustrated by a statement that he made in 1924: "The single most important factor which determines productive efficency is the mental preoccupation (or revery) of the worker as he works." Like other psychologists in the 1920's, he had been eager to justify his profession to management—to convince management that he knew its problems, understood its needs, and sympathized with its goals. By suggesting that the "reason why psychological investigation is necessary to industry is that these pessimistic reveries which culminate in disorder and unrest (absenteeism, high labor turnover, strikes) are relatively easily controlled provided that the management has a means of discovering the nature of the causes," Mayo made quite clear the extent to which he was committed to management, and this commitment was largely responsible for the ways in which the Hawthorne studies were interpreted.

Even during his psychological period, however, Mayo had argued that the "total situation" of the worker must be analyzed if his conduct in the factory was to be understood. To Mayo this meant that the psychologist would have to study the worker in his home as well as on the job.[26] Not until he was exposed to the evolution of the research at Hawthorne did he realize that more than individual psychology was needed to understand human behavior. As he wrote to the dean of the Harvard Business School:

Whereas before the Western Electric experiments one had known the value of the clinical approach and had also known . . . that social changes are somehow related to the extensive maladjustment of our times—whereas this had been known before, the extension of inquiry into the social field had been pre-

vented by defective technique and lack of skilled personnel.
From this moment onwards, the social investigation has been
pressed as actively as the individual. The whole inquiry indeed
has become social.[27]

A most important implication of his research that Mayo
seems not to have fully understood was that the social approach to industrial problems proved to be dangerous.
When it was seen that small groups like the bank wiremen
were sufficiently strong to oppose management, the Hawthorne researchers, in their counseling program, reverted
to an individual approach to the problems of the factory.
Starting from a conviction that individuals had to be dealt
with individually, the Hawthorne researchers and Western
officials swung to the position that human life had meaning
only in social terms, and finally, through counseling, they
returned to the point from which they had started. Using
the tools and frames of reference of sociology, the Hawthorne researchers eventually placed themselves in the
camp of psychology. Nonetheless, sociology was introduced to American industry.

What Mayo meant by the "extensive maladjustment of
our times" was that "in the process of continuously raising
the standard of living American civilization has unwittingly
destroyed all *standards* of living." The scramble for financial success and material acquisition had taken the place
of social life.[28] He pictured a happy preindustrial America and argued that individual isolation, rootlessness, the
"lonely crowd," as characteristic social manifestations were
caused by industrialism. The intense physical and social
isolation of frontier and backwoods existence was left out
of his picture. So were the pathetic, socially isolated lives
of alienated farmers and laborers, of free and indentured
whites of the lower classes, and of parts of the conveniently
forgotten slave population. The dislocation and isolation of
millions of immigrants he did not discuss. But he went on
to say that in this simple and good preindustrial America,

when standards were supposedly clear and obligations and privileges supposedly defined, "the individual lived a full communal life and knew that his services were a necessary social function." The growth of an industrial civilization, with its premium on high mobility, destroyed this satisfying knowledge of social worth. The *established* agrarian America was transformed into an *adaptive* industrial society. According to Mayo, young Americans in the eighteenth and nineteenth centuries had been trained for economic and social life by a form of apprenticeship; in this bewildering twentieth century they either were given no such training or, receiving the same nineteenth-century training, found it irrelevant to their adaptive needs. In short, the social cooperation which Americans had previously been able to achieve in their peaceful corporate society was sadly gone from the modern scene. No longer did they know how to get along with each other.[29]   Mayo ps 9/13

Mayo's commitment to an Agrarian Golden Age throws considerable light on his mind and his works. Standing square in a tradition fathered by Jefferson and supported by the historian Frederick Jackson Turner, Mayo was utterly convinced that there had been magic in the forests and soil of America. Because he believed that there was a mystical but direct relationship between farming and truth, he believed that virtue had been more prevalent in America when her farmers outranked men in other occupations in both numbers and power. An industrial society, by definition, could not be virtuous, for as men lost sight of the soil they lost sight of nature; and in so doing, they lost sight of the meaning of life and fell victim to the glossy gadgetry of modern industrialism. For Mayo, then, the problem of the modern factory was clear: how to make possible the re-creation of Agrarian Virtue, Agrarian Loyalty, and the Agrarian Sense of Community in the twentieth century's world of skyscrapers and subways, of smoke and steam?

Because of his peculiar image of a Garden of America,

Mayo was led into his diagnosis of the ills of industrialism. In a factory society men were uprooted, were alienated from each other and from their own traditions, were bewildered by their lack of belonging. Society became atomized, and a vast mass of isolated individuals took the place of the satisfying and meaningful community characteristic of the Garden; huge institutional associations replaced the former intimate families and communities. Hence, to Mayo, it made sense to look for solutions to the problems of the modern world not in institutions but in the small groups of men working in the factory. If, somehow, these groups would for once be recognized as potential vehicles for recreating the values and spirit of the vanished Garden, a major step toward finding again the necessary means of social cooperation would be taken.

Another conclusion Mayo reached on the basis of his assumptions about the past was that the typical institutions of the industrialized world were organized for conflict instead of cooperation. In the Garden the small and psychologically satisfying communities had literally no basis for conflict; in the twentieth century, because of the way institutions defined their roles, there was literally no basis for cooperation. And this was especially true of the confrontation of capital and labor. If the small group inside the factory could replace the lost but universally necessary community of the Garden, and if institutional conflict could somehow be avoided, Mayo would be well on his way to establishing a new Garden, mechanized to be sure, but the happiest solution under the circumstances. If conflict was unnecessary, and he believed that it was, unions had no function to perform and could easily be dispensed with. Though Mayo never wrote such a prescription, his disciples did; Mayo himself solved the problem of the conflict between labor and management by ignoring organized labor.

Mayo's analysis of industrial society rests on the implicit

assumption that workers act from emotions and generalized feelings, while management responds to logic. In all of his voluminous writings he only twice referred to unions, once when he pointed out that they resist change, and again when he said that unions, like management, organize for industrial conflict rather than cooperation. But "cooperation in the Mayo perspective," wrote one analyst, "is a relationship involving happily unorganized (nonunionized) workers who unthinkingly and enthusiastically comply with the wishes of management toward the achievement and maintenance of its economic objectives. . . . This is also the content of 'morale,' " this writer concluded, "as used by the Mayo group." [30]   To Mayo, in other words, industrial cooperation meant that labor should do as management said.

This cast in his thinking distorted his vision of industrial society and prevented his achieving any empathy with labor. It permanently marked him as a spokesman for management, and it converted the group of disciples that gathered around him into researchers seeking ways and means of making industry, in management's own terms, more effective and more efficient. Not once did the Mayo group, or Mayo himself, indicate that perhaps workers knew what they were doing when they opposed managerial "logic." Never did the Mayo school suggest that perhaps the informal organization of workers, as exposed in the bank wiring room, was a necessary measure established by workers because management was already too effective and too efficient. It would have been more accurate, certainly more scientific, for the Mayo school to insist more strongly than it did that management was itself laced with informal groupings of executives—that managers, exactly like blue-collar labor, acted emotionally and irrationally. But as Mayo spoke, so spoke his Harvard Business School colleagues. This anti-union, pro-management attitude looms large in the thinking of virtually every one of the men who at one time or another were associated with Mayo, and for this reason their work has been severely criticized by a small but increasingly articulate group of social scientists.[31]

To date, the greater part of the American labor movement has not been seriously concerned with the Hawthorne results, and it is possible that most of labor's leadership is even unaware of the research. Despite the potential threat to the policies unions guard most jealously, the vast bulk of organized labor goes about its business of negotiating for higher pay rates, different hours and conditions of work, and, of course, the so-called fringe benefits. The examples of resistance to Hawthorne, though rare, are, however, significant. The Iowa Bell Telephone Company, for example, was forced to abandon its counseling program because its union became convinced that the technique was merely a management tool for prying into the private affairs of the workers.[32]

In 1949 the United Auto Workers' monthly education magazine, *Ammunition,* in an article about Mayo, the Hawthorne results, and the whole human-relations approach to industrial problems, also showed its hostility to Hawthorne, but showed also the general intellectual bankruptcy of American labor in its petulant negativism. Labeling the researchers "cow sociologists" (contented workers will give more "milk"), the union was severely critical:

The Prophet is Elton Mayo, a Harvard University professor who has been prying into the psychiatric bowels of factory workers since around about 1925 and who is the Old Man of the movement. The Bible is his book, the Human Problems of an Industrial Civilization. The Holy Place is the Hawthorne Plant of the Western Electric Company (the wholly owned subsidiary of one of the nation's largest monopolies, the AT and T). At Hawthorne, Ma Bell, when she wasn't organizing company unions, allowed Professor Mayo to carry on experiments with a group of women workers for some nine years. . . .

For these nine years about every kind of experiment a very bright Harvard professor could think of was tried on the women.

Everything you do to white mice was done to them, except their spines and skulls were not split so the fluid could be analyzed. . . .

What did make them produce and produce and produce with ever-increasing speed was the expression of interest in their personal problems by the supervisor; interviews by psychiatrically trained social workers and (later on) the way they were paired off with friendly or unfriendly co-workers.

Now obviously this is the greatest discovery since J. P. Morgan learned that you can increase profits by organizing a monopoly, suppressing competition, raising prices and reducing production.[33]

The theory of managerial trusteeship implicit in the thinking of the Hawthorne social scientists was thus sensed by some. If Mayo's conception of the past and his diagnosis of the present were accurate, it followed that modern industry must provide the now lost satisfactions that once characterized the lives of workers and especially farmers. Thus, if Mayo and his circle were followed, management was encouraged and instructed to enter not only the intellectual, social, and financial lives of its workers, but through counseling, to expose their most personal thoughts and aspirations.

The management of Western Electric has insisted that such thinking and motives did not and do not apply to it. This management showed that many workers expressed real relief from their problems when given the opportunity to talk to a sympathetic listener. Western management strongly maintained that it was interested in neither manipulation nor control of its workers, and that its counseling program was different from the programs used by other companies and institutions. One Western executive rightly cautioned that " 'counseling' in industry has included such a diversity of activities and viewpoints that being 'for' or 'against' counseling has no clear meaning, until such an attitude is related to an actual situation—to a specific program, in a specific context."[34]

But personnel counseling in general, using the tested techniques of the Catholic confessional and the psychiatric couch, has frequently resulted in labor losing control of the nature and conditions of work. It has often meant that the potency of labor organization has been weakened and made less meaningful; and that management has finally found, if it chooses to use counseling as such, a most devastating weapon to employ in its continual struggle for power. Organized labor has no constructive alternatives to offer, but it has finally taken the first hesitant steps in the direction of opposing one of the most seductive levers of social control that the ingenuity of man has ever invented.

CHAPTER 7

Depression
and Repression

AMERICAN INTELLECTUAL life in the 1930's was remarkable for its political vitality. And the big political questions obviously concerned the nature of business and the relations between business and the other public institutions. Rarely have American men of letters or science been personally committed to a political system other than the one to which they were most accustomed, the status quo. During the 1930's, however, some articulate intellectuals moved leftward in their political views, and radical social analyses were heard more and more often as scholars and scientists convinced themselves that Franklin Roosevelt was willing to lead his country along new and exciting paths. Indeed, intellectuals found themselves in the unusual position of being sought after by men of power in the national administration. The political atmosphere and mood of a large part of the nation moved to the left, and in some circles it even became fashionable to criticize the secure world of the self-made man, the heroes of profit-making, and many others of the previously sacred cows of free enterprise.

The New Deal never did make up its collective mind about the power and place of business in America. It seems clear that the early New Deal, characterized by the NRA, was motivated by the idea that business could be made safe for America; but the later New Deal believed that business could not be trusted and that therefore legislation like the Wagner Act and the Social Security Act was needed to protect the people from some of the economic hazards they faced under uncontrolled free enterprise. With war, of course, all such thinking quickly became irrelevant, as American industry became the backbone of national security. Because the government vacillated in its attitude toward business and industry, it was sometimes difficult for the businessmen and managers to determine whether they were in or out of favor. Many took the intellectually easy way out by assuming that F.D.R.'s administration had been consistently opposed to "sound business practices."

Twin horrors, the depression and the CIO, also rose to haunt management during the 1930's. Both would be rendered vulnerable to attack, managers and social scientists agreed, by a fuller understanding of employees' thinking, attitudes, and behavior. "Today, as never before," said one social scientist when the fact of the depression was becoming painfully obtrusive, "the resources, the desires, the motivations, and the capacities of the industrial employee are the subject of major managerial concern"—a concern that was slowly becoming articulate. The failure of some managements to take the human element seriously, according to one plant manager, led to the widening breach between capital and labor. Managers were increasingly warned of the folly of attempting to thwart the aspirations of their workers, even if union-oriented. A major idea was beginning to take shape: managers should learn what employees wanted. By "capitalizing" and "integrating" these wants "into the life and needs of business," managers could funnel human behavior into the most profitable channels.[1]

The characteristic, though not universal, form taken by this increasing managerial concern with the human problems of labor was expanded personnel work. During the 1920's, many managements had considered this activity as an overhead cost, so that, after the depression set in and the frenzied search for ways to cut costs began, personnel work was bound to suffer somewhat. In many firms the work of personnel departments was reduced, and in others it was even wholly abandoned. But the realization that in personnel work industry had found an indispensable tool with which to deal with employees had taken too firm a hold to be entirely eliminated even by the depression. A few companies even increased their personnel activities over the 1929 level.[2]

At the beginning of the depression, it was found that about 31 per cent of 302 companies surveyed had industrial-relations departments or at least directors, and that more than half of the companies that employed over 5000 workers had such departments. Another survey conducted in 1930 disclosed that certain personnel activities were actually increasing: 82 per cent of the firms studied kept records of labor turnover; almost half maintained some kind of employment-expense budget; a sizable percentage conducted job analysis and merit rating. In the next two years the movement toward centralized personnel departments had developed more vigor in the highly industrialized sections of the economy. All of the major automobile manufacturers and their bigger suppliers of parts had established centralized personnel. In the food-products industry, in iron and steel, and in petroleum refining, more than 75 per cent of the firms had done the same. But the Southern textile industry and the boots-and-shoes industry had less than 25 per cent so organized. Over all, about two-thirds of American industry had adopted centralized personnel.[3]

A rather full picture of the personnel and industrial-relations activities of American industry in the middle of the depression can be sketched. In 1935 the National Industrial Labor Relations Act became law, and employers were in greater need than ever of formalizing relations with their employees. Personnel matters, once considered the private prerogative of employers, were becoming part of an insti-

tutionalized pattern that, in certain respects, the depression and some New Deal measures encouraged despite the
increased costs to management. When the NRA became
law, for instance, some personnel men felt that the require-
ment to raise or maintain wages would necessitate greater
labor efficiency and therefore would provide an impetus to
personnel work. The growth of unionism meant that seniority, not necessarily skill, would take precedence in rehir-
ing workers who had been laid off. To many managements
this indicated that greater care would have to be taken in
the original selection of manpower.[4]

A number of devices declined in use from 1927 to 1935,
especially bonuses (except for quality bonuses) and stock-
purchase plans; profit-sharing remained at about the same
level. The use of insurance facilities, mutual benefit associations, pensions, savings plans, apprentice training, and
employee representation all increased. By 1935, of the firms
included in the survey which employed over 5000 workers,
about 80 per cent had personnel departments of some kind,
a significant increase over the 1932 figure.

Treating the nation as a whole and disregarding the size
of the companies, about one-third of the nation's industrial
concerns had personnel departments in 1935. A higher percentage had centralized employment plans though less had
centralized transfer or discharge. Only a little more than
half of American industry kept employment records and
much less than half maintained turnover records. Even
during the depression, no more than 20 per cent of American industry had established definite lay-off procedures.[5]

It is clear that a significant number of managers no
longer considered personnel management as an overhead
cost that could safely be eliminated should business conditions worsen. For example, Procter and Gamble, always
a leader in personnel matters, sounded a typical note when
it said, in 1936, that "enlightened industrial relations are
a matter of sound business, and not of paternalism and wel-

fare." Many other firms agreed that the establishment of formal personnel departments and activities was one means of combating the depression, and some became convinced that by the use of such techniques the growing threat of unionism could be prevented or at least forestalled. Companies that had never made a formal statement of employee-relations policies issued one,[6] and throughout the whole structure of American industry a growing awareness of the business importance of personnel management took hold.

By 1933, one of President Hoover's research committees reported that the over-all attitudes of employers were changing and that personnel management was becoming more positive. The committee believed that this change in attitude was quite as important—in terms of better treatment for labor—as the activities of labor unions. However, the committee stated, the first purpose of much of this personnel activity was still the curtailment of union strength, though much that was being done for the worker did in fact improve the conditions of labor.[7]

Managerial emphasis on the human problems of labor was also good for industrial social scientists, who were, after all, specialists in many of the areas that managers were coming to appreciate as important. But problems still existed. Perhaps most significant was the difficulty managers and social scientists had in communicating. Not only could the managers not understand psychologists and other social scientists, but the social scientists had a hard time grasping the vocabularies of foremen and workers. One proposal was to allow the social scientists to continue their research but to have engineers apply the results in industry, at least until such time as social scientists learned how to speak English.

Social scientists themselves also had a few quiet comlaints. They worried lest the managerial emphasis upon immediate and practical results would destroy research.

Despite the fact that industrial researchers frequently said that they could not "uncover truth on schedule," many managers insisted that if social science increased costs instead of reducing them, industry would have to manage somehow without such aid. The experts came to realize the full implications of this position, and they tried to show management that they really knew how to raise profits by demonstrating ways to cut costs. Special techniques that had won some social scientist a measure of cooperation from a specific management were publicized in the technical journals with as much care as the substantive research itself. Psychologists even took booths at business shows to explain to the milling crowds of executives "the apparatus of their calling."[8]

By the time the depression rolled in, the aims of industrial social science had already been fashioned. Some few industrial social scientists responded to the national political climate, which was now somewhat to the left of Hoover's New Era, and insisted that the guiding purpose of their work should be the welfare of labor, not of management, and that the aims of the two were irreconcilable. But most held to their pro-management orientation. Industrial social scientists were hired by industry to help it realize its own aims—to help the manager do what the manager wanted to do. Those interested in serving industry had to serve industry.

The image of the laborer that some industrial social scientists had provides a clue to their assumptions about the economic system. One psychologist described a job that "could be done by an animal," a job not worthy of his attention. A few years later the same expert clarified his view of the man who labors by writing that such a man "is limited by his heredity to a rather simple type of performance with its attendant modest compensation, his family is too large, and he can seldom do much more than provide necessities." Two other psychologists analyzing dissatisfac-

tion among industrial workers concluded that most industrial unrest is caused by emotional maladjustment of the
worker. The industrial laborer does not know that he is
emotionally maladjusted, so he mistakenly attributes his
dissatisfaction to his job. It is illuminating to note that
these psychologists did not suggest that workers might
have a valid and objective reason for dissatisfaction. Only a
view that completely accepted the status quo could explain
industrial unrest in terms of the personality difficulties of
one party to the conflict. Other psychologists also said that
dissatisfaction was an individual phenomenon, that management could do little if anything about it, and that the
industrial organism of the country was so good that any
worker generally displeased or unhappy needed some kind
of therapy.[9]

The Hawthorne sociologists, too, remained apart from
the political drift to the left. The emphasis with which
Mayo and his colleagues treated the small group, the informal organization that had been discovered in the bank
wiring room, had great appeal to managements concerned
with unionism in the 1930's.[10] T. North Whitehead, one of
the Harvard researchers at Hawthorne, is a good example
of the anti-union interpretation of the Hawthorne results.
In 1936 he spelled out his attitude:

The executive ranks of business contain many of the very best
brains of the country, and it is very possible that they will prove
equal to the task of adapting the organism of industry on lines
more satisfactory for those involved; if this happens, trade
unions may lose their members, because . . . [workers] find in
the direct collaboration within the factory all they need in the
way of personal self-expression and of adequate consideration.[11]

In Whitehead's view unions were merely associations designed to give the worker an opportunity for self-expression and consideration which he could not find at his place
of work. He did not believe that unions had other functions
on an entirely different level, of equal or much greater im-

portance. According to him, unions did not serve labor by
making its bargaining power somewhat equal to that of
employers, or by preventing managements from exercising
their whims to the hurt and danger of employees. The
unions, in Whitehead's perspective, were social clubs designed to meet only the supposed psychological and social
needs of their members.

Whitehead also believed that if management would
assume its prerogatives of "leadership," emphasize the informal organizations of the workers, and persuade those
organizations to think within management's categories, the
need for trade unions would disappear. The way to combat
the depression, according to him, "is to assist working
groups to build and then maintain their own social integra-
tion, and to have these sentiments and customs oriented
towards the policies of the firm."[12] In terms of the Hawthorne experiments, he wanted American management to
encourage such informal organizations as that of the bank
wiremen, but with the management orientation of the relay assemblers.

Most other psychologists accepted and encouraged the
dominant position of their colleagues. One, for instance,
believed that management should keep records of negotia-
tions with employees so that some source of worker attitudes would be available; since attitudes developed slowly,
an alert management could anticipate the demands that
employees were likely to make. By "educational" or other
pressures, management could then avoid situations which
might prove "inconvenient."[13] In other words, if management would study the attitudes of its workers, it could predict and prevent demands that it thought too expensive,
incompatible with its rights, or otherwise uncomfortable.

Social scientists were not satisfied with merely suggesting to management that a study of worker attitudes be
undertaken; they began seriously to investigate methods
of conducting such research. Though only a few firms be-

gan attitude surveys during the 1930's—one study discovered only five out of two hundred firms that did so before 1940—the movement was firmly launched. When one researcher reported that, in 1935, about one-third of all American workers were dissatisfied with their jobs, it seemed to many industrial social scientists that management had better learn what the worker wanted and take steps to see that he got it.[14] The only alternative was to continue to ignore the attitudes of employees and thereby possibly encourage the spread of unionism. To management and most social scientists, this prospect was grim.

Though attitude research was sometimes conducted before the 1930's,[15] it was not until the depression that this became an important personnel device used by a growing number of managements, including, for example, Armstrong Cork and Sears, Roebuck. Early in the depression, a number of firms began to use attitude and interest scales in market and consumer research, and with the success of this technique in those fields, its practicability was demonstrated to personnel men and industrialists.[16]

The Hawthorne research also supported the belief that workers' attitudes were important. The huge number of interviews conducted during the course of that work were used by Western Electric management as source material for supervisory training conferences. Even after the original interviewing program was replaced with counseling, the management of Western Electric made some use of reports from the counseling division as an indication of employee attitudes, and once or twice a year the counselors submitted a general survey of employee morale to management. But, in one counselor's opinion, Western management never made as full use as it could have of this source of information.[17]

The earliest well-developed and direct attitude study was conducted from June to December, 1930, by Arthur W. Kornhauser and Agnes A. Sharp, both of the University of

Chicago, in the Badger-Globe mill of the Kimberly-Clark Corporation, makers of Kleenex and Kotex, at Neenah, Wisconsin. From this study Kornhauser concluded that "an immense part of our industrial discontent is unnecessary. . . . If management knows what its employees are really thinking and feeling, the sources of trouble can usually be greatly reduced in seriousness. . . . Too often," he concluded, "the workers' attitudes are guessed at—or ignored—or damned." It was this piece of research that introduced attitude studies into the domain of industrial psychology, and its inferences about the power situation in industry were consistent with the values implicit in the research other social scientists had conducted.[18]

Procter and Gamble was the next company to begin research aimed at its employees' attitudes. In January, 1933, under the direction of psychologist Richard S. Uhrbrock, almost 4500 factory workers, foremen, and clerical workers were graded on an attitude scale. He felt that, given an opportunity, workers would talk freely about their attitudes, their jobs, and the company; they would disclose their irritations, and the personnel department could then evaluate its policies. But it was important that a continuous sampling of worker attitudes be taken because a long-range program would provide "cues and leads of great value to executives whose success depends upon the cooperation of their employees." Uhrbrock believed that as the labor provisions of the NRA introduced greater employee representation into industry, more companies would come to rely on attitude surveys to learn what was on their workers' minds.[19]

In its own way, General Motors also became interested in employees' attitudes. At first it employed an independent firm to tap the thinking of both the public and its workers. But, dissatisfied with the results, GM turned to the Pinkerton Detective Agency. Subsequently, during a congressional investigation, Senator Robert M. La Follette, Jr., the chairman of the investigating committee, asked Harry W. Anderson, GM's labor relations director, why Pinkerton men were used for this purpose. Anderson answered: "Well, many times men are willing to talk at home, on the street, or various other places, and go into detail as to whether or not they think the foreman is treating them right, whereas in a plant they wouldn't do it." La Follette probed deeper, wanting to know what other purposes GM had in using Pinkerton. Finally Anderson admitted that "we are interested to know if there was any particular labor organization going on in town, and if so, why.... The thing I was interested in," Anderson explained, "was what was there about the plant operation that would give any need for an outside [labor] organization." The assembled brass of GM was told nothing new when one outraged Senator advised them to spend "a little bit of money trying to bring about a knowledge of industrial relations and labor relations," because "profits would flow as a result of that expenditure."[20]

Among the problems uncovered by attitude research was monotony. One view was that the nature of modern industrial work was repetitive, specialized, and necessarily dull. The other and more popular position taken by industrial social scientists was that no job was necessarily monotonous, that some people like repetitive jobs. Monotony, in this second view, inhered not in the job but in the relation between the worker and the job.[21]

Elton Mayo, during his psychological phase, had also been concerned with the nature of monotony. In the 1920's he had stated:

Modern methods of machine production are monotonous; long periods of revery thinking are made inevitable. Life in a city slum and long hours in the factory combine to make such reveries pessimistic or melancholic. Socialism, Syndicalism, Bolshevism—irrational dreams of anger and destruction—are the inevitable outcome.[22]

From Mayo's position grew the argument that dull and repetitive jobs make it possible for the worker to daydream all day long. If those dreams could somehow be made pleasant and happy the worker would like his job, the company, and the economic system in general. For instance, one report told of a girl employed in a British factory who needed only a few minutes each morning to prepare her machine and materials for the day's work. After her machine began to hum, "she married a Duke, took a trip to the Riviera, rented a mansion in West End," and had a most exciting and satisfying day.[23] The most certain way of ensuring that workers thought happy thoughts, according to some social scientists, was for management to provide pleasant working conditions.[24]

This supposedly sophisticated view of monotony implied that management should and could do nothing about the nature of the job. The job was fixed, and management must therefore try to hire people who would not be distressed about working on meaningless and dull activities. This put the problem back where it had been in the 1920's. If management was to locate people who would not merely accept but would prefer monotonous work, the main personnel emphasis would have to be on selection techniques, and psychological testing was still the main prop of the "scientific" personnel department.

Though testing spread more during the depression than it had in the previous decade, it was still far from universal. Psychologists, of course, were generally not satisfied with the extent of testing in industry. In the most thorough survey of American industry in the depression, no more than 7.3 per cent of 2452 companies using any kind of testing program were located. Most of these gave tests to clerical workers; intelligence tests, tests for wage earners, and trade tests followed in that order. The actual number of companies using testing in a relatively thorough and scientific manner was far smaller than the statistics of the total use of tests show, and probably did not exceed a few dozen. Perhaps for reasons of economy, perhaps because the persistence of phrenologists and graphologists resulted in expensive failures, more than 16 per cent of the companies using intelligence tests dropped them when the depression struck. Generally speaking, the more workers a company employed, the bigger and more prosperous the firm was, the more advanced technologically, the greater was the use of psychological tests.[25]

Procter and Gamble remained one of the leaders of the small group of firms that conducted scientific testing programs. Beginning their activity in 1923, this company greatly expanded testing in 1931 when psychologist Richard S. Uhrbrock joined the firm and began testing college graduates. Uhrbrock and his staff, with company engineers contributing the technical items, later developed their own test, composed of one hundred items covering vocabulary, mathematics, physics, chemistry, and general information. It was Uhrbrock's firm conviction that tests could predict group behavior but that a decision about an individual applicant on the basis of his test score alone would be unreliable. This company used tests only to determine achievement, not to assess personality; test results were never used as a sole indication of the potentialities of a job applicant, which were determined through the use of several employment devices, especially interviewing. Uhrbrock was always careful to point out that, even in his company, it had been impossible to establish adequate scientific controls for the testing program. Despite the fact that correlations with criteria of success had been low, the testing program at Procter and Gamble had strong support from top management.[26]

Another example of a scientific industrial testing program was the work done at the Woodward Governor Company, Rockford, Illinois. Late in the 1930's, several executives of this firm attended a lecture on ways and means of reducing production costs, and aptitude tests were mentioned as a promising technique. At just this time the company was growing rapidly in response to increased demands, largely from the aircraft industry, for governors on diesels and change-pitch propellers. Woodward Governor called in the Psychological Corporation to make a study of its requirements and to devise special tests, since there were no ready-made tests that fitted its precise type of machine work. The general manager of the firm concluded that, as a result of the testing program, 85 per cent of the applicants who could not have been profitably trained were eliminated from original selection.[27]

Among the other companies that began or continued to use psychological tests during the depression were Armco Steel, Dennison Manufacturing, Eagle Pencil, Household Finance, Lincoln National Life Insurance, Lockheed Aircraft, Pennsylvania Company, and several textile mills. Especially interesting was Lockheed's use of tests; this firm hoped to discover people who could work in harmony in small groups. Through tests, Lockheed hoped to encourage a "right thinking" informal organization in its plants. The American Transit Association, a national trade association, began a research program on the use of tests to reduce the frequency of accidents.[28]

Though psychologists still argued about the nature of intelligence, its applicability to specific occupations, and the correlation between intelligence and success, many companies, as has been shown, gave intelligence tests. Despite the warnings of some industrial psychologists about the promiscuous use of intelligence and other kinds of tests,[29] some managers were in a hurry to discover among the mass of unemployed workers those who would adjust to the personnel "requirements" of their firms.

The emphasis on speed, dexterity, and ability to conform that resulted from the testing programs in the depression further reduced the concern with human values of many employment departments. While several of the larger industries were being organized by unions, while sit-down strikes, walkouts, and violence characterized several of the important organizing activities of the CIO, some of the employers not yet approached by organized labor were active in their search for "peaceful" employees.

Some of the skills that employers demanded of their workers were considered innate. Thus, training could not transform slow workers into fast workers or make dull ones intelligent. Nor could it be relied on to convert militant union men into "cooperative" workers. Many companies hoped, through their testing programs, to employ only those workers who conformed to the productive and political requirements of the firm.[30] And, as more companies learned that psychological tests could perhaps spot workers who for one reason or another—efficiency, personality, or politics—would become well adjusted to the desires of management, the testing program in American industry achieved a more permanent status.

Many concerns, however, did not abandon their training programs. Though the ideal was to hire only "adaptable" workers, most firms realized that the supply of such men might be limited and that the workers then on the payroll might conceivably be trained into the ways of management. Even if the outcome of a training program could not be predicted, even if the best methods of indoctrination were unknown,[31] still it was better to make an attempt at training than to do nothing at all. Like testing and attitude research, the training program of American industry during the depression was in part implicitly aimed at forestalling the leftward movement of American political and intellectual life.

Regardless of the theoretical approach taken by industrial psychologists,[32] most insisted that their work in training procedures could be among their most significant industrial contributions. But, many hastened to add, training

would have to be "psychological" if it were really to work.
It was not enough merely to appoint a training director or
move some supervisor out of production and give him
the job of teaching new men. Training would be wasted,
and might even do harm to the company, if the right principles of educational psychology were not implemented.[33]

Training programs, of course, did not start in the 1930's.
Men always had been shown what to do by older men,
more experienced workers, in the shop. A form of apprenticeship certainly existed as long as young workers had to
replace old ones. For example, one of the very first companies to install a *formal* training program was the American Steel and Wire Company, a subsidiary of United States
Steel. In 1912 the program was started, though only the
veteran employees (who reportedly responded with un-
qualified enthusiasm) of the total force of between 30,000
and 40,000 workers were included. Workers holding "responsible" jobs were supposedly taught "to *think straight*
in the conception and application of essential fundamentals . . ." and to have "a more intelligent idea of the Company business as a whole."[34] But as a theoretical and
scientific endeavor, as a psychological method, training
programs did not start until well after industrial psychologists had begun their testing work.

Especially did psychologists influence industrial training by insisting that human relations should receive much
attention, though during World War I it was recognized
that the ability to handle and direct men should be an
explicit supervisory skill. But the hard fact that no more
than 300 or 400 of America's 400,000 employers implemented any kind of formal training program during the
war years was publicized as one explanation for the greater
successes of Germany's industrial plant.[35]

Throughout the 1920's, prosperity and a waning labor
movement kept organized training at a low ebb, and,

though a few companies began training programs in that decade, including the Chrysler Corporation, Eastman Kodak, and Swift and Company,[36] most continued to ignore the possibilities of the technique. The main trend in training did not develop until management saw the need of establishing greater control of its workers. That need waited until organized labor began its most serious struggle against the prerogatives of management. That struggle waited for the misery of the severest depression in the nation's history.

Though a few firms reduced their training schedules in the depression as a cost-cutting move, many more learned to place heavy reliance on training. And supervisory training in the skills of human relations received special attention. Beginning early in 1930, foremen at the Edgewater plant of the United States Aluminum Company took a course in industrial psychology. From the interviewing material developed at Hawthorne, supervisors at Western Electric were given intensive training in personal relations, though Western had begun its training program for supervisors as early as 1923. At both Thompson Products and Servel, supervisors and foremen were taught how to "lead" and get along with their men. In January, 1930, 70 of 328 surveyed companies had some kind of formal managerial training. A total of 129 companies conducted systematic training programs for foremen and other first-line supervisors. Five years later, of 30 companies employing 40,000 workers, 67 per cent believed that skills in leadership and personal relations were the most important for foremen.[37]

By 1935, over one-third of almost 2500 companies employing close to 3,000,000 workers had some form of training program. Though only 7.5 per cent of these had started foreman training, they were the large ones, together employing almost 1,500,000 workers. Apprenticeship training was still the most common variety in American industry. A few years later, by the end of the depression, a survey of

2700 companies concluded that almost 19 per cent were using foremen training. By this time, 166 companies even had a special training department.[38]

It is clear that in company after company, a human-relations approach to labor relations was stressed in training programs. Foremen, supervisors, and even managers were told that their ability to "lead" was their key asset. The tradition of authoritarian management began to crumble in the depression as the fear of alienating workers through harsh supervision seeped through the thinking of American personnel men. In those years, because of advancing unionism, it seemed more important than ever to management to keep the loyalty of labor. Industrial social scientists had for many years told management that the first-line supervisor represented the whole company to the worker. As the worker liked or disliked his immediate supervisor, he was either happy or unhappy with the company in general. Thus, supervisors and foremen were instructed in the fine art of commanding men and making them like it. Discipline gave way to "leadership" and persuasion; authority gave way to an "understanding of human behavior."

The faith of many managers that the industrial social sciences could help them in their attempts to repress union thinking laid a firm foundation under the use of social sciences. As managers realized that the attitudes of their workers could control profit and loss, "independence" or unionism, a new vista of the importance of the industrial social sciences was opened. The National Labor Relations Act, passed in 1935, meant that employers no longer could treat employees on an individual basis. Group relations assumed an importance of the first order, and sociologists were told that many virgin areas of research awaited their attention in industry.[39]

But the overarching managerial orientation of much industrial social science did not go entirely unnoticed. Indeed, several social scientists, including Arthur Kornhauser,

themselves bemoaned this drift. Teaching psychology at
the University of Chicago from the mid-1920's through the
1930's, Kornhauser became aware of the wider implications
of industrial social science, as the depression forced itself
on the awareness of the nation. In 1930, he said that the
work of most industrial psychologists in the past had "been
in the interests of the individual business unit." He believed, however, that there was an increasing tendency for
his profession to undertake research of "broader social significance." Despite this confidence, he felt strongly enough
about the past direction of industrial psychology to warn
his colleagues that in the future they would have to decide
whether their discipline would continue to be a tool of
management or become a genuine social science. Floyd H.
Allport, less directly involved in industrial than in social
psychology, was also among the scattered few to protest
about the main drift of industrial psychology. He viewed
with suspicion the dominant theory that psychology should
be used to adjust the worker to his job, because "so long as
the main criterion for that adjustment is increased economic
production . . . personnel work in factories is really only
another method for accelerating the already exaggerated
business segment of human activity." Morris Viteles, too,
was occasionally worried about the management orientation of his fellow practitioners, insisting in 1932 that the
chief concern of industrial psychologists should be to increase efficiency by decreasing the human effort involved in
the job. Doing this, he believed, would automatically increase the efficiency of the factory; but, if efficiency and
human values ever conflicted, as they often must, the industrial psychologist *should* be eager to sacrifice efficiency.[40]

A critique of industrial social science that was genuinely
representative of the leftward-moving *Zeitgeist* did not
emerge until the late 1930's, after the strength of business
opposition to the New Deal was finally appreciated, after
the recession of 1938 demonstrated that the unemployed

were likely to remain without jobs for the foreseeable future, after Roosevelt's concern began to shift away from domestic affairs, and after some criticism of the New Deal took the position that the difficulty with the President and his administration was that their measures were too conservative.

In 1939 was published the first yearbook of the Society for the Psychological Study of Social Issues, an affiliate of the national American Psychological Association. Edited by George W. Hartmann and Theodore Newcomb, this volume, *Industrial Conflict,* claimed to represent the "organized conscience of the profession." Defying the traditional attitude of their colleagues, the editors stated simply that "the present Yearbook is edited from a pro-labor standpoint.... A balanced appraisal of the phenomena of industrial conflict," they continued, "seems to indicate that more and higher values are implicit in the struggles of the workers to achieve a richer and fuller life than can be found in the efforts of owners or their managerial representatives to frustrate these aims." Apparently unsatisfied that they had made themselves sufficiently clear, the editors took an even less equivocal stand:

If this ... Yearbook ... seems on the whole to be more friendly disposed to the workers than to the "bosses," this is far from being the result of any deification of the employees or any conviction of diabolism inherent in employers. The plain facts of conflict indicate that *more* workers than owners are more severely blocked and injured in their activity impulses. Characteristically, a conflict situation may culminate with the owners temporarily losing monetary "profits" or social and political prestige; but the risk of being injured physically, of permanent loss of a job, or of literally seeing one's family starve because of loyalty to one's associates is more frequently borne by the wage-earners.

These convictions so flatly contradicted the main impulses that had characterized the profession for the previous twenty-five years that they took on a luster that would otherwise have been lacking. Several of the contributors to this yearbook also pointed out that the dominant conservative climate of the United States had seriously infected their discipline and made scientific objectivity literally impossible.[41]

Even the American Association of Applied Psychologists, first established in 1937, with a special section devoted to business and industry, was generally dedicated to futhering research potentially useful only to the industrial managers of the country. The statement of purposes of this organization tried to make clear that its members would be just as concerned with "human values" as with industrial efficiency; but the members of the AAAP industrial division were reportedly "concerned with promoting the efficiency and adjustment of workers arising in the production of commodities and with problems involved in the wider distribution of commodities in accordance with human needs and wants."[42] Though the emphasis on distribution was unusual, there were apparently to be no questions about whether workers *should* be adjusted to the status quo of industry, or about how the research results of industrial psychologists were to be controlled. The persistent assumption of this professional association of industrial psychologists, the first such group, was that their only responsibility was to find new knowledge relevant to industrial problems. Questions of power were ignored. Of course the members of such a group would find new knowledge; of course such knowledge would be useful to managers. But what would happen to the research results of such a group of professionals when these findings were turned over to managers?

What in fact did happen is obvious. Social scientists busied themselves in industrial research questions, hired themselves out as industrial consultants, made recommendations to management. Management gratefully accepted the practical contributions of social scientists and went about its business of repressing unionism, controlling the attitudes and thinking of its workers, driving output up, driving costs down, and regaining a firm grip on American social, intellectual, political, and economic life. To the strengthening of this grip almost every industrial social scientist, during the great depression, dedicated his best effort.

CHAPTER 8

War

and Peace

As 1939 BECAME 1940, as war infected a growing number of nations, vital and swift changes marked virtually every aspect of life. Not the least of these changes occurred in industry, as previously undreamed-of technological advances were made, as war ended the depression. Millions of unemployed encountered an overdue and painfully awaited demand for their labor. Manufacturers, after ten dreary and limping years, found themselves with a rapidly mounting backlog of orders that required double and even triple shifts to fill. Material and men became scarce. Firms rapidly doubled and tripled in size and many grew even more, and production quotas began to climb. As the government developed an elaborate system of priorities, as over 15,000,000 men and women left the labor market to join the armed forces, American manufacturers were literally forced to devote an ever increasing amount of time, effort, and money to a search for answers to their material and manpower problems. The tightening of the labor supply, coupled with the almost fantastic demands that the war effort made upon industry, meant that America's managers would have to make increasingly efficient use of the manpower that was available. And personnel departments began their work in earnest.

An example of the breath-taking stresses and strains that American industry had to overcome or at least withstand in the war years can be found in the experience of the Thompson Products Company of Cleveland. Because of the high priority assigned to its valves and other products, the company was in a favorable position when war came. Expansion was swift and dramatic. In December, 1938, Thompson employed about 2700 workers, an increase of more than 1000 since mid-1934; by 1940, some 6200 workers were on Thompson's payroll, and over 4000 more were added in the next year; by the end of 1943, Thompson employed almost 20,000 people. The enormous increase in the size of this firm put intense pressure on the personnel department, whose director wrote to Thompson's president that "it has been impossible for the Employment Office staff to maintain . . . [former] contacts due to the terrific pressure of hiring new people [and] interviewing applicants." He showed that even the appointment of one hundred new supervisors could not keep up with the increasing burden of so many new people. Before the war came, he knew almost all of the workers and they knew something of him; thus "employees had an opportunity to 'blow off steam' to an individual who they knew would keep their confidences and at the same time provide remedial action for any unfair situation." But no longer was this possible. Out of its desperate need for new devices to handle the unmanageable personnel situation, the company tried a number of plans, but the essential problem of dealing with thousands of human beings where only hundreds had been before remained.[1]

Perhaps the aircraft industry was most affected by the gigantic demands of the war. Though it is impossible to convey the hopes and aspirations and fears of human beings by statistics, the problems of the aircraft industry during the years of World War II can at least be illustrated in this fashion. In 1939 this industry was still wallowing in the remaining sludge of the depression, but toward the end of the next year, close to three billion dollars in orders waited to be filled. The industry was asked to raise its production of planes from a prewar figure of two thousand a year to more than nine thousand a month. In 1939 the entire industry employed about 41,000 men, but toward the end of the next year, its manpower needs were estimated at a minimum of 350,000 workers. At the Burbank plant of Lockheed, for example, the number of people on the payroll skyrocketed in less than three years from 3000 to 49,000, and extreme personal and social dislocation resulted. In only nine months of 1943 about 176,000 people left or were fired from their jobs in the aircraft industry in southern California. The human and social problems resulting from this virtually incredible expansion were among the most difficult with which the managers of America's aircraft plants had to contend.[2]

The managerial belief in the importance of understanding human behavior was now reinforced. Early in the war, for example, Cessna Aircraft told its supervisors that human relations comprised three-fourths of their jobs, that even during the war period when such great demands were made upon the engineering and manufacturing skills of the aircraft industry, technical problems were relatively unimportant. "But," declared Cessna's personnel department, "the human side of business becomes increasingly important each passing day."

America's industrial managers were being forced by the necessities of wartime production to accept the idea so long preached by social scientists: that what people think has a direct bearing upon the financial condition of the firm employing them. Journals of management opinion soon began to echo this conviction. "Deep as they are," reported *American Business*, "the factors that 'make a man tick' can be described and analyzed with much of the precision that would go into the making of dies for the . . . side of a Sherman tank." The implications of such a statement were not lost on American management; perhaps in in-

dustrial social science management had found an answer
to its labor difficulties and increasing costs. Psychologists
continued to insist that the psychological problems of employees were at the heart of many business problems, that
a failure to consider the wants of workers would strengthen
the already growing breach betweeen management and
labor. A former president of the National Association of
Manufacturers, president of Thompson Products, agreed
with this by saying that American industry was passing
into a new era, "the age of human relations." "Even the
new role of government," stated the president of an Eastern
investment house a few years later, "and its far greater influence on the economy cannot eliminate the interplay of
human emotions and their effect on business and secu-
rities"; the importance of psychological factors was one of
the "fundamental" lessons he had learned in the previous
twenty-five years.[3]

During this war, industrial social scientists finally came
into their own. In a survey of a number of large corporations in 1946, it was discovered that 30 per cent had a professionally trained psychologist on the staff but over 50
per cent thought it would be a good idea to have one. The
managerial attitude typical of the previous several decades,
the attitude that businessmen were competent to solve by
themselves all of the human problems of their companies,
had changed. It was the experience of World War II that
finally convinced a significant number of America's managers that they needed help to solve the human problems
of industry. Before the 1940's ended, a university dean
reported that "seldom today do we meet the hard-bitten
businessman who asserts belligerently that there is no outside expert or professor who can tell him anything about
running his business.... In fact," he added, "the pendulum
may have swung too far in the other direction."[4] In World
War II, American management became convinced that the
behavior of people—employees and consumers—was the

key variable upon which much of its success or failure rested. For the control of this variable, management increasingly looked to the industrial social scientists.

The use of social scientists by every branch of the armed services contributed to the rising prestige of psychologists and sociologists. Of the 5000 American psychologists in 1945, about 4000 cooperated directly or indirectly with the government; by July, more than 1700 psychologists had been used in the armed forces. Sociologists, too, in increasing number, applied their skills and training to the practical problems of the wartime emergency. In this war, the government used social scientists to improve personnel selection techniques, maintain military and civilian morale, analyze propaganda, develop campaigns to sell war bonds, study and report on the social and psychological characteristics of the enemy, and train personnel to deal with many different peoples and cultures, from Germany to Okinawa. Social scientists were used by the War Manpower Commission to aid in developing and administering training programs that eventually reached almost 2,000,000 supervisors in 16,000 plants; the War Production Board authorized a group of Harvard social scientists to investigate absenteeism and labor turnover. "World War II can . . . be said to have been a social scientist's war," reported one social scientist. "These are thrilling times for applied science," the president of the American Association of Applied Psychology told his Cleveland audience in 1944; "war always drives effort in the direction of utility and service. Whatever enterprises cannot be so classified tend to become outlawed for the duration."[5]

But not merely because the government found social scientists helpful did management turn to them. Several managements had discovered for themselves that some of the most persistent problems of industry did not respond to the traditional engineering approach. Early in 1941 a few industrial social scientists noted this change in the

managerial mentality, and the whole profession became
active in proposing research projects to industry, writing
books and articles, and congratulating one another on the
ultimate justice of the situation. Thompson Products suggested to new supervisors that they read a text in industrial
psychology; International Harvester advised its supervisors
that psychology was not mysterious and that a training
course in "practical psychology" would be made available
to assist in solving their problems of human relations; the
Michigan Bell Telephone Company retained an eminent
psychologist to prepare a training course in human relations
for its supervisors, which, the expert reported, was received
well and "all levels of management . . . [showed] marked
enthusiasm." General Motors, Marshall Field, and the
Chesapeake and Ohio Railroad all had their staff psychologists report to the profession on their research; more than
six hundred executives attended a series of conferences that
the psychologist Robert N. McMurry and his staff gave
under the sponsorship of the Dartnell Corporation; the
Ford Motor Company began a $500,000 research program
in human relations; a growing number of companies hired
social scientists as permanent executives.[6]

Chief among the management problems of the wartime
emergency were absenteeism and turnover. How could
management induce workers to report to work regularly?
How could it hold the workers it had hired? It slowly became clear that patriotic posters showing a grinning Tojo
thanking workers for going to the ball game fell somewhat
short of the desired goal.

By the spring of 1943, these problems were becoming
sufficiently acute for the War Production Board to take
action, and the chief of the resources section of the WPB
decided that there was a chance that social scientists might
shed some light on such problems. Looking for someone
to head his study, he decided that Elton Mayo, of Hawthorne fame, would be ideal. Deciding that the generalized

problem was too vast for meaningful research, a case-study approach was chosen; and the WPB made arrangements, including a promise of union cooperation, with three brass mills in Waterbury, Connecticut, to subject themselves to Mayo's inquiries. From the Harvard Business School a team of sociologically oriented researchers, in the tradition of the Hawthorne studies, descended upon Waterbury.

The over-all conclusion of the final report announced that absenteeism was management's problem. The sheer existence of many absences, said the researchers, proved that management had not taken sufficient interest in the human problems of its employees. Even the obvious difficulties of wartime conditions—housing and transportation problems— could be alleviated by a management sufficiently aware of its responsibilities to the total social and personal situation of the workers. If management was not interested in such matters, this lack of interest would itself become another cause of absenteeism. The few causes of absenteeism beyond managerial control, such as illness or the necessity of hiring marginal and inefficient workers because of the manpower shortage, did not account for a significant proportion of the absences.[7]

A second study in which Mayo was involved corroborated these findings. Attempting to pinpoint and explain the tremendous labor turnover in the West Coast aircraft industry during the war, he and his coresearchers concluded that the marked dislocation and extreme mobility of the area did not explain the high turnover. Factory conditions reflected the unsettlement of the area, but, Mayo concluded, "the only way to achieve control of absenteeism and labor turnover is to study such symptoms *in the situations in which they arise*."[8] Both turnover and absenteeism were related to the precise work experience of the individual worker. Management controlled, to a large degree, this precise work experience; and management, therefore, had within its power the control of both symptoms of dissatisfaction: absenteeism and turnover. Thus, once again, Mayo came to the conviction that the peaceful conditions of the preindustrial Garden of America could be recaptured; since the anonymous System could not be changed, its managers, by assuming personal responsibility for human happiness, could make life meaningful once again.

The central problem around which most studies of turnover and absenteeism revolved was morale. Presumably, both absenteeism and turnover were merely reflections of the state of morale in any given plant. Hence, if the morale of a given plant could be improved, the secondary problems would disappear. Though an explicit concern with morale, in both military and industrial terms, extended back to the First World War, the marked enthusiasm for such studies characteristic of the World War II period was new.

While the war was in progress, several researchers on the problems of morale and job satisfaction concluded that the earlier findings about the significance of the personal relations between the first-line supervisor and the individual worker were valid. They argued that the total plant relationships of the worker determined his satisfaction or dissatisfaction with the company in general. Rejecting the notion that such concrete factors as wages, hours, security, and advancement played a determining role in the level of worker satisfaction and morale, these social scientists believed that the expensive and dangerous demands of labor were not really important to workers. This sophisticated view implied that the demands of labor for higher wages or greater self-determination merely camouflaged the real need of employees for just plain friendliness.[9]

Other social scientists took a somewhat different course. During a wartime investigation of morale and job satisfaction in five shipyards, the researchers insisted that despite critical housing, antagonistic community feeling, and difficult transportation, the feelings of the workers toward their jobs were determined by the conditions inside the plant. Displaying Mayo's influence, these investigators insisted that too much emphasis had been put by management and academicians alike on out-plant conditions. The implication was clear: if the System was omnipotent, the Garden was forever lost. If management could not personalize modern industry, Americans were doomed to fritter away their lives in the impersonal, indeed inhuman, bureaucratic System. Remaining true to Mayo, these men took the only way out of their dilemma: if management wanted to improve morale, it was in its power to do so. Management could not blame conditions beyond its control for general dissatisfaction among its workers. The factors determining morale were inside the plant, within the control of management. Indeed, the specific nature of an individual's job was often said to be the single most important quality influencing his morale.[10]

In the period immediately following the war, a new dimension was introduced into the literature on morale. After a long and painstaking research program at Sears, Roebuck, James C. Worthy concluded that the earlier investigations suggesting that the first-line supervisor determined the morale of his workers were wrong. At Sears, he discovered that the supervisor was himself caught in top-level policy, which influenced or even determined his own behavior. Since the supervisor was not a free agent, he should not be held responsible for the level of morale. Thus, training courses aimed at teaching supervisors how to raise morale would fail. Worthy observed that the total organization of the specific company determined the tone of the company in large degree, and thus directly impinged upon the satisfactions of its employees. Only a fundamental reorganization of the company could change the morale of the work force.[11]

Despite the increasing attention to morale, the satisfaction of workers with their jobs did not increase to a level acceptable to management. Between 15 per cent and 28 per cent of skilled and unskilled labor reported such dissatisfaction in 1945. In the following year, over half of a sizable number of executives reported that decreasing labor productivity was caused by a "general indifference on the part of labor." In 1947, 20 per cent of nonunion and union workers felt that their jobs were either generally uninteresting or completely dull; almost 30 per cent of CIO members felt this way, while only 15 per cent of nonunion workers agreed. In a different survey conducted in the same year, it was learned that almost half of a large number of factory workers believed that their jobs were not satisfying.[12] This was even worse than the depression situation, when one-third of the total working force was reported to have been dissatisfied.

Because a growing number of managers were becoming convinced that morale directly influenced productivity,[13] their alarm at the descending level of employee satisfaction became more marked. Since by this time many thoughtful managers recognized that most unions had castrated themselves by their commitment to Gompersism, the impact of unionism could no longer be blamed for growing dissatisfaction. The answers these managers gave to the problems of the depression were no longer applicable, and, indeed, the problems themselves seemed different in kind. The dissatisfaction of employees during the depression was unlike the dissatisfaction in the postwar world. Merely to assert that employee morale was important, that management, by and large, could control morale, was not to offer a prescription sufficiently concrete to warrant action.

The perception of morale and job satisfaction remained in flux throughout the war period and the peace that followed, as did the assumptions regarding absenteeism and turnover. After 1940, these were the big problems with which personnel-minded companies grappled, and the techniques devised in the 1920's and 1930's for discovering the causes and means of control of human conduct were increasingly used.

Not the least significant of these techniques was still the attitude survey. With the conviction that workers' attitudes, morale, and job satisfaction directly affected productivity, management was ready to make greater use of this procedure than it had ever done before. Refinements in the skill of the attitude researchers also influenced management's decision to place greater reliance on this approach. The war experience proved, more than anything else, that how workers viewed their company was of basic importance to productivity and "labor peace." It was therefore essential for management to learn what was on its workers' minds.

The increasing incidence of strikes resulting from the rising tempo of defense production underlined this need. In 1941, for example, 250,000 workers went on strike in only seven companies: International Harvester, Bethlehem Steel, Ford, GM, North American Aviation, Chrysler, and Carnegie-Illinois Steel. Most of these companies quickly learned to lean on the information supplied by the attitude researchers.

North American Aviation, for instance, before the summer of 1943, questioned some 6000 of its employees about the reasons for absenteeism. Only 14 per cent said that their absences were caused by illness, while as many said that lack of interest accounted for their absences, and others gave different reasons. Eventually, the United Auto Workers, the recognized union at North American, realized that it too could conduct attitude research; from the data thus secured, the UAW hoped to convince management, once and for all, that the union's demands were truly representative of the workers' wants.[14]

In general, labor's official position was either opposed to or unconcerned with attitude surveys. In 1945, however, an unpublished survey disclosed that forty of forty-three labor leaders thought attitude measurement a useful device. But thirty-four of those men insisted that attitude research would be meaningless unless it was conducted by both the company and the union; six thought that the unions alone should measure worker attitudes; none believed that management alone should be allowed to conduct such surveys, because that approach would not result in truthful or representative answers from the workers. If the men knew that their union was sponsoring an attitude survey, however, the results would be useful to all concerned, for an accurate survey would then be achieved.[15]

There were several reasons why at least a part of labor's leadership was hostile to attitude research. One industrial psychologist contended that the attitude researchers—Gallup, Roper, the Psychological Corporation, Opinion Research Corporation, and others—were biased in favor of management. In case after case, it was shown how these organizations loaded questions and misconstrued results to depict management in the best possible light. Organized labor was almost always treated unfairly by the professional pollsters.[16] "The poll takers," concluded the United Auto Workers, "can prove anything they are paid to prove."[17]

Another reason for labor's hostility to attitude research was the conviction that such studies sidestepped the established grievance machinery. Attitude research that was conducted by management fulfilled a deep-seated longing of management: the desire to reach employees directly instead of relying on communication channels established by unions. Attitude research, wrote the research director of the Textile Workers Union, "is a means of stealing the prestige for the solution of problems from the collective bargaining mechanism and arrogating it completely to a management-controlled device."[18]

Labor's general position regarding attitude research was that such studies would be tolerated so long as management was not trying to weaken unionism or to sidestep the machinery of collective bargaining.[19] Since it was rarely clear that such was management's purpose, many unions remained apathetic to this device.

The small amount of labor resistance that did exist did not prevent the increasing use of attitude surveys on the part of management. Most managements were convinced that the right to find out what was on the workers' minds was their prerogative, one which did not need union blessings, though Standard Oil was noteworthy for careful collaboration with its union before an attitude survey was authorized in 1945.[20] Despite the fact that some few firms used this technique during the depression, it was not until the war that attitude research became popular. In 1939, for example, in an industrial survey, the use of attitude research was so limited that no question was even asked about it. By 1944 almost fifty companies reported the use of this device, and by 1947 another two hundred companies were using attitude research—many of them even supplementing the questionnaire type of research with more intensive interviewing.[21]

An example of the use of attitude research by management without the cooperation of nationally organized labor was supplied by Thompson Products. In September, 1943, a suggestion was made to the vice-president in charge of personnel that a poll of the workers' attitudes be taken. By the middle of November the employees were told that they would soon get a questionnaire which, if filled out seriously and intelligently, would result in better jobs.[22] A few days later the questionnaires, prepared by the company, were mailed to the 16,000 salaried and hourly employees of this company, who were told that they need not sign their replies. Thompson's president, Frederick C. Crawford, included a covering letter in which he tried to explain the reasons for such an approach:

The other night, lying awake on a sleeper, bumping along the rails out of Washington, I tried to figure out a way to get out

into the shop and swap ideas with all the men and women who
make up this organization.

We used to be able to do this when the plant was smaller,
before we entered the war. . . . Much good used to come from
our off-the-record discussions; but now, with plants in five cities,
all working on a three-shift basis, it becomes virtually a physical impossibility to make the rounds of the plants and shifts as
frequently as before.

Still, I want and need your ideas, so I had a set of questions
drawn up and printed. I realize, the same as you, that a questionnaire is no substitute for a man-to-man talk, but under today's pressure it might serve as a temporary measure from
which we both can get some good.[23]

The International Association of Machinists, long
unsuccessful in organizing the Thompson plants because
of bitter opposition from top management and from a
company union, replied to Crawford's letter. Signed "A
Thompson Products Worker," the reply outlined the union's
position in its newspaper:

The other night, lying awake after an especially tough day at
the plant, I tried to figure out what is causing the trouble at TP
and why a questionnaire was sent to me.

I agree with you, Fred, that it is a physical impossibility for
me to have a man-to-man talk with you. . . .

There's one sentence in your letter, though, that keeps
bothering me. It's this one: 'Please don't sign your name or
identify yourself in any way.' That sentence set me to wondering. And I guess there are a lot of others who felt like I did
about it.

Now, it's just possible that you haven't been told. Sometimes
a man in your position can't get the truth. So I'm writing this to
let you know that your employees don't trust you. Not even to
the extent of filling out an anonymous questionnaire.

They remember that you have fought against any bonafide
trade union for years. They know about other employers who
use tricks like this one to find out which employees were union-
minded in order to get rid of them at the first opportunity.[24]

By December, not enough questionnaires had been

returned, and pressure was put on supervisors and foremen to get their workers to complete the forms. By February, 1944, the company newspaper, *Friendly Forum*, reported that the results of the survey showed that "the overwhelming majority of Thompson workers like their war jobs." Employees reportedly were content with their salaries, appreciated their supervision, and had a "high regard" for top management. Several months later an even more elaborate report was made, and this time, in an attractive seventy-page booklet, Thompson workers were told by the management that only 4 per cent of their colleagues were dissatisfied with their jobs.[25] The percentage of the total working force that did not answer the questions was not given. How many union men answered? On the basis of the information supplied by the company, a meaningful appraisal of the survey is not possible. But, in the results that it obtained and in the way the results were presented, the management of Thompson Products discovered an extremely useful device that was employed to its fullest extent. Other companes explicitly copied the Thompson approach.[26]

Henry Ford II, after becoming the president of the Ford Motor Company, also decided to make use of attitude research; he was looking for a way to lessen the great gulf between management and employees that had arisen in his company. In October, 1946, a simple questionnaire was mailed to all 124,700 production and salaried employees, of whom 22,000 answered. The published results of this survey were unusual in that a rather unfavorable level of employee morale was disclosed. One item revealed that 18.5 per cent of the men felt that "it would be dangerous for a man at Ford to express his honest opinion." After that first simple survey, the Ford management authorized a series of more sophisticated studies and hired Elmo Roper to do the job. In his surveys the state of morale was shown to be continuously improving.[27]

Since World War II a great number of large corporations have conducted such research and surveys. In virtually all cases, the condition of morale was reported to be high. Obviously, insisted the researchers, the fact of being told that the "overwhelming majority" of one's fellow workers were happy could not but raise the general morale of the plant. If properly handled, in other words, a morale survey could raise morale. It has also been suggested that the decision to conduct attitude surveys indicated to employees that management was really interested in their welfare, which also tended to raise morale.[28]

Most social scientists and personnel men regularly insisted that attitude research was not only scientifically sound but was good business. By surveying and reporting workers' attitudes, management could create "custom made men." A positive correlation between knowledge of "economic fact" and a commitment to free enterprise was discovered, and the extent of this knowledge could be determined through attitude surveys. The pollsters, in other words, not only could assess but could increase the commitment of workers to capitalism and its symbols. Most important, perhaps, was the fact that attitude research could isolate possible sources of "radicalism" in the plant.[29]

Still, a few managements were afraid of attitude surveys. The reasons most commonly expressed for not permitting such research were that polls would suggest dissatisfactions to workers and would upset workers emotionally; that workers would refuse to answer; or that the poll results would provide unions with antimanagement ammunition. The underlying reason for management's opposition, according to one psychologist, was that managers were themselves psychologically insecure. A poll might highlight poor operating methods, weaknesses in supervision, or hostility to top management itself. For this reason another psychologist suggested that surveys of the attitudes of top management as well as of employees seemed to be in order.[30]

Despite the general acceptance of attitude research by both social scientists and management, a number of nagging problems persisted. A very few social scientists suggested that this type of research only aggravated the already swollen commitment to quantification, that a scientific approach to human affairs would have to become more clinical and would have to emphasize the interpretative skills of the social scientist. The point was also made that the assumed relationship between attitudes and productivity had never been fully explored or verified, and the ethics of selling such an assumed relationship to management was therefore questioned.[31] From management's point of view, the essential difficulty with attitude research was that it was at best only therapeutic and could not prevent the "wrong" kinds of attitudes from creeping into the plant in the first place. But proper selection, based upon psychological testing, conceivably could act as such a prophylactic. For this and other reasons, management after World War II also made greater use of testing than it had ever done before.

The war accomplished what psychologists had earlier worked so hard but so vainly to achieve. Fifteen million men and women were tested in the armed services and became familiar with the technique; more managers began seriously to wonder whether psychologists should be allowed to conduct their apparently successful experiments in their factories. The number of surveyed firms making use of testing grew (in approximate figures) from 14 per cent in 1939 to 50 per cent in 1947 and to 75 per cent in 1952.[32] Still, complaints were heard that not enough firms used tests.[33]

The very popularity of the psychological tests sharply reduced one of the factors that had earlier curtailed their use: expense. The United States Employment Service made standard tests available, at no cost and under certain conditions, to employers. Even in cases where special tests were needed, USES would construct and standardize them, but employers who took advantage of this arrangement had to agree to furnish significant data to the government, to use tests scientifically with personnel trained by USES, and to buy this special material from USES. By 1949 over three hundred companies had used this service.[34]   However, commercial tests were still expensive, prohibitively so for the small businessman (indeed, one estimate of the cost of developing and validating a single industrial test was $10,000). After 1950, enough managerial enthusiasm had been generated about testing so that it made sense to think in terms of mass-producing commonly used tests. One psychological consulting firm in Chicago developed a series of package tests that sold for about a dollar each, and only one package was needed for each job applicant.[35]

As the testing movement spread, as an increasing number of managers had to make decisions about the relative merits of various tests, trouble was bound to arise. Perhaps the single greatest pitfall was the unchecked enthusiasm and naïveté with which American industrial managers accepted the principles and practice of psychological testing. As if to compensate for decades of apathy and skepticism, managers now overreacted, as they had in the post-World War I period. There were, however, some objective reasons for managerial confusion, and most bewildering of all was the fact that, in 1947, the staggering total of 783 different kinds of tests were being offered to management. Which to use? Yet, "Most of the errors in industrial psychology," reported *Fortune* magazine, "have been committed by test-happy managements that have not taken the trouble to check up on the tests they use." This overeagerness on the part of America's managers resulted in an ever-growing number of quacks and frauds whom the usual manager could not identify as such. Graphologists, astrologists, palmists, and phrenologists continued their expensive exploitation of the gullible and eager.[36]

At the same time, a few managers began to worry about testing; a few voices were quietly raised to plead for caution —because, they warned, abstract jobs could not be tested, correlations were consistently too low, or tests were not sufficiently scientific. Some managers were afraid of tests, thinking that perhaps they would themselves not make a good enough showing.[37] Even some social scientists attempted to dampen the ardor of management by pointing out mistakes that were made and research that was yet to be done.[38]

Slowly, several managements conceded that such caution deserved respect. Though the testing bandwagon rolled merrily on, this note of hesitation began increasingly to assert itself. Finally, the stance assumed by the National Association of Manufacturers typified the general managerial attitude:

Properly used, psychological tests can be of considerable value in increasing operational efficiency, but it must be emphasized that they do not, in themselves, provide an adequate basis for hiring. . . . Such tests measure only one factor or group of factors. They merely indicate what an applicant is potentially able to do, not whether he *will* do it.[39]

The position of organized labor regarding tests, in the 1940's and early 1950's, was confused. Officially, labor could not have cared less; privately, several of labor's most articulate leaders were worried about the inherent dangers of psychological testing. Solomon Barkin of the Textile Workers expressed his feeling this way:

The increasing influence of trade unions has sharply reduced management's chances of molding workers into the "ideal" form once sought. The use of psychological personnel techniques, and the techniques themselves, must be modified or in some cases abandoned to be in harmony with an era of collective bargaining. . . . Labor's deep dislike and fear of . . . aptitude tests . . . has forced their curtailment. Seniority is far more important than psychological findings in the average industrial plant today.[40]

Another labor official went even further:

I am personally . . . wary of psychological techniques used in industry. They too often turn out to be a device for stifling rather than stimulating self-government. I know of several instances where workers had lost control over collective bargaining because of them.[41]

The general position taken by arbitrators and the National Labor Relations Board was that employers had a unilateral right to use psychological tests on new employees, and under certain conditions on veteran employees. A ruling unfavorable to the union in a case between the United Mine Workers and the Stauffer Chemical Company, in 1947, was typical: "Under contract providing that job vacancies will be filled on basis of seniority where fitness and ability are equal, employer is entitled to use any method, including examination, to test ability so long as the method used is fair and nondiscriminatory."[42]

Most union men granted that testing of job applicants was solely a management function. Testing of veteran employees, however, said the research director of the Steelworkers, would usually be opposed. Because the validity and objectivity of psychological tests used to determine promotions had not been sufficiently established, his union also opposed this use.[43]

Management thought that labor resistance to testing could be overcome by education. The NAM insisted that labor always opposed new personnel techniques but that management had always won, as it had won the scientific-management fight.[44] Indeed, these beliefs may prove accurate, for at least one union has agreed to submit to psychological testing as a substitute for seniority.[45]

Barkin's claim that labor's opposition retarded the testing movement, then, was merely whistling in the dark, for testing assumed ever greater proportions. As almost three-quarters of American industry used tests, as a few unions gave up the struggle, as arbitrators continually ruled in favor of management's use of tests, the time had not come to speak of a retardation of the movement. Indeed, it seems certain that the use of testing will continue to grow, especially if management becomes convinced that testing can be used as a substitute for seniority.

One particular type of test proved especially dangerous to organized labor, and indeed to society as a whole. This was the long-sought-after personality test. Though social scientists and personnel men regularly reported their dissatisfaction with the various personality tests that psychologists devised, all insisted on the great importance of assessing the temperamental and personality factors of job applicants.[46]

One of the earliest applications of personality testing to industry occurred at Lockheed Aircraft. The Humm-Wadsworth Temperamental Scale, developed by two California psychologists, was used early in the war by Lockheed to locate and weed out "possible troublemakers from among employment applicants." It was reported that before its testing program, Lockheed made only six successful hirings out of ten, and after the program was started the company made better than nine successful hirings out of ten.[47]

Other firms used personality tests to eliminate political liberals and radicals from the labor force. Still another company used personality tests to find out if the job applicant's wife dominated his family decisions, because it was believed that such a man would likely do what he was told to do, and this was just the type of man this company was looking for.[48] Without inquiring into the assumptions of such a position, without searching the social implications of such a test, the psychologists who devised and sold this technique to industry continued in their search for "scientific objectivity."

Another personnel device developed by social scientists was given a new birth during World War II. Merit-rating plans, in use since the pioneering efforts of Walter Dill Scott, now became standard equipment in all but a very few companies. The Chrysler Corporation was perhaps the most notable nonconformer; toward the close of the 1940's, it concluded that "rating scales are an obstruction and no more reliable than the person who is doing the rating."[49] From 1939 to 1946, however, the percentage of factory workers subjected to rating rose from 16 per cent to almost 29 per cent and the use of this technique increased with the size of the company.[50]

Again, Thompson Products provides a meaningful example. Early in 1939 Thompson's foremen were told that they would soon conduct a quarterly rating of their men. This was not a new procedure in that company, but the management felt that the foremen were insufficiently aware of the implications of rating. At the time these instructions were issued, the company was struggling with several unions and was hopeful that it could prevent the organization of a national union in its Cleveland plants. It had successfully resisted both the CIO and the AFL and had organized a company union, which the NLRB repeatedly ruled illegal but which, through repeated appeals and litigation, Thompson managed to keep.

Looking forward to the day when Thompson Products would no longer be worried by the national unions, the management of that company told its foremen that the "PURPOSE behind these periodic ratings is to clearly determine employees' QUALITIES, ATTITUDES and PERFORMANCES." This faith in the utility of rating was supported by the opposition to the national unions. "Ratings will provide authentic, recorded information upon which to base promotions, transfers and discharges, and will be of untold value IF at some future date SENIORITY rules are tempered with a consideration of MERIT." This management instructed its foremen that merit rating was useful as a defense against union charges of discrimination, while several unions were to claim that rating was itself discriminatory. The final benefit from rating that Thompson's management expected was an increase in the efficiency of its employees. Foremen were told that "there is a *psychological* effect upon the employee being rated."[51] Thompson Products, in other words, aside from an evaluation of merit, expected that merit rating might provide a substitute for seniority, as well as an increase in individual productivity.

Because the opposition of organized labor to merit rating was more explicit than its attitude toward testing, the position of the National Labor Relations Board became important. In 1941 the NLRB upheld the Interlake Iron Corporation's use of merit rating to determine the order of layoffs. The protest of the Steelworkers that rating was used as a discriminatory device supposedly was proved to have been without foundation. In the course of the testimony it was found that Interlake Iron was vigorously anti-union and that the supervisors who were required to do the rating did not understand the instructions. The rating system was secretly installed. But the ruling held that the company did not use merit rating as a discriminatory device. Many personnel men were delighted with this decision and felt that other managements should be encouraged to make greater use of formal rating systems. Under the pressure of employers and the NLRB, a few unions felt that they had to become resigned to merit rating.[52]

The general point of view taken in NLRB and arbitration cases about the legitimacy of merit rating was that under contracts making seniority controlling in layoffs and promotion, where skill and ability were approximately equal, the employer had the right to use merit rating. But such a device could not be used to discriminate against union members, and where proof of such use was available, the NLRB decisions ordered management to abandon or change the merit-rating procedure. In determining skill and ability through merit rating, employers could not use such factors as cooperation, adaptability, safety habits, personal habits, and attendance records; ability, an arbitrator ruled in 1948, was not the same as willingness to conform to company rules.[53] The sense of several cases involving merit-rating plans was that the device itself was weak, that under certain conditions employers had the right to use it, and that labor must offer evidence of discriminatory use or intention when it protested against rating schemes.

However, several of the most powerful unions have insisted that merit rating is "incompatible with collective bargaining." The Steelworkers, for example, have believed that when wage rates are related to the scores of a merit-rating device, the union loses its grip on wage policy, and that therefore a single wage rate should be negotiated for a specific job. If the Steelworkers were successful in securing a single rate for a specific job, all of the men holding that job got the same rate. But even where this union has been unable to negotiate a single rate, it has refused to accept merit rating as an alternative, trying instead to negotiate predetermined wage rates at specified time intervals.[54]

Merit rating, from 1914 onward, has remained a controversial subject. Even now ratings depend on the judgment of the rater. Because of this obvious shortcoming, most unions and a few managements have refused to have anything to do with rating schemes. Some managements, however, have found that merit rating is a weapon which can be used against their employees, unionized or not. Some companies have hoped that the simple knowledge that he was being rated in a systematic way by his superiors would force the worker to increase his output. And some companies have seen in merit rating, as in psychological testing, a device that might be used to subvert the seniority principle so important to organized labor.

Not content to rely on such impersonal techniques as attitude surveys, testing, and merit rating, management had still another device that social scientists had supplied. This was counseling. Stemming directly from the Hawthorne research, counseling intimately engaged the individual personalities of employees.

From Hawthorne to the Second World War, the industrial use of counseling was quite limited. With the tremendous production and engineering demands of the war, however, more and more companies turned to counseling as the best method of solving personnel problems. Women workers, especially, troubled managers who had neither the time nor the skill necessary to deal with their problems. The traditional personnel office was simply not equipped to deal with individual personality problems. Elton Mayo and the other Hawthorne researchers had shown that non-directive counseling was the answer.

By 1944 several hundred of America's leading companies used the services of counselors, and many agencies of the government showed an interest, including the office of the Secretary of War, many branches of the armed forces, the Department of Agriculture, TVA, and the Social Security Board. About fifty shipyards employed counselors, though about half of the industrial firms using counselors were aircraft manufacturers. Wherever the pressures of the labor shortage proved to be the most relentless, there was a counseling program to be found. Most of the firms using counseling agreed that the technique reduced turnover and absenteeism and kept grievances at a minimum.[55]

The postwar industrial world continued counseling on a somewhat reduced basis. Because the proportion of women workers declined as peace returned, because of the high cost of well-trained counselors (though agreement was never reached about the necessary training or qualifications of counselors), and because of the feeling that supervisors should do their own counseling, many companies eliminated or curtailed their programs.[56] This is not to suggest, however, that counseling ceased to be a significant personnel technique. On the contrary, several firms began their counseling programs only after the war was over.

Standard Oil of New Jersey, under R. L. B. Roessle's guidance, was among the companies to begin counseling after the war. In 1947 Roessle asked for and got permission to begin a counseling program in Jersey Standard. By 1952 Roessle and his assistant had listened to 1500 workers "blow their tops," and three years later about 6000 interviews had been held. Described as "a safety valve for the angry, a stimulant for the bored, an escape for the frustrated, a refuge for the fearful," Roessle became an important cog in Standard's personnel machinery.

Though counseling was still considered experimental in 1948, by 1955 it was firmly imbedded in Standard's personnel program. The company, according to an official report, had several objectives in mind in this program. One was a "humanitarian" reason: "to help people to analyze their problems and help themselves." The other reasons were "corporate objectives," including the reduction of friction, improvement of morale, proper placement, improvement of public relations, and the creation of an outlet permitting employees to "vent resentments before they add up and trouble results."[57]

The position of labor concerning counseling, like its position concerning most other personnel procedures, was confused. One author, in 1945, found that national committees of both the CIO and the AFL favored counseling programs; another writer, at about the same time, discovered that labor was apathetic on this score.[58] The attitude of labor, of course, depended on its views of the implications of counseling. Was this device a management technique for molding human personality, frustrating union purposes, and maintaining the power relations of American society? Since the social scientists themselves could not agree on the answers to these questions,[59] labor's confusion is at least understandable. With the passage of a few years, however, a growing number of union leaders took the position that counseling was perhaps the most dangerous weapon that management had in its personnel arsenal. The United Auto Workers, for instance, looked forward "to a happy day when the NLRB will declare the use of the deep interview an unfair labor practice and will at the same time award the worker concerned a back-frustration up until the time he was talked out of his grievance by a company-employed industrial psychologist."[60]

From the beginning of World War II to the present, management has learned to place greater and greater reliance on the work of industrial social scientists. Through attitude surveys, testing, rating, counseling, and training, personnel men, managers, and social scientists hoped to realize the benefits of a controlled labor force, and the goal of "custom made men" seemed to be coming closer to realization. Problems of turnover, absenteeism, morale, and unionism were all subjected to the techniques of industrial social science. Managers became increasingly satisfied. Most labor leaders became increasingly suspicious and alarmed. Almost all of the social scientists concerned themselves with how to improve and refine their techniques, without troubling themselves about the effects of what they were doing.

Despite all of the research and application of social science in industry, however, the work force still seemed to be capable, occasionally, of exerting its own will. The day had not yet come when managers could relax in the knowledge that human will or caprice would prove incapable of upsetting their plans. But, at the same time that these formal personnel policies were being implemented, a new approach to the problems of human behavior was started. The "human relations approach" to industrial problems rounded out the personnel man's dream of a more complete reservoir of plans whose implementation would effectively force labor to respond to the demands of management.

CHAPTER 9

Human Relations
and Power

EARLY IN 1957 the McGraw-Hill organization reported that America's manufacturers expected that by 1959 new products would account for 11 per cent of their sales. So thoroughly had Americans become accustomed to product development through research that the forecast caused hardly a ripple in the nation's press. Spending for physical research, at the time the statement was made, averaged around five billion dollars a year, an annual increase of over four billion since the early 1940's. By the middle of the 1950's research had become increasingly characteristic of a growing number of firms, small as well as large. The 2800 corporations conducting research in 1950 grew to 4000 seven years later; the five billion spent in 1957 would grow to twenty billion by 1975, forecast one research institute.

The increasing utility and therefore prestige of the physical sciences in industry reinforced the growing managerial faith in the social sciences. In fact, the industries spending the most money on research in the physical sciences came to be the leaders in conducting and implementing social-science research. The chemical, electrical equipment, and aircraft industries were those most committed to support of basic physical research, and these same industries also became increasingly oriented to social science. Social scientists became aware of this correlation, and began to assure each other that their future was bright because of the growing involvement of American industry in basic research in physical science.[1]

New developments in industrial personnel work also encouraged the social scientist. No longer content to use mechanically the devices long cherished by "professional" personnel men, a growing number of managers turned to research to find out the effects of standard programs, to check the results of usual techniques, and to discover, if possible, new methods of achieving their old aims. After World War II, the number of firms using research as a part of their personnel work grew markedly, and by the late 1950's the movement was deeply entrenched.[2]

After the Second World War, a new trend in social science made its way into industry. Alongside of the psychological and sociological techniques of which industry now made use, the so-called human-relations approach to industrial problems offered the manager still another personnel tool to use in his efforts to deal with the human problems of the postwar industrial world.

This field of human relations was, as the name suggests, interdisciplinary; borrowing from both psychology and sociology, human-relations experts frequently were also trained in anthropology and other related fields. In industrial terms these experts made use of the psychology of the 1920's and the sociology of the Hawthorne experiments. The new element was their focus, as they put it, not on the isolated individual or on the dehumanized milieu but on the interrelationships between the individual and his several environments. Believing it was possible to isolate the internal and external pressures on the individual which would explain his conduct and thought, the human-relations experts concerned themselves with motivation and with small groups in their search for clues to the enigmas of human behavior. Interested also in the processes of human relationships, they studied such phenomena as leadership and communication. Making use of relatively new techniques such as role-playing and sociometry, the human-relations specialists carved out for themselves what they believed was a distinct professional domain whose industrial significance they hoped would be apparent to the nation's managers.

After 1946, the managerial conviction that problems of human relations were important knew virtually no bounds. "Human-relations" courses were begun in an increasing number of firms. Skill in human understanding, according to the American Management Association, was the most important ingredient in the executive's talents; in the coal industry "human engineering becomes a vital factor in higher productivity . . ."; the most significant industrial problem, others said, was human relations.[3] Even the trend toward automation was believed to place greater demands on human understanding because, it was argued, machines could never completely replace people. "No matter how fancy the equipment," said *Business Week*, "output takes a wallop unless the worker gets a kick out of his job."[4]

A Standard Oil executive, in September, 1954, summed up the reasons for which his company, at least, had come to believe that an understanding of human behavior was so important. It was interesting to read the many academic arguments insisting that the nature of the modern corporation was social. Interesting also were the reformers' pleas that human dignity must be preserved in the increasingly anonymous industrial world. But more than just interesting was the fact that "the biggest competitive advantage that Esso can gain lies in continuing to build initiative, cooperation, and the will to work within our people." There was a boundary to the leadership that Esso could maintain in wages and benefits for its workers. But the extent to which they could be better motivated was said to be limitless.[5]

Given this attitude and its financial resources, it follows that Standard Oil of New Jersey most completely embraced the human-relations approach to its post-World War II problems. In the convictions of this management was reflected the new stature that industrial social science had achieved. According to one of Standard's consultants, this management was forced to accept social science for the same reasons as many other firms, but because of Standard's intimate involvement with foreign cultures it had a special compulsion. As social scientists began to spell out the implications of dealing with people in different cultural settings, Standard of New Jersey became convinced of the industrial applicability of social science.

Early in 1948, at a conference of affiliates called to discuss the practicability of using psychological tests, Standard's employee-relations manager reported that the board of directors "has given its blessing" to research on the use of social science. As the research got under way Standard decided that it could itself make a contribution to general knowledge. The company decided to publish all the results of its social-science research because there was "no reason why such information should be kept secret." The speaker went on to say that "if other companies would adopt the same attitude perhaps much more could be accomplished in developing data which would be of great assistance to industry and the country in making the best use of its human resources." Around 1951 Standard established an Advisory Committee on Human Relations, which was authorized to advise the various staff departments that were concerned with any phase of human relations, and to give its opinions about projects undertaken. "Among the reports and projects which have been given to this committee have been some involving social science research, both in the company and outside the company. . . . The Committee was so impressed with what they heard that they suggested that the information be made available to as many members of management as possible." In the opinion of Douglas McGregor, M.I.T. psychologist and consultant to Jersey,

Standard management was convinced of the "desirability of encouraging social science research." He pointed out to Standard executives some of the dangers and pitfalls of expecting too much or too little from this activity, but he apparently believed that the management of Standard Oil knew what it was doing.[6]

By 1954 social research in industry had become a highly lucrative business. By this time, as a number of firms invited academic social scientists and other professors to visit their plants in order to get a first-hand view of what industry was really like, the acceptance of social science had become "an established part of the industrial scene." The place of the psychologist in industry was secure, and the United States Bureau of Labor Statistics could finally point out that there would be a "slow but steady growth in employment opportunities" for sociologists in industry.[7]

Despite the deepening involvement of most of America's industries in human-relations research, a number of firms persisted in their skepticism; proof, in clear cash terms, of the achievements of industrial social science was still lacking. "Time and cost," said the personnel supervisor of the Cleveland Electric Illuminating Company, "are factors which are frequently overlooked by 'human relations' experts." Some managers believed that most social scientists were wild-eyed radicals, and others worried that sociologists especially would be led by their research into delicate areas of management philosophy and motivation, suggesting perhaps the need for unwanted changes. Responding to this managerial mood, one Adlerian psychologist said that managers wanted to maintain the status quo in their firms but wanted to "find a kind of magic that will change the results of their mistakes."[8]

An example of this countercurrent of managerial hostility was reported by a team of California sociologists who had proposed a research project to an executive of a firm that planned to open a new Los Angeles branch. Trying to get an answer from this man, the sociologists kept writing letters even though the executive refused to answer. Finally, in a fit of pique, he replied:

Well, wasn't my silence answer enough? What do you think we are trying to do here? We can't be a bunch of guinea pigs for you fellows. We don't want people asking us a lot of silly questions. Frankly, we are moving out here to run a factory, and we just can't be bothered with this sort of thing.[9]

Social-science jargon certainly was an obstacle to even the most well-disposed manager. Though social scientists might have the answers to any or all of industry's problems, the answers were worthless so long as managers could make no sense out of them. The belief that social scientists would "never really 'arrive' in industry as long as they require interpreters" was shared by a growing number of experts who attempted to speak and write in more intelligible terms. "Social sciencese" was called a "weird jargon," "the strangest language ever penned by man." It was thought by one observer that social scientists had developed their inimitable jargon as a "pretentious attempt to borrow the successes of natural science by imitating the precision of its vocabulary." Whatever the case, the executive's head was sure to spin as he listened to the social scientists discuss sociodrama, communication engineering, nondirective therapy and counseling, group-action laboratories, field theory, group dynamics and group therapy, spontaneity theory, and so on and on. An early justification of this language mentioned the necessity for precision; it would be silly to make the obvious complicated but, the argument went on, the subtleties of human nature demanded a technical vocabulary capable of distinguishing between finely drawn nuances. The extremes to which some social scientists went, however, could not be justified on any grounds. The sneaking suspicion, for instance, that "a detachable inclement weather device" bore a close resemblance to an umbrella forced even fellow social scientists to lose patience. In his language alone, some managers found ample reason to label the industrial social scientist as impractical, ignorant of industry, and possibly crazy. With time, however, even executives joined in the sport and used the jargon themselves.[10]

This antagonistic strand of the managerial mentality served only to highlight the ready acceptance of social science by most American managers. As the human-relations aproach gathered steam, fewer and fewer managers had the necessary conviction or will to resist the fad. One either authorized human-relations research or was made to feel like an anachronism left over from the Neolithic epoch. The human-relations approach to industrial personnel at last seemed to have almost universal managerial approval.

One of the key concepts of the human-relations specialists was motivation. To find out what made workers work or regulate output, rebel or obey, was still a desideratum of progressive managements. Both social scientists and managers had long discussed various devices calculated to spur workers to greater efforts. Though most managers had assumed that money was the greatest incentive for employees, many social scientists insisted that workers needed other, less tangible rewards.[11] The idea that workers were really less interested in hard cash than most managers had long assumed had obvious and attractive implications for management.

After about 1950, some industrial social scientists, worrying about the managerial bias of most of their colleagues, reversed the traditional position. Instead of trying to show management how to induce workers to work harder for less money, these men insisted that money was the single greatest incentive. "Human-relations programs," this argument went, "are never a substitute for sound economic relationships. Geraniums in the plant windows and a turkey for Christmas do not make up for substandard pay."[12]

Among the conclusions of motivation research in industry was the finding that wages were important to workers, perhaps not as things in themselves but for what they represented. Even in cases where workers said that wages were relatively unimportant, the researchers concluded that this indicated merely that wages were on an acceptable level and were taken for granted. Similarly, researchers who insisted that items like "security" were nonfinancial factors were criticized for not asking why workers wanted security; the answers to such a question might show that this, after all, was a financial factor.[13]

Regardless of the lack of a theoretical base upon which an acceptable and workable concept of motivation could be fashioned, regardless of the bitter disputes among the social scientists, a growing number of America's managers agreed that motivation studies were of the utmost importance. Especially when the sensational successes of advertising agencies using motivation research were popularized[14] did the less glamorous industrial managers find reinforcement for their conviction about the importance of such studies. It was true that through attitude surveys management could learn the views, desires, and aspirations of its workers. But how to change these attitudes if they were unacceptable to management? Counseling proved to be one answer to this problem, but it had to proceed on a person-to-person basis, it was expensive, and because it had to be voluntary if it were to work, many employees could not be approached at all. If, however, some way could be found to install a system of incentives that would touch universal chords of human motivation, management would be in the invincible position of being able to predict and control the thinking of its men. Both managers and social scientists reported their approval of such a procedure.[15]

The entire field of motivation research as applied to

industrial personnel problems was bitterly opposed by men committed to organized labor. One such observer summed up the movement this way:

The anti-democratic 'human relations' experts misuse psychological findings. One of them is the conclusion that workers are animated by other needs than high wages. Dr. Robert McMurry . . . reports that workers kept telling him and his associates that they joined unions for greater job security and higher pay; but the McMurry psychologists decided that the workers' real if unconscious motive 'was a craving to improve the emotional situation surrounding their jobs.' So, the practitioners conclude, if you can use psychology to give the workers 'emotional release' and 'ego involvement' they will forget about their pay.[16]

The United Auto Workers, too, became aware of the implications of motivation research as applied to industry. A cartoon in the educational magazine of the UAW showed hanging on a wall a sign, signed by "the Boss," which read: "Even if we do cut your pay and break you down with speed up, we still love you."[17] The point is simply that many industrial human-relations specialists still concluded that pay was less important to workers than "fair treatment." Thus management apparently could lower wages with impunity if it became concerned with workers as men, treated the labor force with so-called dignity, and replaced fear with the promise of (nonfinancial) rewards.

At least since the Hawthorne researchers became convinced that the small circle of his intimate fellows exerted a tremendous influence on every member of the group, industrial researchers as well as managers devoted increasing time and thought to a search for methods of control. Granting the premise of the significance of the small group, the importance of psychological testing began to dwindle. Tests, psychologists in the postwar period agreed, merely indicated those job applicants who were technically incapable of performing the work. The attitudes, expectations, commitments, and shared motivations of the group of men with whom the applicant would work would certainly influence and perhaps even determine whether he would conform to managerial expectations.[18]

Management had limited alternatives when dealing with the small group. As the Hawthorne researchers demonstrated in the bank wiring room, the small group was organized in defiance of and for protection against management. Such a group had to be either destroyed or changed. Perhaps management could replace hostile groups with friendly ones of its own creation, or perhaps it could convince the members of a group that hostility to management was pointless. In any case, management, by and large, understandably refused to allow these informal associations to emerge without "guidance," without control. The bank wiring room experiment at Western Electric had shown that the power of the group was superior to that of management. It was unlikely, therefore, that many researchers or managers would attempt to attack the problem frontally. The least dangerous method seemed to be the encouragement by management of friendly informal associations.[19] One personnel man told how, in 1944, he advised a company employing 25,000 workers to organize its employees into small groups. The company ignored his advice "and the CIO got them, and they still have plenty of troubles."[20]

Some social scientists worried about such an antilabor application of the theories of the small group. If, for example, small groups were to be given some responsibility for maintaining production quotas, according to one social scientist, they must also be given a voice in the determination of the quota. Anything short of this, he continued, would be "a manipulative device for getting more out of the workers without giving them more."[21] Sharing these feelings, several union officials went on record as being opposed to the formation and possible manipulation of the small industrial group.[22] But labor leaders, like managers, were powerless to frustrate the formation of such groups. The question was, toward which goals would the small groups be directed? Thus it was clearly advantageous for management to attempt to get the many small groups in its employ to think "constructively," to act in accordance with managerial desires.

To satisfy this managerial urge, some industrial social scientists applied a technique borrowed from Jacob L. Moreno. Since 1934, when he introduced the technique called sociometry, his influence had steadily increased. As a psychiatrist, Moreno was concerned with the impact of group life on the individual members. His technique led the study of groups back to the individual and away from the perception of the group as a separate entity with its own sociological existence. Because sociometry also shed light on the nature of groups, Moreno was influential in weakening the barriers between psychology and sociology. Personnel men frequently were told of the importance of sociometry and advised that the use of this technique would significantly raise production and reduce absenteeism.

Sociometry is a technique for measuring the personal relations among the members of a group, who are asked to list the persons with whom they like to work best and least. A map of the bonds holding the group together, holding certain individuals in and expelling others, can then be drawn. It is the belief of the sociometrists that their technique can quantify the personal relations of the group. Regardless of validity, it is clear that sociometry provides a technique for studying the kinds of informal, primary group associations that the Hawthorne researchers discovered at Western Electric. With Moreno's tool it becomes possible to speak of the degree of cohesiveness of a specific group and to make comparisons between one group and another.[23]

Related to the concern with small groups in industry was the range of problems clustering around the phenomenon of leadership, industrial and otherwise. This concern antedated the work with small groups, since it was one of the earliest industrial problems investigated by psychologists. The early formulation, and one which partly persists to the present day, insisted that leadership was an art, a subjective quality, something vague and even mystical that could not be reduced to a science or communicated to others. According to this view, good leaders are born and not made; training courses for future leaders may be of some small help, but because it is so subjective, leadership generally cannot be taught. Social scientists who took this position have argued that the formulation of concrete criteria of leadership success was impossible, that no one really knew just what made a successful leader.[24]

Closely allied to this position was the belief that leadership was a function of personality. Thus, strength of character, "*intensity* of . . . *thought-forces,*" self-confidence, "humanness," sensitivity, integrity, imagination, and so on, were frequently listed as necessary qualifications for the industrial leader.[25] Only one psychologist, Donald A. Laird, found that successful business executives lacked the hackneyed list of virtues so frequently depicted by sanguine biographers; according to him, "about half of the successful executives studied had a noticeable dislike of their associates, had man-sized tempers, did not know or care much about the home conditions or troubles of their employees, were argumentative and inclined to fly off the handle."[26]

Clinical methods, including the Thematic Apperception Technique, have been used for isolating some of the personality traits of the successful industrial leader. Confronting the subject with a series of pictures whose content could be interpreted in an infinite number of ways, the psychologist could learn a good deal from the responses elicited in the subject by these nondirective stimuli. According to the proponents of the industrial application of the T.A.T., their technique could successfully isolate the necessary qualifications of successful leadership. But the list of personality traits that successful leaders shared, according to T.A.T. advocates, was fundamentally similar to the older lists of personality characteristics, including, for example, firmness of conviction, realism, aggression, and other such amorphisms. The T.A.T. experts did insist that their approach greatly increased the proportion of successful leaders among candidates for executive positions in industry. Several companies, including General Electric, Sears Roebuck, Standard Oil (N.J.), Inland Steel, and Union Carbide, authorized such studies of the personality characteristics of their executives.[27]

Despite the general agreement among social scientists about the importance of leadership in industry, discussion of key personnel was rarely held in a random sample of industrial boards of directors.[28] If profit and production figures were satisfactory, if "labor troubles" were kept at a minimum, if a competitive advantage was maintained, the top level of industrial management was satisfied with its operating executives. Questions of leadership as social scientists conceived of them troubled America's industrialists but rarely.

With the emergence of the human-relations approach to personnel problems, however, a few managers did become concerned with the social-science approach to leadership. The president of General Mills, for instance, in 1949 asked whether candidates for management positions had a "sufficient understanding of the factors which motivate individuals to work together efficiently?"[29] There was the magic word, "motivate." Implied in the question was the assumption that leadership meant something other than dictation. This assumption was to grow significantly.

Though a few social scientists and managers in the 1920's and 1930's believed that authoritarian leadership would produce nothing but trouble, that the consent of the governed was essential to leadership success,[30] it was not until the Second World War that this belief spread. In 1946 a survey of America's "well-paid successes" showed that almost half agreed that handling people skillfully was the most important part of their jobs.[31] But handling people did not mean merely getting along with them and being pleasant. It meant, according to General Foods, the ability to *persuade* people of the wisdom of managerial decision. Authority was not to be used where persuasion had a chance of working. American Telephone & Telegraph, too, argued that the successful leader instilled in his people the desire to do what they were told. "Now, I don't want you to do it my way because I say, 'Do it my way,' " said the friendly executive to a white-collar subordinate in a *New Yorker* cartoon. "I want you to do it my way because you *see* it my way."[32]

Among some managers this concern with leadership became a fetish. At almost all meetings of executives, speeches were given on the importance of leadership, the nature of leadership, and so on. According to two sociologists, this fixation derived from the fact that managers wanted to believe that their power over millions of people resulted from the recognition by their followers of their superior ability. Because of this recognition, the tale continued, workers were eager to follow. Power was left out of the story. Managers evidently liked to think that men obeyed them because they were "gifted to lead," not because they had the power to force obedience.[33]

Out of the desire of executives to be respected as persons rather than as powers grew the discussion of democracy in industry. Some social scientists concluded that democratic leadership in industry would in fact raise productivity. The kind of leadership characteristic of a particular plant would determine the way employees would respond. Thus, it was believed that democratic leadership would elicit cooperation from the workers and autocratic leadership would result merely in obedience, while a laissez-faire policy would encourage self-reliance and initiative.[34]

But, said a labor official, "It is about time that the psychologist and the so-called social scientist scrapped the notion that freedom and democracy exist in the authoritarian environment of the factory." Industrial democracy was a myth. Arthur Kornhauser, one of the leaders of socially conscious industrial social science, agreed with this attitude by saying that industry was simply and clearly authoritarian, and that any attempt to explain away its power or dilute its effects by teaching "democratic leadership" to executives was bound to fail. Power, insisted Kornhauser, must be recognized for what it was. And because so many industrial social scientists and managers refused to admit the power of management, they viewed the problem of the distribution of power in industry in terms of human relations, terms that stressed motivation, participation, democracy, and so forth.[35]

The debate about the nature of leadership was also related to the problems of the workers' motivations. What did workers work for? As has been shown, most social scientists believed nonfinancial rewards were more important than money. These nonfinancial needs of workers could be stimulated and then satisfied by "correct" industrial leadership. "Management," said one eminent industrial psychologist, "can anticipate continuing pressure for higher wages, enlarged benefits, improvements in working conditions, and other changes which 'cost money.'" If these demands could be anticipated, they could be forestalled. "Management of every plant," this expert continued, "has at its disposal media for stimulating production and raising morale . . . which do not call for substantial increases in out-of-pocket expenditures." Chief among such media was "effective" leadership.[36]

The advantages of such leadership were presumably

clear. Management could reduce substantially its personnel expenditures including wages, reduce its labor trouble,
and raise morale, all by learning to instill in its employees the desire to follow men of allegedly greater wisdom.
Whether employees were in fact motivated more by eti-
quette, pleasantness, and kind words than by hard cash
remained a disputed point. The tremendous advantages
to management, however, in assuming that this kind of
"constructive leadership" would result in at least some
of the benefits outlined by so many industrial social scientists were vital enough to make for a continued effort to
improve leadership.

The brunt of this increasing conviction that leadership
had to be improved and that methods of leading men had
to be changed was aimed at the foreman. Virtually all
managements and social scientists, as well as a few labor
leaders, agreed that the foreman was the key figure in
labor relations. The degree to which the worker was satisfied with his foreman was the degree to which he was
satisfied with his job. Foremen and other first-line supervisors were told that they needed to have clearly in mind
the rules of persuasion. No longer could they use blunt
authority to accomplish a given task. They had to convince
their men that doing the job would be to everyone's advantage. No longer could the foreman tell a worker: "Do it—
now!" He had to convince the worker that the worker himself would be happier if the job was done, and the sooner
it was done the happier the worker would be. The underlying assumption of this position was that workers could
be made happy or unhappy by the human relations between them and their immediate supervision. Human
relations and the social system of the factory were at stake,
and to "progressive" management nothing was as important. Foremen, therefore, had to become highly skilled in
the arts and techniques of sophisticated leadership.[37] "It
is in keeping with the managerial demiurge and the

changed nature of the foreman's role that he is led into the ways of manipulation," said C. Wright Mills, the Columbia sociologist; the foreman "is to develop discipline and loyalty among the workers by using his own personality as the main tool of persuasion."[38]

The Ford Motor Company was among those most committed to training foremen in human relations. Henry Ford II called his approach "human engineering," and through a series of conferences with foremen his company "hoped to help foremen to develop a clearer understanding of the principles of leadership, because the whole tone and morale, the general atmosphere, the physical output per man and the personal satisfaction foremen derive from their work in our plants is affected in marked degree by the quality of leadership which they give the rank and file in the organization."[39] To this Ford's union responded:

The profit possibilities of human engineering, as it is called by Henry Ford II, are fantastic.

As the result of this discovery, foremen are attending schools throughout the country to receive training in the art of convincing workers that they really are deeply beloved by the boss.

Employers are trooping to special classes at Harvard, where they learn workers are not the least bit mercenary, and that while it is true that the boss is in business for an honest, or at least a fast, dollar, workers report to the plant each morning for love, affection, and small friendly attentions.[40]

Many other "progressive" companies began foreman training in an organized manner after the close of the Second World War; even by 1946 one-third of a large sample of American industry had organized such programs. Making use of techniques like sociometry, industrial psychology and sociology, and the case method of instruction so cherished by the human-relations people at the Harvard Business School, industrial trainers faced a growing sea of first-line supervisors. Such training in human relations was thought to be necessary because, as industrial consultant Peter Drucker put it, "the skills of the new mass-produc-

tion society are different from those of traditional society."
The new skills demanded of foremen were skills in dealing
with people.[41]

As usual, a few social scientists dissented, questioning
the human-relations training being given to foremen and its
effectiveness. One psychologist concerned with problems
of leadership reported that "training . . . in leader behavior
must be examined much more broadly than we in psychology have been accustomed to do."[42] Despite such professional doubts, industry went on its determined way of
finding out whether or not more highly trained foremen
could in fact increase output, morale, and loyalty while
reducing costs, grievances, and conflict.

To compound the difficulties of the foreman was the
confused nature of his job. Obviously it was necessary for
him to maintain the loyalty of his men. Just as clear was
his obligation to remain loyal to the goals and purposes of
management. Was the foreman a part of management or
a part of the working force? A man in the middle, the
modern foreman was torn between two conflicting sets
of expectations. He had to protect both his men and his
management.

Still another device used in supervisory training in
human relations was role-playing. Moreno is generally
credited with explaining the full usefulness of this procedure and Kurt Lewin's "group dynamics" circle at M.I.T.
brought it to the attention of management. Like other
aspects of the human-relations approach to industrial personnel, role-playing made its impact on industry only after
the conclusion of World War II.[43]

Role-playing is a method of showing an individual how
someone else would feel in a given situation. For instance,
a foreman is asked to play the role of an aggrieved worker
in order to get the feel of the worker's emotions when dealing with a strict foreman. As a training device, role-playing
was said to be "equal to the difficult task of altering and

improving the attitudes of rank-and-file employees, supervisors, and higher management personnel."[44] Again management was presented with a powerful tool of social and
individual control by industrial social scientists. It is believed that the Harwood Manufacturing Company, where
"labor unions seem unable to make headway," was the
first to make use of the device. Other companies to follow
Harwood's lead included American Steel and Wire, Bristol-
Myers, Chrysler, General Foods, Johnson and Johnson,
Michigan Bell, Procter and Gamble, and Swift.[45]

One shrewd observer has said that most corporations
have made only infrequent use of these advanced techniques: "a bit of role playing here, a sociodrama there, and
perhaps some thematic apperception tests now and then."
But another device was completely accepted by management. "Group conference techniques," he continued, "have
been taking such hold that in some companies executives
literally do not have a moment to themselves."[46] Of course
management has always made use of groups to solve
problems, but the conscious and deliberate creation of
"problem-solving groups" did not occur until the human-
relations approach to industrial personnel got under way.
By the end of World War II companies without experience
with executive conferences were said to be "unusual."[47]

The leader of such a conference was merely to precipi-
tate discussion and summarize results. He was not to direct
the discussion, and he did not necessarily have to know the
answers to the problems because of which the conference
was called. He did have to know, according to General
Foods, *"how* to get a group *to think."* The success or failure
of the conference seemed to depend on the personality of
the group leader.[48] He was to so stimulate the group that
a group answer to the problem would emerge.

Group thinking was the goal, and individual domination of the discussion was considered the worst failure of
a problem-solving group.[49] The fear of a willful executive

was pressing in industry. Evidently management had to have assurance that its executives would toe the mark. And the group conference seemed to be the single most effective instrument for realizing this end.

Of even greater interest was the conference in which employees were told to participate. The concept of participation, like motivation, became a fundamental prop of the human-relations approach. Several psychologists and sociologists studied the effects of participation on the behavior of workers, and concluded that the more workers participated in decisions concerning their welfare, the happier and the more productive they would be.[50] One group of social scientists, however, proved that equal participation was not related to member satisfaction.[51] But the notion that participation directly influenced morale persisted, and after 1945 the human-relations specialists began to sell the idea of participation to an increasing number of firms.

Not until H. H. Carey, a management observer, described "consultative supervision" in 1937 was the full meaning of participation, in the human-relations sense, understood by most American managers. "Consultative supervision," he wrote, "may be defined as the procedure whereby supervisors and executives consult with employees or their representatives as equals on all matters affecting the employees' welfare or interest prior to formulating policies or taking action."[52]

Making it possible for employees to participate in decisions affecting their behavior was frequently said to be the final and democratic industrial answer to personnel problems. Here at last, argued several companies, was the way to humanize and democratize industry. Of course, management pointed out, employee participation increased productivity, reduced costs, reduced grievances and resistance to change, and increased morale. But these were supposedly less meaningful than the sense of importance and belonging felt by participating employees. One company, a subsidiary of Bethlehem Steel, reported that employee participation in management descisions actually converted radical workers into "sound" management-oriented employees. Standard Oil reported a 20 per cent increase in production. Detroit Edison told of increased benefits in virtually every aspect of its business. General Foods reduced costs and believed that the ability to think was stimulated in every employee, from the chairman of the board to the janitor. American Telephone & Telegraph said that its workers accepted "restrictions" more willingly when they had a hand in formulating them. Carnegie-Illinois Steel reduced grievances. Western Electric and Caterpillar Tractor both were convinced of the necessity of participation and training in human relations, but were cautious about evaluating results.[53]

Atlantic Refining was most explicit. The advantage of participation, according to this company, was that an individual tended to accept the decisions of a group of which he was a member. Group pressures were so relentless that, regardless of personal convictions, conformity to a group decision was virtually guaranteed. Cessna Aircraft advised that "the group leader's job is to mould the human weaknesses of his men and women in the proper direction." And Alfred J. Marrow, president of the Harwood Manufacturing Company, a Ph.D. in psychology himself, said that the leaders of group decision conferences in his company "must be prepared to channel discussion so that the group decision springs from the persons in the group and is agreed to unanimously by them."[54]

A few labor spokesmen and sympathizers took a less favorable view of the participation fad that swept American industry. Lewis Corey, a professor of political economy at Antioch College, described the Harwood system of participation as "vicious." As workers were divided into small groups, into "teams," the effect, said Corey, was to "*frag-*

mentize the labor force and make managerial control of it easier." Because only management had the whole view of the many conferences in which employees participated, management gave up none of its control. And, Corey continued, "the objectives of this use of 'group dynamics' are to get the workers to accept what management wants them to accept *but* to make them feel *they* made or helped to make the decision." The system was "at best paternalistic and at worst despotic."[55] William H. Whyte, an assistant managing editor of *Fortune*, with his characteristic bite, summarized the movement:

Now one no longer need be ashamed of going along with the herd; indeed, with the aid of the new jargon he can be articulately proud of the fact. He is not just conforming, he is using 'group skills.' He is maintaining 'equilibrium.' He is 'participating.'[56]

The essential difficulty with the participation studies of the industrial social scientists and the participation plans installed by many managements was the confusion over the meaning of participation. If the conclusions of the social scientists concerning participation were implemented in industry merely to induce conformity and greater satisfaction with unchanged and undesirable working conditions, including wages, then this was merely another in the long string of personnel devices that have been used by management further to control labor.

As part of the human-relations approach to industrial personnel, communication techniques completed the social-science contribution to American industry. Several social scientists and management spokesmen argued that misunderstanding was at the root of most labor-management conflicts. Better communication, both up and down the line, would facilitate the kinds of understanding necessary for cooperation. But the atmosphere of the plant was thought to be important. Labor-management equality and trust were said to be absolute requirements for effective communication.[57] Under these conditions innumerable advantages would be realized, presumably by both labor and management. In 1946, for instance, Henry Ford II said that "informed employees are more productive than uninformed employes [*sic*]."[58]

In general, the social scientists concerned with communication stressed the narrowest side of the problem. Much of their work was on the level of a cookbook, as they devised intricate lists of do's and don'ts and carefully prepared tables of what should and what should not be communicated. Focusing, in short, on content and technique, most of the social scientists concerned with the problem ignored its broader and more vital aspects. With this approach management generally was enthralled.[59] But, according to two social scientists, the principles of effective communication would never be found as long as most of their colleagues busied themselves in the search for specific remedies for specific management problems.[60]

An example of one kind of benefit management hoped to realize from more conscious communication programs was provided by an incident at Thompson Products. Late in 1939 this company was being threatened with union organization by both the CIO and the AFL. Foremen of the company were told that they should communicate more directly with the workers:

While industry does continue to hum, organization activities of unions will be pushed hard. During that period great care should be taken that employees are kept in an attitude in which they will not be receptive to 'crack-pot' theories of economics, on which labor agitators thrive.... Drive home sound economic thought, now. Don't miss any opportunity to make friends with employees. Make them realize you are their friend.[61]

The position of the foreman was recognized as crucial to effective communication. A trade journal, in 1948, reported that workers wanted more information about the company but did not trust first-line supervision as a source of that information. Social scientists pointed out that especially in communicating upward the foreman was an unreliable source for management. He usually would be loath to report bad news and eager, perhaps too eager, to send up good news. The amount of distortion as a result of the foreman's desire to protect himself was large.[62]

As with every other personnel device that social scientists supplied to industry, communication plans were clouded by the assumptions and biases of a management orientation. Finally, even some executives, their spokesmen, and journals realized this. In 1951 *Fortune* reported, for example: "Control communication and you control." Because the industrial social scientists were almost always unwilling to admit that the managers of American industry constituted a power elite, they were forced to put their research and explanations in unreal terms. Unwilling to admit the class divisions in American society, they failed to see what *Fortune* saw. In refreshingly simple terms one of the editors of that magazine wrote the single best summation of all the enthusiasm over communication: "All the communication in the world is not going to make a coal miner think like a coal operator, or, for that matter, eliminate that great block to communication, the s.o.b."[63]

Because the editors of *Fortune* were relatively uncrippled by the clichés of liberalism about industrial democracy and other misleading assumptions of industrial social scientists, the editors were able to see communication plans clearly. Regardless of content and technique, regardless of the atmosphere of the plant, communication plans that ignored the power relationships of American society were bound to fail.

Because the underlying assumptions of the industrial social scientists gave direction to so much of their work, these assumptions warrant a closer look.

CHAPTER 10

The Servants
of Power

HENRY FORD, II, 1946: "If we can solve the problem of human relations in industrial production, we can make as much progress toward lower costs in the next 10 years as we made during the past quarter century through the development of the machinery of mass production."[1] By the middle of the twentieth century, industrial social science had become one of the most pregnant of the many devices available to America's managers in their struggle with costs and labor, government and the consuming public. But, even then, industrial social science remained richer in its promise than in its accomplishments, impressive as these had been. It was often what social science *could* do in the next five, ten, or twenty years that justified to managers their current support of its practitioners. Thus far, social scientists had contributed to management a useful array of techniques, including testing, counseling, attitude research, and sociometry. All to the good, certainly; but much was left to do. And most of what was left, as Henry Ford correctly pointed out, was centered in the area of human relations. The reason that an understanding of human relations assumed such monumental proportions was that, in an age of governmental regulations and more powerful unions, costs continued to rise. American management came to believe in the importance of understanding human behavior because it became convinced that this was one sure way of improving its main weapon in the struggle for power, the profit margin.

The promise of industrial social science has not been a subject about which America's managers have had to guess. The industrial social scientists themselves have, throughout their professional history, made explicit their aspirations, their hopes for the future, and their unbounded faith in the centrality of their discipline to the problems of modern life. The history of this explication of faith began, appropriately enough, with Walter Dill Scott, who argued in 1911 that a knowledge of the laws of psychology would make it possible for the businessman to control and therefore raise the efficiency of every man in his employ, including his own. At about the same time, a lecturer at the University of Wisconsin's School of Commerce assured his students that a knowledge of psychology would increase their "commercial proficiency by fifty per cent." Workers, according to Hugo Münsterberg's 1913 statement, would have their wages raised, their working hours reduced, mental depression and dissatisfaction with work eliminated, all through the application of psychology to industry. He assured Americans that a "cultural gain . . . will come to the total economic life of the nation." A knowledge of psychology, reported another psychologist, would provide the business executive with the skills needed to influence the behavior of his workers. Psychologist G. Stanley Hall went all out: "Our task," he said, "is nothing less than to rehumanize industry."[2]

During the 1920's and 1930's psychologists reported that "the fate . . . of mankind" depended on the help they could give to managers. Indeed, according to James McKeen Cattell, the founder of the Psychological Corporation, "The development of psychology as a science and its application to the control of human conduct . . . may in the course of the coming century be as significant for civilization as has been the industrial revolution." Specific tasks were also outlined for the psychology of the future. For example, General Motors' sit-down strikes of 1937 could have been avoided through the use of psychology, said a psychologist. If psychologists were as effective in industry as they had been in education, said another, "something akin to an industrial Utopia would arise." Over and over again these men assured anyone who cared to listen that many of the world's problems would disappear if only executives would be more receptive to the advances of psychology.[3]

Even problems of general moment were thought to be solvable through the work of industrial psychologists; the factory, said M.I.T. psychologist Douglas McGregor, "is a microcosm in which we may well be able to find answers to some of the fundamental problems of modern society." Industrial conflict would disappear, reported other psychologists, if their conclusions were implemented in industry. In fact, said still another, if psychology were more widely accepted by management, "the advancement of our emotional, social, and economic life" would be more certain. *"Potentially the most important of sciences for the improvement of man and of his world-order"* is the way Robert M. Yerkes, a psychologist at Yale, described his discipline in 1946.[4]

Sociologists, too, tried to make clear what they could do if they were given the chance, though they were usually more restrained than the psychologists. They recognized that managers determined the kinds of opportunities the sociologists had, and hence, if the claims of sociology were frustrated, the managers themselves would be at fault. If all was in order, however, if managers cooperated, sociologists could "provide useful analytical tools and profitable guides for activity." Other sociologists believed that they could help managers "think more effectively about their human problems." Perhaps this was why one sociologist accepted employment with a petroleum company in 1943 to explain why the CIO was able to organize its men. Margaret Mead thought her colleagues could help make the anonymous industrial worker feel important. Focusing on the top echelon of the business hierarchy, some sociologists were dissatisfied with what they saw. A different type of social control was needed, and they believed that they were the men to point the way to the future. The powers of the sociological elite would be concentrated on the subelite of managers who needed to be led and "clarified." All that was needed was some cooperation from those who wielded managerial power.[5]

It was precisely this need for managerial cooperation that made the social scientists' conception of what they could do in the future seem at best a trifle grandiose and at worst silly. As part of the bureaucratization of virtually every aspect of American life, most industrial social scientists labored in industry as technicians, not as scientists. Not professionally concerned with problems outside the delimited sphere which management had assigned to them, not daring to cross channels of communication and authority, they were hemmed in by the very organization charts which they had helped to contrive. And the usual industrial social scientist, because he accepted the norms of the elite dominant in his society, was prevented from functioning critically, was compelled by his own ideology and the power of America's managers to supply the techniques helpful to managerial goals. In what should have been a healthful tension between mind and society, the industrial social scientist in serving the industrial elite had to abandon the wider obligations of the intellectual who is a servant of his own mind.

Casting his characteristically wide net, sociologist C. Wright Mills pointed out that "the intellectual is becoming a technician, an idea-man, rather than one who resists the environment, preserves the individual type, and defends himself from death-by-adaption." Unless psychologists raised their sights and became concerned with broader social problems, said another observer, they would not "rise to the level of professional persons but will degenerate into mere technicians."[6]

The technician's role was literally forced upon industrial social scientists by the nature of their industrial positions. Hired by management to solve specific problems, they had to produce. The problem was best stated by two of the most astute psychologists of the 1920's: "Research, to be successful, has to be carried out under the most favorable conditions, and only the business man himself can say whether these conditions shall be provided."[7]

A few industrial social scientists learned that they could not even rely on the much touted practicality of business executives. One psychologist employed by an advertising agency said in 1955 that he "had expected that the businessman would be hard headed and practical. . . . To my surprise and frustration," he went on, "they have accepted an awful lot of research mish mush. . . . Hard headed businessmen hell!"[8] Managers, however, have usually been sufficiently practical, from their own point of view, to realize that controls over research programs were necessary. Demanding that the social scientists in their employ concentrate exclusively on the narrow problems of productivity and industrial loyalty, managers made of industrial social science a tool of industrial domination. Some social scientists warned that this procedure would result in a "distorted view of industry," but failed to see that this was precisely what sophisticated managers wanted.[9]

Even Elton Mayo, of Hawthorne fame, feared that the forced status of technician would seriously limit the effectiveness of industrial social scientists, whose science would thereby be strangled. Because of the control of management over the nature and scope of their work, Mayo said, "the interesting *aperçu*, the long chance, may not be followed: both alike must be denied in order that the [re-

search] group may 'land another job.'" The long-range
effects would be even worse, because the "confusion of
research with commercial huckstering can never prosper:
the only effect is to disgust the intelligent youngster who
is thus forced to abandon his quest for human enlighten-
ment."[10]

Management, in short, controlled the industrial social
scientists in its employ. Managers did not make use of
social science out of a sense of social responsibility, but out
of a recognized need to attack age-old problems of costs
and worker loyalty with new weapons designed to fit the
needs and problems of the twentieth century. Thus the
recent arguments that American industry has entered a
new era of social obligations and responsibilities[11] have
missed the main point in the motivation of managers.
When fulfilling putative social obligations became smart
business, smart managers became socially conscious. Walter Reuther is characteristic of the small group that has
refused to be seduced by the sophisticated rhetoric of
managers, their spokesmen, and the articulate academicians who insist that the American business civilization is
the best of all possible worlds. Trying to educate a congressional committee, Reuther said that his extensive experience with employers had taught him that "the one sure
way of making them [employers] socially responsible is to
make them financially responsible for the social results of
what they do or fail to do."[12] Because of the general climate of opinion today, it is perhaps necessary to repeat
what in previous years would have been a cliché unworthy
of serious argument: managers, as managers, are in business to make money. Only to the extent that industrial
social scientists can help in the realization of this goal will
management make use of them.

Managers are forced by the necessities of the business
world to measure their personal success or failure by the
yardstick of the balance sheet; they have occasionally made

considerable effort to clarify the thinking of industrial social scientists who just might be of help in improving the financial condition of the firm and therefore improving the position of the manager. It will be recalled that one of the main obstacles to easy interchange between managers and social scientists had long been the managers' conviction that social scientists were ignorant about the nature and purposes of industry. To employ an expert who did not recognize either the values or necessities of business might prove dangerous. Articulating what many managers felt, an executive of a large utility company, for example, in 1951 laid down the law to social scientists specifying the attitudes business expected of them:

First—a willingness to accept the notion that businessmen perform a useful function in society, and that their methods may be necessary to accomplish this function. . . .

Second—a willingness to accept the culture and conventions of business as necessary and desirable. . . .

Third—a willingness to obtain personal satisfaction from being a member of a winning team, perhaps an anonymous member.

Fourth—a willingness and ability to practice the good human relations principles that he knows.[13]

How unnecessary was this managerial fear of the industrial social scientist. The popular image of the impractical and absent-minded professor who was either a political liberal or perhaps even worse blurred the perception of the hard-headed managers of the business life of the nation. For, throughout their professional history, industrial social scientists, without prodding from anyone, have accepted the norms of America's managers. If this attitude had not tended to influence their work, it would deserve merely passing mention. But this commitment to management's goals, as opposed to the goals of other groups and classes in American society, did color their research and recommendations. These men have been committed to aims other than those of their professional but nonindustrial colleagues. Though the generalization has weaknesses, it seems that making a contribution to knowledge has been the essential purpose of only a few industrial social scientists. Reducing the pressures of unionism while increasing the productivity of the labor force and thereby lowering costs have been among their most cherished goals, because these have been the goals which management has set for them.

Managers, of course, had the power to hire and fire social scientists. If a social scientist was to be kept on the payroll, he had to produce. The judge of whether he was producing was his boss. His boss was interested in the specific problems of the business including those that threatened managerial control. Thus industrial social scientists have usually been salaried men, doing what they were told to do and doing it well—and therefore endangering those other personal, group, class, and institutional interests which were opposed to the further domination by the modern corporation of the mood and direction of American life. Endangered most have been the millions of workers who have been forced or seduced into submission to the ministrations of industrial social scientists. For these men and women there has been little defense, because organized labor generally has been apathetic to the movement, and because, even had labor been more active, management has played the game from a dominant position. Recently, however, there have been a few hints indicating that organized labor is beginning to make use of social-science techniques itself.[14] In any case, to date nothing seems to stand in the way of increased industrial exploitation of social science, and the industrial social scientists themselves have been especially willing.

The position these social scientists have taken regarding the ethics and politics of power obtrudes as a red thread in the otherwise pallid canvas on which they have labored.

From the pioneers in industrial psychology to the sophisticated human-relations experts of the 1950's, almost all industrial social scientists have either backed away from the political and ethical implications of their work or have faced these considerations from the point of view of management. Aptly, it was Hugo Münsterberg who first formulated the comfortable and self-castrating position that industrial psychologists should concern themselves with means only, not with goals, aims, or ends, which could and should be determined only by the industrial managers themselves. Scientific method was clearly on Münsterberg's side, for science cannot solve political problems, and psychology, he argued, was a science which must be impartial. Thus he insisted that his colleagues should not pander "to selfish fancies of either side"—that is, capital or labor—but should remain detached and scientific observers of the industrial situation. Other early leaders in the development of industrial psychology quickly picked up Münsterberg's cue and explicated his position: "Psychology will always be limited by the fact that while it can determine the means to the end, it can have nothing to do with the determination of the end itself."[15]

During the 1920's the political stance desirable for social scientists was made even more clear. Moving from the justification by objectivity to a recognition of the industrial facts of life, psychologists were told that "business results are the main object." Objectivity was lifeblood to a true science, but the industrial manager would instruct his hired specialists about those problems or subjects that required analysis. "The pursuit and enlargement of psychological knowledge is merely a by-product of business efforts," psychologists were further cautioned. Confusion was compounded when, late in the decade, another industrial psychologist explained his position: workers who were justifiably dissatisfied were not fit subjects for psychological analysis because such a situation was an "economic or ethical problem." The obverse held: where workers were treated fairly and still were dissatisfied, there was the spot for psychological inquiry.[16] The controlling question of who determined the justification of employee dissatisfaction was unanswered, as of course it had to be. Moving from the academic to the industrial world, it seemed relatively clear that managers would at least suggest where psychological analysis should occur, which is to say that the decision about the justification of employee satisfaction or dissatisfaction was one that management made. The social scientist applied his tools where he was told to apply them.

Of major importance in this subordination of industrial social science to the pleasure of management were the assumptions made by the Hawthorne researchers. Perhaps this was the area in which the work of Elton Mayo was the most significant. For Mayo, more than any other single individual, directed the course of industrial research—obliquely, to be sure, through the statement of his attitudes and assumptions, which proved so comfortable that many disciples made them their own.

Mayo's unshakable conviction was that the managers of the United States comprised an elite which had the ability and therefore the right to rule the rest of the nation. He pointed out, for instance, that many of America's managers were remarkable men without prejudice.[17] According to one of his critics, Mayo believed that "management is capable, trained, and objective. Management uses scientific knowledge, particularly engineering knowledge, for making decisions. Political issues are illusions created by evil men. Society's true problems are engineering problems."[18] With this frame of reference, Mayo throughout his inquiring and productive life ignored labor, power, and politics. Indeed, he ignored the dignity that is possible in the age of the machine, despite his contrary arguments idealizing what for him was the soothing past, the preindustrial America. And in his myopia his colleagues and the larger movement of industrial human relations shared.[19]

But the commitment of social science to management derived not alone from Mayo's assumptions about the nature of the industrial world and of American civilization. Quite as important were the implications of the substantive research done at the Hawthorne Works of the Western Electric Company. The counseling program developed there, for example, led most industrial social scientists to conclude that, because workers felt better after talking to a counselor, even to the point of commenting about improved pay rates which the company had not changed, most workers did not have compelling objective problems. Much of industrial unrest was simply a function of faulty perception and conceptualization on the part of labor. One counselor, also an industrial consultant, put it this way:

At least half of the grievances of the average employee can be relieved merely by giving him an opportunity to 'talk them out.' It may not even be necessary to take any action on them. All that they require is a patient and courteous hearing, supplemented, when necessary, by an explanation of *why* nothing can be done. . . . It is not always necessary to yield to the worker's requests in order to satisfy them.[20]

More and more industrial psychologists heeded the injunction of one of their colleagues who, in 1952, said that "the psychologist must reorient his thinking from what is good management of the individual to what is good personnel management and, ultimately, good business."[21]

The industrial social scientists' view of labor and unionism adds further depth to our understanding of their sweeping commitment to management. What kind of man is he who labors and why does he join a union? He is the kind of man, the early industrial psychologists agreed, who is stupid, overly emotional, class conscious, without recreational or aesthetic interests, insecure, and afraid of responsibility. He is a man who, when banded together in a union with others of like sort, is to be distrusted and feared. This blue-collar man joins a union, psychologists and sociologists eventually postulated, because of a personality maladjustment, one that probably occurred early in life.[22] The need for an equalization of power between labor and management, the need for economic sanctions, were not seen as the real reasons why men join unions. Rather, said psychologist Robert N. McMurry:

The union also serves the worker in another way. Being somewhat authoritarian, *it may tell him what to do. He no longer has to think for himself*. . . . Once he has been relieved of personal responsibility for his actions, *he is free to commit aggressions which his conscience would ordinarily hold in check*. When this is the case, his conscience will trouble him little, no matter how brutal and anti-social his behavior may be.

Granting such premises, solely for the sake of discussion, one is forced to conclude with McMurry, whose position was rather typical, that "where management is fair and is alert to discover and remove sources of employee dissatisfaction, a union is not necessary."[23]

The social scientists' view of industrial conflict further illuminates their commitment to management. Throughout their professional history, the majority of industrial social scientists insisted that as soon as management took the trouble to study or to authorize studies of its workers, to learn their wants, instincts, desires, aspirations, and motivations, management would be able to do something about the demands of labor before such demands tied up the lifeline of industry and resulted in a strike. Understanding human relations, in short, was the only certain way to avoid conflict. Thus the demand of labor for wages was merely camouflage, argued the social scientists, masking more real and human needs of appreciation, understanding, and friendliness.[24]

Because of his impact, Elton Mayo's formulations have always been important, and his statement of the problem of conflict was no exception. His early approach to conflict, and one that was to become rather representative of a large segment of industrial social science, was based on the postulate of the primacy of the individual in all social processes, including labor-management conflict. Before the Hawthorne researches broadened his vision, Mayo believed that " 'industrial unrest' has its source in obsessive preoccupation." And again: "There is a real identity between labor unrest and nervous breakdown."[25] Conflict to Mayo was neither inevitable nor economic. It was a result of the maladjustment of a few men on the labor side of the picture. Even after Hawthorne forced Mayo to grow, he remained firm in his conviction that conflict was an evil, a symptom of the lack of social skills. Cooperation, for him, was symptomatic of health; and, since there was no alternative in the modern world, cooperation must mean obedience to managerial authority. Thus collective bargaining was not really cooperation, but merely a flimsy substitute for the real thing.[26]

The nature of the social sciences in the twentieth century was, and is, such as to encourage the type of thinking of which Mayo is a good representative. His illusions of objectivity, lack of integrative theory, concern with what many have called the "wrong problems," and, at least by implication, authoritarianism, virtually determined the types of errors he committed. Such errors are built into modern social science.

The problem of objectivity has proved to be especially troublesome to modern social scientists. During the depression of the 1930's, for instance, some social scientists warned that a rigid insistence on objectivity would place power in the hands of partisans who would not trouble themselves with such matters. In other words, social scientists, by providing, without interpretation or advocacy, techniques and concepts useful to men engaged in struggles for power, became by default accessories to the power politics of American government and industry, while insisting that they were innocent of anything of the sort. The insistence on objectivity made an impartial *use* of their research findings virtually impossible.[27]

Only after World War II did many social scientists, including Mayo, blame their difficulties on a lack of theory.[28] But the more general belief that "the chief impetus to the field of industrial sociology has come from observational studies in industry rather than inference from theoretical principles"[29] discouraged a concentrated effort to tie together the many dissociated studies with some kind of underlying theory. Data were piled on data; statistical analyses were pursued with increasing vigor.

Only rarely was any attempt made to explain, in a broader framework, the significance and relationships of psychological and sociological research. "Lacking an objective scale of values," said one industrial psychologist, "we have accumulated a vast body of data on what some of us suspect are either the wrong problems, or false or misstated questions, or altogether minor ones."[30] In 1947 the criticism was fully developed:

The human problems of industry and economic relationships lie at the very heart of the revolutionary upheavals of our century. One might expect industrial psychologists to be fired by the challenge of these issues. But most of us go on constructing aptitude tests instead—and determining which of two advertising slogans "will sell more of our company's beauty cream."[31]

This concentration on wrong or trivial problems was a result of the fact that social scientists, especially those who applied their science to the desires or needs of power groups, were not in command of their activities. They have not been, and are not, free agents. Clearly, however, industrial social scientists have not been forced to accept the assumptions, biases, and frames of reference of America's industrial elite. These specialists, like virtually every other group in American society, freely shared the assumptions of this elite. Most managers have had no trouble in getting social scientists to grant managerial premises because such premises have also been assumed by the social scientists. According to some analysts, this acceptance and sanction of America's power status by social scientists can most easily be explained by reference to the social scientists themselves. Said a sociologist, "American social scientists have seldom, if ever, been politically engaged; the trend towards the technician's role has, by strengthening their a-political professional ideology, reduced, if that is possible, their political involvement, and often, by atrophy, their ability even to grasp political problems." Hence industrial social scientists have had no qualms about serving "the needs of the business side of the corporation as judged by the business manager." This, another sociologist believed, made "something less than a scientist" of any social scientist directly involved in the power relationships of the modern bureaucracies.[32]

The classic statement of the position of the industrial psychologist in relation to the powers for which he worked was made, in 1951, by the eminent industrial psychologist W. V. Bingham, who said that industrial psychology "might be defined as psychology directed toward aims other than its own."[33] Who, then, should set the aims for industrial psychologists? Obviously, managers would have no scruples against telling the social-science specialists on their payrolls how they should earn their money. With Bingham's definition in mind, most industrial social scientists did not hesitate to do what they were told. "The result," reported one of *Fortune's* editors, "is not a science at all; it is a machine for the engineering of mediocrity.... Furthermore," he continued, "it is profoundly authoritarian in its implications, for it subordinates the individual to the group. And the philosophy," he concluded, "unfortunately, is contagious."[34]

A handful of industrial social scientists bitterly complained of this willing acceptance by almost all of their colleagues of the control of their science and their research by the managers and spokesmen of that ubiquitous concentration of power: the modern corporation. The psychologist Arthur Kornhauser was one of the first, when in 1947 he called industrial psychology a management technique rather than a social science, and complained that "psychological activities for industry . . . are characterized by the fact that business management constitutes a special interest group which manifests its special viewpoint in respect to research as in other matters. . . . Certain areas of research are tabu," he went on. "Certain crucial variables must not be dealt with. We must avoid," he concluded, "explicit analysis of the broad and basic problems of *power and authority* in economic life." On rare occasions an industrial sociologist expressed similar attitudes. In the same year, for instance, Wilbert E. Moore, then of Princeton, warned his audience of sociologists that the persistent managerial assumptions underlying so much of their work would reduce their profession to a refined type of scientific management dedicated to the exploitation of labor.[35] But such expressions were unusual and not representative of the opinions of most industrial social scientists. Most of these specialists remained content to develop and refine further the techniques in which management expressed an interest, and either did not bother about or approved of the implications of their research.

Despite the avowed or implicit hostility of virtually all industrial social scientists to organized labor, union leaders traditionally have been either unaware of or indifferent to the work of these specialists. With time, however, at least since the Second World War, a few labor leaders have spoken against the entire social-science movement as it was then implemented in industry. No major union has, however, taken action on the national level to counteract this movement.[36]

One labor leader has been especially troubled about the industrial use of social science; his formulation of the problem serves to highlight the basic difficulties of labor in a social-science world that is built on the assumptions of management. First of all, he wrote, social scientists so complicate the bargaining relationship that control is taken out of the hands of the inadequately informed workers and their representatives; experts are required to get through the maze of confusion, and democracy becomes impossible. "The essence of unionism," he continued, "is not higher wages, shorter hours or strikes—but self-government. If, as some unions apparently believe, higher benefits are the essential objective, then unionism becomes another, and more subtle, form of paternalism. . . . As for me," he concluded, "I would prefer to receive lower benefits than to lose control of my bargaining relationship. Unfortunately, and this is the nub of the problem, many workers prefer higher benefits to democracy."[37] The issues at stake in this man's dilemma are profound, and the impotence of all unions, including his own, to resist, as well as the general apathy of other labor leaders, causes rot at the heart of American unionism. But the industrialist's keen awareness of the problems pushes him forward in his use of social scientists to complicate and confuse bargaining, to reduce grievances, and to squelch militant unionism.

A final question remains. What difference does it make if social scientists have found a place in industry and generally have shared the points of view of management? Are not social scientists an esoteric group of academicians with little or no contact with reality? What if they have been hostile to interests other than those that pay them?

The difference is great. Many managers have not hesitated to make explicit the point that their use of social scientists and their skills is for the purpose of human control. Through group conferences, management hopes to pressure the recalcitrant individual into conforming with his more right-thinking colleagues. Cessna Aircraft and Atlantic Refining have furnished good examples of this approach. American Telephone & Telegraph has been convinced that it is possible through an understanding of motivation to "influence" a given employee. The Life Insurance Sales Research Bureau said that "in learning to shape people's feelings and control their morale, we shall be doing nothing more difficult than we have already done in learning how to fly. . . . We need not 'change human nature,' we need only to learn to control and to use it." General Foods took the position that "leadership" and persuasion would prove most effective in directing the thinking and conduct of its workers. Other businessmen and social scientists have agreed that the main business of business is the control of human conduct.[38]

A few social scientists were concerned, however, about the implications of their growing effectiveness with a science of behavior. Would this not lead to the most insidious and relentless form of exploitation ever dreamed of? One industrial social scientist argued that control in a complex and interdependent society is inevitable:

Society has always outlawed certain techniques for getting people to do what one wants them to do. As our understanding of behavior becomes more and more refined, we will have to refine equally the moral judgment on the kinds of coercion—however subtle—that are approved and disapproved.[39]

Control, in other and more simple words, is a given; what needs to be changed is the system of morals that disapproves of control. Slim hope for the future, this. But *Business Week* has assured us that there is nothing to worry about. "There's no sign," reported this organ of business interests, "that the science of behavior is getting ready to spawn some monster of human engineering, manipulating a population of puppets from behind the scenes."[40]

Business Week is wrong. Social scientists by now have evolved a series of specific techniques whose results have delighted management. Especially through the use of group pressures has management shoved its people into line. Majority opinions, even when directly contrary to visual fact, sway the attitudes of others who would rather not trust their own eyes than suffer the stigma of being unusual. This social scientists have proved.[41] "If a manager's superior," said the personnel director of Continental Oil, "has had difficulty in developing a cooperative attitude within that manager, the group technique can frequently help in developing the appropriate attitude." Even *Business Week* was forced to admit that the pressures of the group on the individual members were so relentless that this was "one good way to change what they [managers] want." The Harwood Manufacturing Company and American Cyanamid both learned to lean heavily on group techniques to assure the continuation of management control.[42]

Through motivation studies, through counseling, through selection devices calculated to hire only certain types of people, through attitude surveys, communication, role-playing, and all the rest in their bag of schemes, social scientists slowly moved toward a science of behavior. Thus management was given a slick new approach to its problems of control. Authority gave way to manipulation, and workers could no longer be sure they were being exploited. Said C. Wright Mills:

Many whips are inside men, who do not know how they got there, or indeed that they are there. In the movement from authority to manipulation, power shifts from the visible to the invisible, from the known to the anonymous. And with rising material standards, exploitation becomes less material and more psychological.[43]

Many industrial social scientists have put themselves on auction. The power elites of America, especially the industrial elite, have bought their services—which, when applied to areas of relative power, have restricted the freedom of millions of workers. Time was when a man knew that his freedoms were being curtailed. Social scientists, however, are too sophisticated for that. The fires of pressure and control on a man are now kindled in his own thinking. Control need no longer be imposed. It can be encouraged to come from within. Thus the faith that if "people develop propaganditis" the effectiveness of control would be weakened[44] seems to miss the point. A major characteristic of twentieth-century manipulation has been that it blinds the victim to the fact of manipulation. Because so many industrial social scientists have been willing to serve power instead of mind, they have been themselves a case study in manipulation by consent.

Over the years, through hundreds and hundreds of experiments, social scientists have come close to a true science of behavior. They are now beginning to learn how to control conduct. Put this power—genuine, stark, irrevocable power—into the hands of America's managers, and the work that social scientists have done, and will do, assumes implications vaster and more fearful than anything previously hinted.

References

THE FOLLOWING abbreviations are used in the notes:

AJS American Journal of Sociology
Annals Annals of the American Academy of Political and
Social Science
ASR American Sociological Review
BLS Bureau of Labor Statistics
BTS Bulletin of the Taylor Society
CBR Conference Board Reports
FMM Factory Management and Maintenance
HBR Harvard Business Review
JAP Journal of Applied Psychology
JCP Journal of Consulting Psychology
JPR Journal of Personnel Research
NICB National Industrial Conference Board
SPP Studies in Personnel Policy

CHAPTER 1:

The Need for Knowledge

1. Quoted in Frederick L. Nussbaum, A History of the Economic Institutions of Modern Europe (New York, 1933), 379.
2. John L. McCaffrey, "The Objective of Business Education," in The Challenge of Business Education (Chicago, 1949), 52.
3. Cf., however, Reinhard Bendix, "Bureaucracy: The Problem and Its Setting," ASR, XII, 5 (Oct., 1947), 493.
4. H. K. Hathaway, "Discussion," BTS, III, 6 (Dec., 1917), 9.
5. James Burnham, The Managerial Revolution (New York, 1941), 74, 78, 85.
6. Wilbert E. Moore, Industrial Relations and the Social Order (New York, 1946), 86–88.
7. George Katona, Psychological Analysis of Economic Behavior (New York, 1951), 197. Cf. Hans H. Gerth and C. Wright Mills, "A Marx for the Managers," in Robert K.

Merton *et al.* (eds.), *Reader in Bureaucracy* (Glencoe, Ill., 1952), 168, 172: "One error which pervades this [Burnham's] interpretation of the chances at power of managerial elements of the new middle class is the assumption that the technical indispensability of certain functions in a social structure are taken *ipso facto* as a prospective claim for political power. . . . Where Marx had the coupon-clipping parasites expropriated by the exploited proletariat, Burnham has them expropriated by their junior partners and social colleagues, the managers. The Marxist class struggle has shifted its stage from the barricades to the Social Club."

8. *Boston Globe*, Jan. 22, 1956, 26; Sylvia F. Porter, "Era of Research," *New York Post*, Jan. 7, 1957, 28.

9. President's Research Committee, *Recent Social Trends in the United States* (New York, 1933), I, xxvii.

10. Solomon Barkin, "A Trade Unionist Appraises Management Personnel Philosophy," *HBR*, XXVIII, 5 (Sept., 1950), 62.

11. W. Lloyd Warner and J. O. Low, "The Factory in the Community," in William Foote Whyte (ed.), *Industry and Society* (New York, 1946), 44–45.

12. Daniel Katz, "Employee Groups," *Advanced Management*, XIV, 3 (Sept., 1949), 120.

13. American Telephone & Telegraph Co., Personnel Relations Dept., "Leadership," *Human Relations in Management: Conferee Outline* (New York, 1949), 2, AT&T Co. MSS.

14. Peter F. Drucker, *Concept of the Corporation* (New York, 1946), 21–22, 25.

15. Daniel Bell, "Adjusting Men to Machines," *Commentary*, III, 1 (Jan., 1947), 79.

16. See, e.g., F. C. Crawford to Earl Harding, May 17, 1937, Thompson Products Co. MSS; Douglas McGregor in Standard Oil Co. (N.J.), Employee Relations Dept., *Employee Relations Research in Standard Oil Company (New Jersey) and Affiliates* (New York, 1955), I, 5.

17. E. Wight Bakke, *Bonds of Organization* (New York, 1950), 2.

18. See, e.g., D. R. Kennedy, "Horse Sense in Human Relations," *Industrial Management*, LVII (Jan., 1919), 68; A. M. Rochlen, "Industrial Relations," *Aero Digest*, XLI, 3 (Sept.,

1942), 138; testimony of Alfred Marshall in U.S. Congress, Senate, Subcommittee of the Committee on Education and Labor, *Hearings, Violations of Free Speech and Rights of Labor,* part 6, "Labor Espionage, General Motors Corporation," 75th Cong., 1st Sess., 1937., 2044.

19. Harold E. Burtt, *Principles of Employment Psychology* (Boston, 1926), 499; Wayne Dennis, "The Background of Industrial Psychology," *Current Trends in Industrial Psychology* (Pittsburgh, 1949), 7–8; Burleigh B. Gardner, *Human Relations in Industry* (Chicago, 1945), iii; Harry W. Hepner, *Psychology in Modern Business* (New York, 1931), 647–648; F. J. Roethlisberger, *Management and Morale* (Cambridge, 1942), 114; J. L. Rosenstein, *Psychology of Human Relations for Executives* (New York, 1936), viii; Winthrop Talbot, "The Human Element in Industry," *Iron Age,* XCI, *6* (Feb. 6, 1913), 366; Wallace H. Wulfeck, "Psychology and Management," *Personnel Journal,* XIX, *2* (June, 1940), 51.

20. E.g., Clarence J. Hicks, *My Life in Industrial Relations* (New York, 1941), 140–141; H. L. Hollingworth and A. T. Poffenberger, *Applied Psychology* (New York, 1917), 327; Alfred Marrow, "Group Dynamics in Industry," *Occupations,* XXVI, *8* (May, 1948), 472; Morris S. Viteles, "Caveat Emptor," *JCP,* V, *3* (May-June, 1941), 122.

21. H. S. Person, "The Manager, the Workman, and the Social Scientist," *BTS,* III, *1* (Feb., 1917), 7.

22. Eliott Frost, "Should Psychology Bake Bread," *JAP,* IV, *4* (Dec., 1920), 305.

23. Marion A. Bills, "Psychology Applied to Problems of Office Personnel," *JCP,* VIII, *3* (May-June, 1944), 163–164; Max Freyd, "The Statistical Viewpoint in Vocational Selection," *JAP,* IX, *4* (1925), 352; Douglas Fryer, "Applied and Professional Attitudes," *JCP,* III, *1* (Jan.-Feb., 1939), 9; John H. Gorsuch, "Industrial Psychology's Growing Pains," *Personnel,* XXIX, *2* (Sept., 1952), 153; H. S. Person, "The Reaction of Workers to Machine Work and Working Conditions," in Henry C. Metcalf (ed.), *The Psychological Foundations of Management* (New York, 1927), 134–135.

24. Gwilym A. Price, quoted in Eugene Staley *et al.* (eds.), *Creating an Industrial Civilization* (New York, 1952), 15.

CHAPTER 2:

The Birth of Industrial Psychology

1. See, e.g., Thorstein Veblen, *The Instinct of Workmanship and the State of the Industrial Arts* (New York, 1914), *passim*; Ordway Tead, *Instincts in Industry* (Boston, 1918), ix–x: "*Human conduct tends to become not only more intelligible but more amenable to control as we view it in the light of an understanding of the instinctive mainsprings of action*"; Carleton H. Parker, *The Casual Laborer and Other Essays* (New York, 1920), 133, 137: "Man is born into his world accompanied by a rich psychical disposition which furnishes him ready-made all his motives for conduct, all his desires. . . . All human activity . . . is untiringly actuated by the demand for realization of the instinct wants."

2. William McDougall, *An Introduction to Social Psychology* (15th ed., Boston, 1923), 30.

3. Gardner Murphy, *Historical Introduction to Modern Psychology* (rev. ed., New York, 1949), 403–405.

4. Oscar Herzberg, "Human Nature as a Factor in Advertising," *Printers' Ink*, XIII, *14* (Oct. 2, 1895), 4. It is common to read that social scientists began to concern themselves with advertising only in the 1920's; cf., e.g., Vance Packard, *The Hidden Persuaders* (New York, 1957), 26.

5. "Editorial Comment," *Printers' Ink*, XLV, *11* (Dec. 9, 1903), 34.

6. Walter Dill Scott, *The Psychology of Advertising* (Boston, 1908), 2, 56–78, 205–206; Henry C. Link, *The New Psychology of Selling and Advertising* (New York, 1934), 82. For other examples of the use made of the instinct theory, see, e.g., Charles H. Griffitts, *Fundamentals of Vocational Psychology* (New York, 1925), 122; John A. Stevenson, "Psychology in Salesmanship," *Annals*, CX (Nov., 1923), 148.

7. Herbert Moore, *Psychology for Business and Industry* (New York, 1939), 6–7.

8. Walter Dill Scott *et al.*, *Personnel Management* (5th ed., New York, 1954), 244–245, 250; Wayne Dennis, "The Back-

ground of Industrial Psychology," *Current Trends in Industrial Psychology* (Pittsburgh, 1949), 6–7.

9. Milton J. Nadworny, *Scientific Management and the Unions, 1900–1932* (Cambridge, 1955), 1, 4–5, 13, 17–18.

10. Hornell Hart, "Changing Social Attitudes and Interests," in President's Research Committee, *Recent Social Trends in the United States* (New York, 1933), I, 431.

11. L. M. Gilbreth, *The Psychology of Management* (New York, 1914), 18–23, 219, 331.

12. Nadworny, *Scientific Management*, 25–26, 125–126.

13. E.g., "Certain Limitations in the Application of Scientific Management," *HBR*, IV, 1 (Oct., 1925), 106–111; Lillian M. Gilbreth, "Discussion," *BTS*, X, 3 (June, 1925), 162.

14. E.g., Paul S. Achilles, "Some Psychological Aspects of Scientific Management," *Society for the Advancement of Management Journal*, I, 3 (May, 1936), 68; R. M. Fox, "Psychology of the Workshop," *Nineteenth Century*, XCIX (June, 1926), 805–812; Frederic S. Lee, *The Human Machine and Industrial Efficiency* (New York, 1918), 95; Morris S. Viteles, *Industrial Psychology* (New York, 1932), 437.

15. Nadworny, *Scientific Management*, 5.

16. Morris L. Cooke, "Who Is Boss in Your Shop?" *BTS*, III, 4 (Aug., 1917), 5; Gilbreth, *Psychology of Management*, 3–4, 22–23, 31; Morris S. Viteles, *Motivation and Morale in Industry* (New York, 1953), 18.

17. NICB, *Some Problems in Wage Incentive Administration*, by E. S. Horning (CBR, SPP No. 19; New York, 1940), 17.

18. Viteles, *Industrial Psychology*, 18.

19. H. Addington Bruce, "Psychology and Business," *Outlook*, XCIX (Sept. 2, 1911), 32–36; "Psychological Tests for Accident Prevention," *Electric Railway Journal*, XXXIX, 10 (March 9, 1912), 394; Walter Dill Scott, "The Scientific Selection of Salesmen," *Advertising and Selling*, XXV, 7 (Dec., 1915), 11.

20. Samuel M. Levin, "Ford Profit Sharing, 1914–1920," *Personnel Journal*, VI, 2 (Aug., 1927), 75–82; Allan Nevins with Frank E. Hill, *Ford: The Times, the Man, the Company* (New York, 1954), 517, 523, 527, 533–539, 541, 554–556.

21. Samuel M. Levin, "The End of Ford Profit Sharing," *Personnel Journal*, VI, 3 (Oct., 1927), 161–166.

22. Nevins and Hill, *Ford*, 567.

23. Ernest M. Hopkins, "The Supervisor of Personnel," *Bulletin of the Society to Promote the Science of Management*, I, 2 (Jan., 1915), 9–15; James Hartness, "The Human Element," *Iron Age*, XCIV, 23 (Dec. 3, 1914), 1297; "Human-Being Management," *Industrial Management*, LII (Dec., 1916), 398–400; James Logan, "Can Human Beings Be Standardized?" *Factory*, XV, 1 (July, 1915), 11; Fred H. Rindge, Jr., "Solving the Problems of 'Human Engineering,'" *Engineering News*, LXX, 20 (Nov. 13, 1913), 962–963; Harry Tipper, "The Need for a New Incentive for the Industrial Worker," *Automotive Industries*, XXXIX, 14 (Oct. 3, 1918), 582-584.

24. William F. Kemble, "Testing the Fitness of Your Employees," *Industrial Management*, LII, 2 (Nov., 1916), 149.

25. Hugo Münsterberg, *Psychology and Industrial Efficiency* (New York, 1913), 3–7, 27, 55–56, 116–117, 308–309.

26. Münsterberg, *Business Psychology* (Chicago, 1915), 182.

27. E.g., Arthur W. Kornhauser and Forrest A. Kingsbury, *Psychological Tests in Business* (Chicago, 1924), 2; Moore, *Psychology for Business*, 10; Viteles, *Industrial Psychology*, 41.

28. P. W. Gerhardt, "Scientific Selection of Employees," *Electric Railway Journal*, XLVII, 21 (May 20, 1916), 945; Münsterberg, *Business Psychology*, 282; "Scientific Selection of Workmen," *Engineering Record*, LXVII, 7 (Feb. 15, 1913), 171.

29. Viteles, *Industrial Psychology*, 45.

30. Walter V. Bingham, "Today and Yesterday," *Personnel Psychology*, II, 4 (Winter, 1949), 557; J. M. Bruce, "Discussion," *Bulletin of the Society to Promote the Science of Management*, I, 2 (Jan., 1915), 13; Walter Dill Scott, "The Scientific Selection of Salesmen," *Advertising and Selling*, XXV, 5 (Oct., 1915), 5; Scott, *ibid.*, 6 (Nov., 1915), 11, 55.

31. Richard A. Feiss, "Personal Relationships as a Basis of Scientific Management," *Bulletin of the Society to Promote the Science of Management*, I, 6 (Nov., 1915), 10–11; Mary B.

Gilson, *What's Past Is Prologue* (New York, 1940), 63, 65; Henry C. Link, "Psychological Tests in Industry," *Annals*, CX (Nov., 1923), 34.

32. W. V. Bingham, "Coöperative Business Research," *Annals*, CX (Nov., 1923), 180–183; Bingham, "Psychology Applied," *Scientific Monthly*, XVI, 8 (Feb., 1923), 148–150, 153; Moore, *Psychology for Business*, 16–17.

CHAPTER 3:

War

1. H. L. Hollingworth and A. T. Poffenberger, *Applied Psychology* (New York, 1917).
2. R. A. Wentworth, "Discussion," *BTS*, III, 6 (Dec., 1917), 12.
3. Donald G. Paterson, "Applied Psychology Comes of Age," *JCP*, IV, 1 (Jan.-Feb., 1940), 3.
4. Clarence S. Yoakum and Robert M. Yerkes (comps. and eds.), *Army Mental Tests* (published with the authorization of the War Dept.; New York, 1920), viii–ix, 2, 5, 12, 21, 27.
5. Henry C. Link, "Personal Opinion Records and Rating Scales," *Industrial Management*, LXVII, 2 (Feb., 1924), 78.
6. Walter Dill Scott, "Selection of Employees by Means of Quantitative Determinants," *Annals*, LXV (May, 1916), 192.
7. Norman G. Shidle, "Incentives to Better Workmanship Appeal to a Variety of Instincts," *Automotive Industries*, XLIV (March 31, 1921), 712–714.
8. E.g., Link, "Personal Opinion," *Industrial Management* (1924), 78.
9. H. S. Person, "Industrial Psychology," *BTS*, IX, 4 (Aug., 1924), 163.
10. Lewis M. Terman, "The Status of Applied Psychology in the United States," *JAP*, V, 1 (March, 1921), 1–4.
11. Hornell Hart, "Changing Social Attitudes and Interests," in President's Research Committee, *Recent Social Trends in the United States* (New York, 1933), I, 393.
12. Yoakum and Yerkes, *Army Mental Tests*, iii.
13. "Army Personnel Work—A War Gift to Industry," *Factory*, XXII, 4, (April, 1919), 687.
14. "Mental Tests in Industry," *Bulletin of the American In-

stitute of Mining and Metallurgical Engineers, CXLVIII (April, 1919), 681.

15. Hart, "Changing Social Attitudes," *Recent Social Trends,* I, 433.

16. Willard E. Hotchkiss, "Industrial Relations Management," *HBR,* I, 4 (July, 1923), 439; U.S. Federal Board for Vocational Education, *Employment Management* (Employment Management Series No. 1, Bull. No. 50; Washington, Jan., 1920), 9.

17. U.S. Federal Board, *Employment Management,* 15.

18. Harry D. Kitson, "Making Employees Interested in Their Work," *American Machinist,* LII, 19 (May 6, 1920), 983.

19. Herbert Moore, *Psychology for Business and Industry* (New York, 1939), 17; J. David Thompson, *Personnel Research Agencies* (BLS Bull. No. 299; Washington, 1921), 150.

20. Paul S. Achilles, "Commemorative Address on the Twentieth Anniversary of the Psychological Corporation," *JAP,* XXV (1941), 609–618; Achilles, "The Consulting Services of the Psychological Corporation," *JCP,* X, 3 (May-June, 1946), 120–126; Walter V. Bingham, "Today and Yesterday," *Personnel Psychology,* I, 3 (Autumn, 1948), 399n; J. McKeen Cattell, "The Psychological Corporation," *Annals,* CX (Nov., 1923), 165–171; "Psychology's a Business, Too," *Business Week,* Nov. 16, 1932, 11; "The Tests of Management," *Fortune,* XLII (July, 1950), 94.

21. Among the early companies to use the services of this organization were Western Electric, American Telephone & Telegraph, Boston Elevated Railway, Eastman Kodak, Colgate, Dennison, and White Motor. W. V. Bingham, "Personnel Research Federation," *JPR,* III, 3 (1924–1925), 103–104; Bingham, "The Personnel Research Federation in 1928," *Personnel Journal,* VII, 4 (Dec., 1928), 300; Alfred D. Flinn, "Development of Personnel Research Federation," *JPR,* I, 1 (May, 1922), 7–13; Charles S. Slocombe, "The Personnel Research Federation," *Personnel Journal,* XII, 6 (April, 1935), 334; Thompson, *Personnel Research Agencies,* 5.

22. E.g., Morris S. Viteles, "Psychology in Business—In England, France and Germany," *Annals,* CX (Nov., 1923), 211–212.

23. *Ibid.*, 207–208; George H. Miles, "The Extent and Application of Psychology and Psychological Method in English Industrial Life," *HBR*, IV, 2 (Jan., 1926), 138–144; Henry J. Welch and Charles S. Myers, *Ten Years of Industrial Psychology* (London, 1932), *passim*.
24. Donald A. Laird, *How to Use Psychology in Business* (New York, 1936), 9.
25. Bruce V. Moore and George W. Hartmann (eds.), *Readings in Industrial Psychology* (New York, 1931), 7–8.
26. Viteles, "Psychology in Business," *Annals* (1923), 208–209.
27. J. McKeen Cattell, "Psychology in America," *Scientific Monthly*, XXX (Feb., 1930), 126; Arthur W. Kornhauser, "Industrial Psychology in England, Germany, and the United States," *Personnel Journal*, VIII, 6 (April, 1930), 430.
28. Viteles, "Psychology in Business," *Annals* (1923), 212–215.
29. *Ibid.*, 209–210; "First Russian Conference on Technopsychology," *Personnel Journal*, VII, 1 (June, 1928), 70–71; "Industrial Psychology in Japan," *JPR*, I, 1 (May, 1922), 39–40; May Smith, *An Introduction to Industrial Psychology* (London, 1943), 241–249.

CHAPTER 4:

In Search of a Science

1. Harry W. Kimball, "Fellow Feeling in the Factory," *Industrial Management*, LXII, 1 (July 1, 1921), 59.
2. F. G. Buffe, "The Human Element in Industry," *Aera*, XVI, 2 (Sept., 1926), 279–286; Charles R. Hook, "The Human Side of Production Management," *Printers' Ink*, CXXII, 12 (March 22, 1923), 80; Clarence H. Howard, "Business Success and Human Relations," *Machinery*, XXV (Sept., 1928), 20; Sam A. Lewisohn, "What Human Organization Means to Industry," *Printers' Ink Monthly*, VII, 2 (Aug., 1923), 26; E. J. McDonnell, "The Human Factor in Paper Manufacture," *Paper Trade Journal*, LXXVIII (May 1, 1924), 42, 44; Glenn G. Munn, "The Human Equation in Business," *Printers' Ink*, CXIV, 7, (Feb. 17, 1921), 149–150; Martin L. Pulcher, "Friendship in Business," *Forbes*, XXI (April 15, 1928), 25–26; Harry Tipper, "Personal Aspirations More

Important to Worker than Economic Laws," *Automotive Industries*, XLVII (Oct. 5, 1922), 683; Robert R. Updegraff, "Trend and Tempo," *Business Week*, Nov. 16, 1929, 50; Whiting Williams, *Mainsprings of Men* (N.P., 1923), 95–96, 233. Cf. J. David Houser, *What the Employer Thinks* (Cambridge, 1927), 84–85, 91.

3. See, e.g., H. M. Somers, "Methods of Harmonizing Capital and Labor," in George W. Hartmann and Theodore Newcomb (eds.), *Industrial Conflict* (New York, 1939), 349–350.

4. J. Walter Dietz, "New Trends in Personnel Policies," *Personnel*, XVI, 3 (Feb., 1940), 100; "Personnel Research Federation," *Personnel Journal*, XVIII, 5 (Nov., 1939), 195.

5. Richard A. May, "The Trade Association and Its Place in the Business Fabric," *HBR*, II, 1 (Oct., 1923), 94.

6. NICB, *Industrial Relations* (New York, 1931), 84–85.

7. "Industrial Plants *Abandoning* Many Personnel Activities," *Automotive Industries*, LIX, 5 (Aug. 4, 1928), 163.

8. NICB, *Industrial Relations Programs in Small Plants* (New York, 1929), 57.

9. NICB, *Industrial Relations* (1931), 84–85.

10. Eliott Frost, "What Industry Wants and Does Not Want from the Psychologist," *JAP*, IV, 1 (March, 1920), 20; C. S. Yoakum, "Conditions of Research in Industrial Psychology," in Henry C. Metcalf (ed.), *The Psychological Foundations of Management* (New York, 1927), 21; Yoakum, "Applications of Psychology to Industry and Business," *JPR*, I (1922), 318.

11. Edgar J. Swift, *Business Power Through Psychology* (New York, 1925), 57.

12. Max Freyd, "The Statistical Viewpoint in Vocational Selection," *JAP*, IX, 4 (1925), 349–350; Harry W. Hepner, *Psychology in Modern Business* (New York, 1931), 208; Arthur W. Kornhauser and Forrest W. Kingsbury, *Psychological Tests in Business* (Chicago, 1924), 3.

13. E. L. Godkin, "The Duty of Educated Men in a Democracy," *Forum*, XVII (March, 1894), 43; H. J. Hapgood, "College Men in Business," *Annals*, XXVIII, 1 (July, 1906), 59.

14. Eugene J. Benge, quoted in NICB, *The Use of Tests in Em-*

ployment and Promotion (CBR, SPP No. 14; New York, June, 1939), 13; Henry C. Link, *The New Psychology of Selling and Advertising* (New York, 1934), 170.

15. Gardner Murphy, *Historical Introduction to Modern Psychology* (rev. ed., New York, 1949), 362.

16. Harold E. Burtt, "Employment Psychology in the Rubber Industry," *JAP*, IV, *1* (March, 1920), 1, 8.

17. John G. Jenkins, *Psychology in Business and Industry* (New York, 1935), 108; Morris S. Viteles, "Tests in Industry," *JAP*, V, *1* (March, 1921), 60.

18. Robert M. Yerkes, "What is Personnel Research?" *Monthly Labor Review*, XIV, *1* (Jan., 1922), 15.

19. W. V. Bingham and W. T. Davis, "Intelligence Test Scores and Business Success," *JAP*, VIII, *1* (1924), 1–3, 22; Bingham, "Intelligence Test Scores and Business Success," *Psychological Bulletin*, XXI, *2* (Feb., 1924), 105.

20. George C. Brandenburg, "Personality and Vocational Achievement," *JAP*, IX, *3* (1925), 292; "Business Can't Judge Recruits on Business School Marks," *Business Week*, Oct. 1, 1930, 28; Henry C. Link, "Psychological Tests in Industry," *Annals*, CX (Nov., 1923), 43; C. S. Yoakum and Marion A. Bills, "Tests for Office Occupations," *ibid.*, 73.

21. Harold E. Burtt, *Principles of Employment Psychology* (Boston, 1926), 86–87, 292.

22. Walter V. Bingham and Max Freyd, *Procedures in Employment Psychology* (Chicago, 1926), 71; A. J. Snow, *Psychology in Business Relations* (Chicago, 1925), 519–521.

23. E.g., Reynold A. Spaeth, "Prevention of Fatigue in Industry," *Industrial Management*, LIX, *4* (April, 1920), 311.

24. "Army Trade Skill Tests Applicable in Construction," *Engineering News-Record*, LXXXII, *12* (March 20, 1919), 554.

25. "Industrial Democracy Not a Panacea," *Iron Age*, CIII, *22* (May 29, 1919), 1443.

26. Kornhauser and Kingsbury, *Psychological Tests in Business*, 165n; NICB, *Experience with Psychological Tests* (CBR, SPP No. 92; New York, 1948), 4; U.S. Federal Board for Vocational Education, *Employment Management* (Employment Management Series No. 1, Bulletin No. 50; Washington, Jan., 1920), 11.

27. William F. Kemble, "Choosing Employees by Test," *Industrial Management*, LII (Jan., 1917), 447–460; Kemble, "Testing the Fitness of Your Employees," *ibid.* (Nov., 1916), 150; Herbert Moore, *Psychology for Business and Industry* (New York, 1939), 13.

28. C. O. Weber, "The Psychology of Employment," *Administration*, III, 6 (June, 1922), 674.

29. J. P. Lamb, "Intelligence Tests in Industry," *Industrial Management*, LVIII, 1 (July, 1919), 21.

30. E. D. Bartlett, "A Test to Gauge Business Knowledge," *Personnel Journal*, VI, 3 (Oct., 1927), 199; Elsie O. Bregman, "A Study in Industrial Psychology," *JAP*, V, 2 (June, 1921), 127; Glenn C. Compton, "Aptitude Tests," *Inland Printer*, CXVII (May, 1946), 40; Donald A. Laird, *The Psychology of Selecting Men* (2nd ed., New York, 1927), 274–275; U.S. Federal Board for Vocational Education, *Employment Management*, 8; C. S. Yoakum, "Can Executives Be Picked by Mental Tests?" *Forbes*, IX, 8 (Jan. 21, 1922), 259.

31. Cf. Lorine Pruette, "What Mental Tests Can Do for Industry," *Industrial Management*, LXX, 5 (Nov., 1925), 270–271.

32. See, e.g., Josephine R. Glascock, "Are Psychological Tests Here to Stay?" *American Management Review*, XIII, 9 (Sept., 1924), 6–7; A. W. Kornhauser and A. W. Jackson, "A Note on the Extent to which Systems of Character Analysis Are Used in the Business World," *JAP*, VI (1922), 302.

33. Katherine M. H. Blackford, "Scientific Selection of Employees," *Iron Trade Review*, LII (Feb. 20, 1913), 463; Blackford and Arthur Newcomb, *The Job, the Man, the Boss* (Garden City, 1914), 86, 110, 117; Myron A. Lee, "Character Analysis by the Observational Method as Used in the Selection of Employees," *Sibley Journal of Engineering*, XXXV (Feb., 1921), 22-28.

34. Frost, "What Industry Wants," *JAP* (1920), 22; Hugo Münsterberg, *Business Psychology* (Chicago, 1915), 238.

35. Mary B. Gilson, *What's Past Is Prologue* (New York, 1940), 64.

36. Daniel Starch, "The Use and Limitations of Psychological Tests," *HBR*, I, 1 (Oct., 1922), 71–72.

37. L. K. Frank, "Industrial Patent Medicine," *BTS*, V, *1* (Feb., 1920), 11.

38. Henry Bruère and Grace Pugh, *Profitable Personnel Practice* (New York, 1929), 380; Herman Feldman, *A Survey of Research in the Field of Industrial Relations* (mimeographed; New York, June 8, 1928), 71; Lillian M. Gilbreth, "The Present State of Industrial Psychology," *Mechanical Engineering*, XLVII, *11A* (Nov., 1925), 1039; Louis L. McQuitty, "Psychologists in Industry," *Personnel Journal*, XXVI, *5* (Nov., 1947), 178; "News Notes," *JPR*, III, *12* (1925), 485; Morris S. Viteles, "The Clinical Viewpoint in Vocational Selection," *JAP*, IX, *2* (1925), 131.

39. Feldman, *Survey of Research*, 75; Henry C. Link, *Employment Psychology* (New York, 1919), 20, 195; Snow, *Psychology in Business Relations*, 539–540; John B. Watson, "Can Psychology Help in the Selection of Personnel?" *Printers' Ink*, CXXXIX, *3* (April 21, 1927), 72.

40. Walter V. Bingham, "Today and Yesterday," *Personnel Psychology*, I, *1* (Spring, 1948), 127.

41. Gilson, *What's Past Is Prologue*, 63; Link, "Psychological Tests in Industry," *Annals* (1923), 34.

42. W. V. Bingham, "The Personnel Research Federation in 1928," *Personnel Journal*, VII, *4* (Dec., 1928), 302; Walter T. Blake and John H. Gander, "Organization and Techniques of a Modern Personnel Department," (unpublished thesis, School of Industrial Management, M.I.T., 1937), 92; Feldman, *Survey of Research*, 72; "Grading of General Electric Employees," *Iron Age*, CXII, *18* (Nov. 1, 1923), 1195; Hepner, *Psychology in Modern Business*, 210–211; Franklin B. Kirkbride, "About Aptitudes," *Trusts and Estates*, LXIX, *2* (Aug., 1939), 196; Donald A. Laird and Eleanor C. Laird, *Practical Business Psychology* (New York, 1951), 19–20; George E. MacIlwain, "How G.E. Fits Square Pegs into Square Holes," *Forbes*, XIX (May 15, 1927), 40; "News Notes," *JPR*, V, *9* (1927), 372–373; *ibid.*, V, *4* (1926), 174; Frank W. Persons, "The Psychologist Takes a Hand in Personnel Selection," *Aera*, XX, *8* (Aug., 1929), 462–467; Millicent Pond, "Scientific Selection of Industrial Labor," *Advanced Management*, VI, *1* (Jan.-March, 1941), 29–30;

Charles S. Slocombe, "The Personnel Research Federation," *Personnel Journal*, XIII, 6 (April, 1935), 334; Snow, *Psychology in Business Relations*, 531n–532n; Richard S. Uhrbrock, Procter and Gamble, to L. Baritz, March 26, 1956; Kornhauser and Kingsbury, *Psychological Tests in Business*, 83n, 96. The following firms used relatively scientific tests as an aid to the better selection of clerical employees: American Rolling Mills, American Tobacco, Armstrong Cork, Atlantic Refining, Burroughs Adding Machine, Continental and Commercial National Bank, Curtis Publishing, Marshall Field, Goodyear Tire and Rubber, Macy's, Metropolitan Life, National Cash Register, National Cloak and Suit, Phoenix Mutual Life Insurance, Sears Roebuck, Swift and Company, Western Union, and Westinghouse.

43. Walter Dill Scott *et al.*, *Personnel Management* (5th ed., New York, 1954), 250.

44. Link, *Employment Psychology*, 184–185, 374–375.

45. Harold E. Burtt, *Psychology and Industrial Efficiency* (New York, 1929), 385–386; Kornhauser and Kingsbury, *Psychological Tests in Business*, 170–171; Laird, *Psychology of Selecting Men*, 276.

46. Feldman, *Survey of Research*, 13.

Chapter 5:
Hawthorne

1. Burleigh B. Gardner and William F. Whyte, "Methods for the Study of Human Relations in Industry," *ASR*, XI, 5 (Oct., 1946), 512; Charles S. Slocombe, "Million Dollar Research," *Personnel Journal*, XVIII, 5 (Nov., 1939), 162. There are now dozens of reports of the Hawthorne studies; the standard account has remained F. J. Roethlisberger and William J. Dickson, *Management and the Worker* (Cambridge, 1939). Other full accounts by members of the Harvard Business School include L. J. Henderson and Elton Mayo, "The Effects of Social Environment," *Journal of Industrial Hygiene and Toxicology*, XVIII, 7 (Sept., 1936), 401–416; Mayo, *The Human Problems of an Industrial Civilization* (New York, 1933); Mayo, *The Social Problems*

of an Industrial Civilization (Boston, 1945); F. J. Roethlisberger, *Management and Morale* (Cambridge, 1942); T. N. Whitehead, *The Industrial Worker* (Cambridge, 1938). The health and hygiene aspects of the study are best discussed in C. E. Turner, "Test Room Studies in Employee Effectiveness," *American Journal of Public Health*, XXIII, 6 (June, 1933), 577–584. Among the best descriptions of the study from the viewpoint of management are American Telephone & Telegraph Co., Personnel Relations Dept., "An Interviewing Method: Outline of Certain Principles and Procedures Developed from the Harvard-Hawthorne Research," (N.P., June 30, 1941), mimeographed, AT&T MSS; G. A. Pennock, "Industrial Research at Hawthorne," *Personnel Journal*, VIII, 5 (Feb., 1930), 296–313; M. L. Putnam, "Improving Employee Relations," *ibid.*, 314–325. For examples of how the Hawthorne research has been incorporated into standard textbooks, see Delbert C. Miller and William H. Form, *Industrial Sociology* (New York, 1951); Wilbert E. Moore, *Industrial Relations and the Social Order* (New York, 1946). Also see Henry A. Landsberger, *Hawthorne Revisited* (Ithaca, 1958), 4–27. Because the Hawthorne research has been reported in such detail, the following discussion of the substantive research will be as brief as possible.

2. Elton Mayo to G. A. Pennock, Oct. 28, 1929, Mayo MSS; Stuart Chase with Marian T. Chase, *Men at Work* (New York, 1945), 9.

3. See, e.g., H. L. Hollingworth and A. T. Poffenberger, *Applied Psychology* (New York, 1917), 215; Hugo Münsterberg, *Business Psychology* (Chicago, 1915), 192; Walter Dill Scott, *Increasing Human Efficiency in Business* (New York, 1911), 9.

4. W. J. Dickson to L. Baritz, Oct. 19, 1956.

5. Roethlisberger, *Management and the Worker*, 14–19. For Elton Mayo's concept of a control group, see E. M. to M. L. Putnam, May 21, 1930, Mayo MSS.

6. V. Bush to L. Baritz, March 16, 1956.

7. C. G. Stoll, in Roethlisberger, *Management and the Worker*, vii.

8. W. J. Dickson to L. Baritz, Oct. 19, 1956; personal interview with C. E. Turner, April 11, 1956; C.E.T. to L.B., April 13, 1956; C.E.T., "Test Room Studies," *American Journal of Public Health* (1933), 577.

9. Roethlisberger, *Management and the Worker*, 3, 30.

10. Turner, "Test Room Studies," *American Journal of Public Health* (1933), 578.

11. Roethlisberger, *Management and the Worker*, 30, 75, 77, 85, 87–88, 128, 133–134, 160.

12. Harold E. Burtt, *Psychology and Industrial Efficiency* (New York, 1929), 387; Rex B. Hersey, "Rests—Authorized and Unauthorized," *JPR*, IV, 2 (1925–1926), 37; Elton Mayo "Revery and Industrial Fatigue," *JPR*, III, 8 (1924-1925), 277–278; Münsterberg, *Business Psychology*, 201; *Philadelphia Public Ledger*, Dec. 8, 1927, Mayo MSS; George H. Shepard, "Effect of Rest Periods on Production," *Personnel Journal*, VII, 3 (Oct., 1928), 186–202.

13. Roethlisberger, *Management and the Worker*, 82.

14. Personal interview with I. P. Leseth, Superintendent, Western Electric Co., Aug. 1, 1955; Roethlisberger, *Management and the Worker*, 184–185; "What Makes Gertrude Give," *FMM*, CIX, 3 (March, 1951), 76. The results in the test room in regard to rest periods were caricatured in a skit called "What Makes Gertrude Give," presented at a conference on morale for the manufacturing management of the Bigelow-Sanford Carpet Co. in 1950:

> Then the girls did suggest we change conditions of test,
> That they could do best and work with new zest,
> If given a five-minute rest. We accepted with glee
> Their justified plea for periods at ten and at three.
> We realize that all you guys
> May well surmise without surprise
> That output continued to rise.

15. Elton Mayo to G. A. Pennock, Feb. 9, 1931, Mayo MSS.

16. Herman Feldman, *A Survey of Research in the Field of Industrial Relations* (mimeographed, New York, June 8, 1928), 85; Mayo, *Human Problems*, 27; B. Muscio, "Is a Fatigue Test Possible?" *British Journal of Psychology*, XII, 1 (June, 1921), 31–46; Scott, *Increasing Human Efficiency*, 10–11; Joseph Tiffin, *Industrial Psychology* (New York,

1942), 219–220; Morris S. Viteles, *Industrial Psychology* (New York, 1932), 441, 463. Cf., however, Donald A. Laird, "The Influence of Noise on Production and Fatigue," *JAP*, XVII (1933), 32ff.

17. Roethlisberger, *Management and the Worker*, 117, 127.
18. Mayo, *Human Problems*, 69.
19. Pennock, "Industrial Research," *Personnel Journal* (1930), 309; Whitehead, *Industrial Worker*, I, 239, 241.
20. T. K. Stevenson to Elton Mayo, March 15, 1928; E. M. to T.K.S., March 19, 1928; G. A. Pennock to E.M., April 17, 1928; Mayo MSS.
21. Elton Mayo to G. A. Pennock, May 9 and Nov. 27, 1928; G.A.P. to E.M., Nov. 20, 1928; T. K. Stevenson to E.M., May 11, 1928; Mayo MSS. For an illustration of the Harvard Business School's interest in the physiological basis of efficiency, see O. S. Lovekin, "The Quantative Measurement of Human Efficiency Under Factory Conditions," *Journal of Industrial Hygiene*, XII, 3 (March, 1930), 99–119.
22. Personal interview with F. J. Roethlisberger, April 2, 1956.
23. W. J. Dickson to L. Baritz, Oct. 19, 1956; M. L. Putnam to E. Mayo, May 28, 1930; Mayo MSS.
24. Personal interview with F. J. Roethlisberger, April 2, 1956.
25. Roethlisberger, *Management and the Worker*, 385, 523, 525, 554, 559, 568.
26. See, however, Elton Mayo, "Industrial Research," *Harvard Business School Alumni Bulletin*, XVI, 2 (Feb., 1940), 87.
27. Roethlisberger, *Management and the Worker*, 445–446.
28. Mayo, *Social Problems*, 111.

CHAPTER 6:

Hawthorne and Managerial Sociology

1. Eugene J. Benge, "Grouping Workers to Get Best Results," *Factory*, XXIV, 8 (May 1, 1920), 1332–1333; Harold E. Burtt, *Psychology and Industrial Efficiency* (New York, 1929), 290; Lorine Pruette and Douglas Fryer, "Group Problems of the Executive," *JPR*, III, 2 (1924–1925), 39, 45;

"Team System Is Thought to be Best Labor Solution," *Electrical World*, LXXII, 7 (Aug. 17, 1918), 298.

2. Ordway Tead, *Human Nature and Management* (2nd ed., New York, 1933), 184.

3. Quoted in Milton J. Nadworny, *Scientific Management and the Unions, 1900–1932* (Cambridge, 1955), 8; L. M. Gilbreth, *The Psychology of Management* (New York, 1914), 117.

4. Stanley B. Mathewson, *Restriction of Output Among Unorganized Workers* (New York, 1931), 68, 73–74.

5. "Holding Back on Production," *BTS*, IV, 5 (Oct., 1919), 3.

6. Whiting Williams, *What's On the Worker's Mind by One Who Put On Overalls to Find Out* (New York, 1921), 15. Cf. *ibid.*, 129; Whiting Williams, *Mainsprings of Men* (N.P., 1923), 494.

7. Mathewson, *Restriction of Output*, 6n, 11, 86, 103, 146, 166; Williams, *What's On the Worker's Mind*, 283–284. Cf. "What the Factory Worker Really Thinks about Productivity, Nationalization of Industry, and Labor in Politics," *FMM*, CIV (Jan., 1946), 81–82.

8. Quoted in Mathewson, *Restriction of Output*, 126–127.

9. William M. Leiserson, "The Economics of Restriction of Output," in *ibid.*, 166–168; Wilbert E. Moore, *Industrial Relations and the Social Order* (New York, 1946), 261. Cf. Reinhard Bendix, "Bureaucracy: The Problem and Its Setting," *ASR*, XII, 5 (Oct., 1947), 494.

10. See, e.g., H. A. Wright to Elton Mayo, Feb. 22, 1932, and G. A. Pennock to E. M., March 11, 1932, Mayo MSS; F. J. Roethlisberger, *Management and Morale* (Cambridge, 1942), 81–83; T. N. Whitehead, *Leadership in a Free Society* (Cambridge, 1936), 18; T. N. Whitehead, "Leadership within Industrial Organizations," *HBR*, XIV, 2 (Winter, 1936), 170. Cf. Eugene V. Schneider, *Industrial Sociology* (New York, 1957), 201–202.

11. Elton Mayo, *Human Problems of an Industrial Civilization* (2nd ed., Boston, 1946), 115.

12. Mason Haire, "Group Dynamics in the Industrial Situation," in Arthur Kornhauser *et al.* (eds.), *Industrial Conflict* (New York, 1954), 374. Cf., however, Roethlisberger, *Management and the Worker*, 536.

13. M. L. Putnam, "Improving Employee Relations," *Personnel Journal*, VIII, 5 (Feb., 1930), 320–322; F. J. Roethlisberger and William J. Dickson, *Management and the Worker* (Cambridge, 1939), 189, 197, 200, 200n. Cf. M. E. Mitchell, "Getting the Worker's Side of the Picture," *System*, LVIII (Oct., 1930), 306–307.

14. Roethlisberger and Dickson, *Management and the Worker*, 374–375.

15. Fritz Roethlisberger to Elton Mayo, July 20, 1931, Mayo MSS; Roethlisberger and Dickson, *Managment and the Worker*, 536; B. M. Selekman, "Discussion," *Proceedings of the First Annual Meeting, Industrial Relations Research Association, Cleveland, Ohio, Dec. 29–30, 1948* (N.P., 1949), 231.

16. C. W. M. Hart, "Industrial Relations Research and Social Theory," *Canadian Journal of Economics and Political Science*, XV, 1 (Feb., 1949), 56–57.

17. W. J. Dickson to L. Baritz, Oct. 19, 1956; personal interview with I. P. Leseth, Superintendent of Personnel Administration, Western Electric headquarters, Aug. 1, 1955; American Telephone & Telegraph Co., Personnel Relations Dept., "An Interviewing Method," June 30, 1941, mimeographed, 1, 6–7, and AT&T Co., Personnel Relations Dept., "Personnel Counseling," Oct. 20, 1941, mimeographed, 1, 5, 8, AT&T Co. MSS; Western Electric Co., Kearney Works, *Personnel Counseling* (Allentown, Pa., 1948), 3, 8, 11–14; John A. Bromer, Prudential Insurance Co., "A New Approach to Employee Counseling" (mimeographed speech to graduate seminar in industrial engineering, Columbia University, March, 1950), 4–6; Jeanne L. and Harold L. Wilensky, "Personnel Counseling," *AJS*, LVII, 3 (Nov., 1951), 266, 269.

18. Western Electric Co., *Personnel Counseling*, 15.

19. Wilensky, "Personnel Counseling," *AJS* (1951), 275–276.

20. Sylvia B. Gottlieb, CWA, CIO, to L. Baritz, Dec. 2, 1955; U. S. Congress, Senate, *Labor-Management Relations in the Bell Telephone System*, Hearing before Subcommittee on Labor-Management Relations of the Committee on Labor and Public Welfare, U. S. Senate, 81st Cong., 2nd Sess. (Washington, 1950), *passim*.

21. W. J. Dickson to L. Baritz, Oct. 19, 1956; American Telephone & Telegraph Co., "Personnel Counseling," 11, AT&T Co. MSS; Walter Dill Scott *et al.*, *Personnel Management* (5th ed., New York, 1954), 83n; Wilensky, "Personnel Counseling," *AJS* (1951), 267, 278.

22. W. J. Dickson to L. Baritz, Oct. 19, 1956; personal interview with E. C. Tessman, Chief of Personnel Counseling and Research Dept., Western Electric Co., Hawthorne Works, May 9, 1956; personal interview with F. B. Shannon, Western Electric headquarters, Aug. 1, 1955; Elton Mayo to G. A. Pennock, Oct. 28, 1929, Mayo MSS; J. W. Dietz, "Some Aspects of Personnel Research in a Manufacturing Organization," *Annals*, CXIX (May, 1925), 103; Mayo, *Human Problems*, 74–75; G. A. Pennock, "Industrial Research at Hawthorne," *Personnel Journal*, VIII, 5 (Feb., 1930), 311; Whitehead, *Leadership in a Free Society*, 104. Cf., however, Wilensky, "Personnel Counseling," *AJS* (1951), 280.

23. Frank W. Braden to L. Baritz, Sept. 13, 1955; R. K. Greenleaf to L. B., Nov. 4, 1955; E. C. Tessman to L. B., Dec. 30, 1955.

24. Personal interview with F. J. Roethlisberger, April 2, 1956; [Western Electric Co.], "Impact of Hawthorne Studies and Counseling," (N.P., [1955]), *passim*, W. E. Co. MSS.

25. Elton Mayo, *Social Problems of an Industrial Civilization* (Boston, 1945), 20; Roethlisberger, *Management and the Worker*, 604.

26. Mayo, "The Basis of Industrial Psychology," *BTS*, IX, 6 (Dec., 1924), 249, 256; Mayo, "Revery and Industrial Fatigue," *JPR*, III, 8 (1924–1925), 273.

27. Mayo to Wallace B. Donham, [N.D.], Mayo MSS.

28. Mayo, "Economic Stability and the Standard of Living," *Harvard Business School Alumni Bulletin*, VII, 6 (July 1, 1931), 293; Mayo, "Research in Human Relations," *Personnel*, XVII, 4 (May, 1941), 269.

29. Mayo, *Social Problems*, 9, 13, 30–31; Mayo, "What Every Village Knows," *Survey Graphic*, XXVI, 12 (Dec., 1937), 695–698. Cf. C. Wright Mills, *White Collar* (New York, 1953), 144; Harold L. Sheppard, "The Social and Historical Philosophy of Elton Mayo," *Antioch Review*, X, 3 (Sept.,

1950), 403.

30. Reinhard Bendix and Lloyd H. Fisher, "The Perspectives of Elton Mayo," *Review of Economics and Statistics*, XXXI, 4 (Nov., 1949), 316n; Sheppard, "Social and Historical Philosophy of Elton Mayo," *Antioch Review* (1950), 399. Cf. Delbert C. Miller and William H. Form, *Industrial Sociology* (New York, 1951), 78; Harold L. Sheppard, "The Treatment of Unionism in 'Managerial Sociology,'" *ASR*, XIV, 2 (April, 1949), 310.

31. See, e.g., F. J. Roethlisberger *et al.*, *Training for Human Relations* (Boston, 1954), 116; Sheppard, "The Treatment of Unionism," *ASR* (1949), 310–313; Whitehead, *Leadership in a Free Society*, 80, 102–103, 155. The process by which empiricism leads to an acceptance of the assumptions of the dominant group is admirably outlined in Robert S. Lynd, *Knowledge for What?* (Princeton, 1939), 119–120. For summaries of recent criticisms, see Henry A. Landsberger, *Hawthorne Revisited* (Ithaca, 1958), 28–47; Harold L. Wilensky, "Human Relations in the Workplace," Industrial Relations Research Association, *Research in Industrial Human Relations* (New York, 1957), 26n2.

32. Personal interview with F. B. Shannon, Aug. 1, 1955.

33. "Deep Therapy on the Assembly Line," *Ammunition*, April, 1949, 47–48.

34. W. J. Dickson to L. Baritz, Oct. 19, 1956.

Chapter 7:
Depression and Repression

1. M. G. Demougeot, "Management and the Human Element," *American Machinist*, LXXVIII, 1 (Jan. 3, 1934), 7; Harry W. Hepner, *Psychology in Modern Business* (New York, 1931), 503; Ordway Tead, "Trends in Industrial Psychology," *Annals*, CXLIX, part I (May, 1930), 110. Cf. "Defaulted Bonds," *Business Week*, May 18, 1932, 40; "Management Group Sees Need for Human Engineering," *Steel*, C (May 3, 1937), 37; Saunders Norvell, "The Human Side of Management," *Sales Management*, XXXII, 6 (March 15, 1933), 246, 271–272; Frederic Oakhill, "The Human Factor

in Maintenance," *FMM*, XCIV, 3 (March, 1936), 117–118.

2. See, e.g., L. M. Clegg, vice-president, to F. C. Crawford, president, March 6, 1936, Thompson Products Co., Inc. MSS: "We are budgeting an appreciable amount of money for personnel work and for other department activities that were not in effect in 1929." See also Samuel N. Stevens, "The Applications of Psychology to the Problems of Business and Industry," *Personnel*, XII, 4 (May, 1936), 228; Edwin E. Witte, *The Evolution of Managerial Ideas in Industrial Relations* (New York State School of Industrial and Labor Relations, Cornell University, Bull. No. 27; Nov., 1954), 10.

3. "Hiring and Separation Methods in American Factories," *Monthly Labor Review*, XXXV, 5 (Nov., 1932), 1006; NICB, *Industrial Relations* (New York, 1931), 54; Walter D. Scott *et al.*, *Personnel Management* (5th ed., New York, 1954), 615, 631.

4. "Coming: A Boom in Personnel Management," *Forbes*, XXXII, 10 (Nov. 15, 1933), 13; Delbert C. Miller and William H. Form, *Industrial Sociology* (New York, 1951), 21; Morris S. Viteles, "Caveat Emptor," *JCP*, V, 3 (May-June, 1941), 119.

5. NICB, *What Employers are Doing for Employees* (New York, 1936), 23, 26, 60–61.

6. E.g., Northwestern Mutual Life Insurance Co., "Labor Policy," June 12, 1939, N.M.L.I. Co. MSS; "How Procter & Gamble Do It," *Business Week*, July 4, 1936, 22.

7. Leo Wolman and Gustav Peck, "Labor Groups in the Social Structure," President's Research Committee, *Recent Social Trends in the United States* (New York, 1933), II, 843.

8. Walter V. Bingham and Max Freyd, *Procedures in Employment Psychology* (Chicago, 1926), 42; Harold E. Burtt, *Principles of Employment Psychology* (Boston, 1926), 186–188; Burtt, *Psychology and Industrial Efficiency* (New York, 1929), 386; Charles A. Drake and Holger D. Oleen, "The Technique of Testing," *FMM*, XCVI, 3 (March, 1938), 72; B. V. Moore, "Interpreting Psychological Data to Those Who Must Use Them in Industry," *JCP*, IV, 3

(May-June, 1940), 106–109; "Personnel Research Federation," *Personnel Journal*, XVIII, 5 (Nov., 1939), 193; "Psychology's a Business, Too," *Business Week*, Nov. 16, 1932, 11; "Rating Tests Shown at Business Show," *Management Methods*, LXI, *11* (Nov., 1932), 612. Cf. Robert E. Schwab, "Putting Human Relations Research to Work," *Public Utilities Fortnightly*, LIII, 5 (March 4, 1954), 284.

9. Burtt, *Principles of Employment Psychology*, 7–8, 189; Burtt, *Psychology and Industrial Efficiency*, 389; V. E. Fisher and Joseph V. Hanna, *The Dissatisfied Worker* (New York, 1931), vii–viii; Harry W. Hepner, *Human Relations in Changing Industry* (New York, 1934), 237–239; R. N. McMurry, "Mental Factors in Labor Disputes," *Personnel*, XII, *1* (Aug., 1935), 153, 160.

10. Witte, *Evolution of Managerial Ideas*, 14–15.

11. T. N. Whitehead, *Leadership in a Free Society* (Cambridge, 1936), 155.

12. Whitehead, *Leadership in a Free Society*, 80, 100-101, 119. Cf. C. Wright Mills, "The Contribution of Sociology to Studies of Industrial Relations," *Proceedings of the First Annual Meeting, Industrial Relations Research Association, Cleveland, Ohio, Dec. 29–30, 1948* (N.P., 1949), 209n.

13. See, e.g., Alex Brule, "Human and Psychological Aspects of Management," *FMM*, XCVI (Oct., 1938), 140; "How to Learn Worker Attitudes," *Personnel Journal*, XVI, 7 (Jan.-Feb., 1938), 260–261; Donald A. Laird, *How to Use Psychology in Business* (New York, 1936), 24–25; Rensis Likert, "What Psychology Can Contribute to Industrial Stability," *Mechanical Engineering*, LVI, *4* (April, 1934), 206; Henry C. Link, "The Future of Consulting Psychology," *JCP*, I, *1* (Jan.-Feb., 1937), 12–13; Charles S. Slocombe, "Meet C.I.O. on Its Own Ground," *Personnel Journal*, XVI, *1* (May, 1937), 1–8.

14. D. H. Ewing, "Employee-Attitude Interviews as Tools of Personnel Management," *HBR*, XII, *1* (Oct., 1933), 106–107; Hepner, *Human Relations*, 41; Robert Hoppock, *Job Satisfaction* (New York, 1935), 6; "How to Learn Worker Attitudes," *Personnel Journal* (1938), 261; NICB, *Experience with Employee Attitude Surveys* (CBR, SPP No. 115;

New York, 1951), 7; "Psychology of Attitudes," *Personnel Journal*, XVI, 7 (Jan.-Feb., 1938), 243.

15. E.g., J. David Houser, *What the Employer Thinks* (Cambridge, 1927), 84–85, 177, 182; Milton J. Nadworny, *Scientific Management and the Unions, 1900–1932* (Cambridge, 1955), 79–80; Whiting Williams, *What's on the Worker's Mind by One Who Put on Overalls to Find Out* (New York, 1921), 117.

16. Personal interview with Douglas McGregor, Jan. 26, 1956; Roy Dickinson, "Building a Labor Policy," *Printers' Ink Monthly*, XXXV (Nov., 1937), 39, 42; Rex B. Hersey, "Employees Rate Plant Policies," *Personnel Journal*, XVI, 3 (Sept., 1937), 71–72, 74; John G. Jenkins, *Psychology in Business and Industry* (New York, 1935), 314; James C. Worthy, "Factors Influencing Employee Morale," *HBR*, XXVIII, 1 (Jan., 1950), 61.

17. Western Electric Co., General Personnel Dept., "History of Supervisory Conference Training in the Western Electric Company," 1932, mimeographed, 11, W.E. Co. MSS; Jeanne L. and Harold L. Wilensky, "Personnel Counseling," *AJS*, LVII, 3 (Nov., 1951), 269n.

18. Arthur H. Brayfield and Walter H. Crockett, "Employee Attitudes and Employee Performance," *Psychological Bulletin*, LII, 5 (Sept., 1955), 397; Arthur W. Kornhauser, "The Technique of Measuring Employee Attitudes," *Personnel*, IX, 4 (May, 1933), 99; Kornhauser and Agnes A. Sharp, "Employee Attitudes," *Personnel Journal*, X, 6 (April, 1932), 393–404.

19. Personal interview with R. S. Uhrbrock, Oct. 27, 1955; Uhrbrock, "Attitudes of 4430 Employees," *Journal of Social Psychology*, V, 3 (Aug., 1934), 365–366; Uhrbrock, "Getting Facts for Administering Personnel Policies," *Personnel*, XII, 1 (Aug., 1935), 133.

20. U. S. Congress, Senate, *Violations of Free Speech and Rights of Labor,* Hearings before Subcommittee of the Committee on Education and Labor, U. S. Senate, 75th Cong., 1st Sess., on S. Res. 266, Part 6, "Labor Espionage, General Motors Corp.," Feb. 15–19, 1937 (Washington, 1937), 1876–1877, 1907, 1945.

21. Burtt, *Psychology and Industrial Efficiency*, 193, 387; "Fatigue and Boredom," *Engineering*, CXLIV (July 23, 1937), 108; Herman Feldman, *A Survey of Research in the Field of Industrial Relations* (New York, 1928), 77; Lillian M. Gilbreth, "Monotony in Repetitive Operations," *Iron Age*, CXVIII, 20 (Nov. 11, 1926), 1344; Jenkins, *Psychology in Business*, 202; Donald A. Laird, "Hands, Heads and Hearts," *Printers' Ink*, CXLV, 2 (Oct. 11, 1928), 88; H. S. Person, "The Reaction of Workers to Machine Work and Working Conditions," in Henry C. Metcalf (ed.), *The Psychological Foundations of Management* (New York, 1927), 139; Yoichi Uyeno, "Discussion," *BTS*, VII, 3 (June, 1922), 96; Morris S. Viteles, "Man and the Machine," *Power Plant Engineering*, XLIII, 1 (Jan., 1939), 51.

22. Elton Mayo, "The Irrational Factor in Human Behavior," *Annals*, CX (Nov., 1923), 122–123.

23. Quoted in Bruce V. Moore and George W. Hartmann (eds.), *Readings in Industrial Psychology* (New York, 1931), 391. Cf., however, Daniel Katz, "Satisfactions and Deprivations in Industrial Life," in Arthur Kornhauser *et al.* (eds.), *Industrial Conflict* (New York, 1954), 90–91.

24. Ordway Tead, *Human Nature and Management* (2nd ed., New York, 1933), 241.

25. Eugene J. Benge, "Tests in Selecting Employees," *Society for the Advancement of Management Journal*, III, 2 (March, 1938), 72–73; Hepner, *Psychology in Modern Business*, 227, 434–435; Jenkins, *Psychology in Business*, 52, 73; Moore and Hartmann, *Readings in Industrial Psychology*, 42–92; NICB, *Personnel Activities in American Business* (Conference Board Management Record Supplements, SPP No. 20; New York, 1940), 8; NICB, *What Employers are Doing for Employees*, 24, 63, 65; J. L. Rosenstein, *Psychology of Human Relations for Executives* (New York, 1936), 128; Tead, *Human Nature*, 199; Morris S. Viteles, *Industrial Psychology* (New York, 1932), 190–322.

26. Personal interview with Richard S. Uhrbrock, Oct. 27, 1955; R.S.U. to L. Baritz, Dec. 6, 1955.

27. Irl C. Martin, "How and Why Woodward Governor Co.

Uses Aptitude Tests for Employees," *Sales Management*, XLVIII, 5 (March 1, 1941), 18.

28. Otto W. Bitzenhofer, "Testing the Applicant," *Textile World*, LXXXIV (Aug., 1934), 1600–1601; J. B. Delaney, "Tests: Psychology Sifts Out Misfits," *Iron Age*, CLXXI, 8 (Feb. 19, 1953), 61; Henry S. Dennison and John S. Keir, "The Selection, Assignment and Training of Workers," *Personnel*, VII, 2 (Aug., 1930), 42–51; Charles A. Drake, "Aptitude Tests Help You Hire," *FMM*, XCV, 6 (June, 1937), 55–57, 92; Edward N. Hay to Margaret L. Plunkett, April 8, 1939, Industrial Relations Library, Massachusetts Institute of Technology MSS; R. Randell Irwin, "Lockheed's Full Testing Program," *Personnel Journal*, XXI, 3 (Sept., 1942), 103–106; NICB, *Experience with Psychological Tests*, 20; Joyce Oliver, "Our Experience with Aptitude Tests in Hiring Salesmen," *Sales Management*, XXXIII, 11 (Nov. 15, 1933), 485–486, 509; Elizabeth L. O'Rourke, "Pros and Cons of Employment Tests," *System and Business Management*, LXIII, 12 (Dec., 1934), 582–583, 598.

29. See, e.g., Eugene J. Benge, "Maladjustment of Abilities and Interests," in George W. Hartmann and Theodore Newcomb (eds.), *Industrial Conflict* (New York, 1939), 149; Hepner, *Psychology in Modern Business*, 219; Jenkins, *Psychology in Business*, 95; Arthur W. Kornhauser, "Overcoming the Barriers to Industrial Testing," *Personnel*, XII, 4 (May, 1936), 239; Laird, *How to Use Psychology in Business*, 18, 59, 103–104; Howard K. Nixon, "Your Likes Reveal What You Are," *System*, LIX (Jan., 1931), 19–20.

30. Floyd H. Allport *et al.*, "Psychology in Relation to Social and Political Problems," in Paul S. Achilles (ed.), *Psychology at Work* (New York, 1932), 247–248.

31. NICB, *Training Solutions of Company Problems* (CBR, SPP No. 15; New York, 1939), 77.

32. Cf. George Katona, *Psychological Analysis of Economic Behavior* (New York, 1951), 43–49, 57–58; Gardner Murphy, *Historical Introduction to Modern Psychology* (rev. ed., New York, 1949), 264–267, 275–277; Viteles, *Industrial Psychology*, 423–427.

33. See, e.g., Burtt, *Psychology and Industrial Efficiency*, 86;

Moore and Hartmann, *Readings in Industrial Psychology*, 244; Tead, *Human Nature*, 233; Viteles, *Industrial Psychology*, 393.

34. Charles R. Sturdevant, "Training Course of the American Steel and Wire Company," *JAP*, II, 2 (June, 1918), 140–147.

35. "Community Vestibule School a Growing Factor in American Industry," *American Gas Engineering Journal*, CIX, 26 (Dec. 28, 1918), 583; "Teaching Foremen Human Factors," *Iron Trade Review*, LXIV (April 17, 1919), 1030.

36. Chrysler Corp., "Functions and Activities of Supervisory Training in Chrysler Corporation," [1949 (?)], mimeographed, 3, C.C. MSS; Eastman Kodak Co., "Educational Courses for Kodak Employees," *Personnel Journal*, XVI, *1* (May, 1937), 9–11; "Kodak Executive Recruits Will Learn as They Go," *Business Week*, July 30, 1930, 18; NICB, *Training Solutions*, 6.

37. R. S. Livingstone to Messrs. Cox, McBride, and Kerwin, Sept. 30, 1935, Thompson Products Co. MSS; Western Electric Co., "History of Supervisory Conference Training," 2, 11, 14, W.E. Co. MSS; R. O. Beckman, "Employee Training in Wide-Spread Organizations," *Personnel Journal*, XIII, *1* (June, 1934), 16; Walter T. Blake and John H. Gander, "Organization and Techniques of a Modern Personnel Department," (unpublished thesis, School of Industrial Management, M.I.T., 1937), 13; Henry Bruère and Grace Pugh, *Profitable Personnel Practice* (New York, 1929), 68–69; Byron F. Field, "Industrial Training," *Personnel*, VII, 2 (Aug., 1930), 57–64; "Human Relations Win," *FMM*, XCII, *12* (Dec., 1934), 536; Homer L. Humke, "Teaching How to Teach," *Personnel Journal*, XVI, *3* (Sept., 1937), 99–101; "Industrial Psychology for Foremen," *Personnel Journal*, VIII, 5 (Feb., 1930), 360; Moore, "Interpreting Psychological Data," *JCP* (1940), 106–107; F. J. Roethlisberger and William J. Dickson, *Management and the Worker* (Cambridge, 1939), 189–190, 203.

38. NICB, *What Employers Are Doing for Employees*, 15, 40–41; NICB, *Personnel Activities* (1940), 29–31. Cf. NICB, *Training Solutions*, 8, 19, 27, 40, 48, 60.

39. Henry P. Fairchild, "Business as an Institution," *ASR*, II, *1* (Feb., 1937), 4–5.
40. Allport *et al.*, "Psychology in Relation to Social and Political Problems," in Achilles (ed.), *Psychology at Work*, 247; Arthur W. Kornhauser, "Industrial Psychology in England, Germany, and the United States," *Personnel Journal*, VIII, 6 (April, 1930), 422; Kornhauser, "The Study of Work Feelings," *ibid.*, VIII, 5 (Feb., 1930), 351; Viteles, *Industrial Psychology*, 19, 465.
41. Hartmann and Newcomb, *Industrial Conflict*, vii–viii, 15–17, 103, 464, 541.
42. H. E. Burtt, "Reports of the A.A.A.P.," *JCP*, II, 3 (May-June, 1938), 79–80; *ibid.*, X, 3 (May-June, 1946), 178; *ibid.*, X, 6 (Nov.-Dec., 1946), 335n.

CHAPTER 8:

War and Peace

1. R. S. Livingstone to F. C. Crawford and L. M. Clegg, Aug. 20, 1940, Thompson Products Co., "Outline—Industrial Relations Conference," Dec. 6, 1940, T. P. Co. MSS; *Moody's Industrial Manual* (New York, 1939), 1370; *ibid.* (1944), 2770; *ibid.* (1954), 2636; *Forty First Annual Report of Thompson Products, Inc. and Subsidiaries for the Year Ended Dec. 31, 1942* (N.P., N.D.), 21; Thompson Products, Inc., *Foremen's Bulletin*, III, *10* (Oct., 1941), 1.
2. "America Trains Her Industrial Army," *FMM*, XCVIII, *11* (Nov., 1940), 42; Elton Mayo and George F. F. Lombard *et al.*, *Teamwork and Labor Turnover in the Aircraft Industry of Southern California* (Boston, Harvard Business School, Business Research Studies, No. 32, Oct., 1944), 4–5.
3. Cessna Aircraft Co., Personnel Dept., *How to Win Workers (Or—Hosswhippin' Won't Work)*, (Wichita, Kansas [1942 (?)]), [2]; Ted Cox, "Fitting the Right Man to the Right Job," *American Business*, XX, 2 (Feb., 1950), 44; Frederick C. Crawford, *Humanizing Labor Relations* (N.P. [1944 (?)]), 9; Maurice T. Freeman, Loomis-Sayles Mutual Fund, Inc., *Twenty-Fifth Annual Report* (New York, 1954), 9; Douglas McGregor, "Management Rights and Collective

Bargaining," *Mechanical Engineering,* LXVII, 9 (Sept., 1945), 610; Daniel Starch, "What Psychologists Can Do in Business," *JCP,* VI, 2 (March-April, 1942), 92.

4. Howard R. Bowen, "Future of Business Education," in *The Challenge of Business Education* (Chicago, 1949), 36; Ross Stagner, "Attitudes of Corporate Executives Regarding Psychological Methods in Personnel Work," *American Psychologist,* I, *11* (Nov., 1946), 541.

5. George B. Holderer, WPB, to Elton Mayo, March 12, 1943, and E.M. to G.B.H., March 18, 1943, Mayo MSS; John G. Darley, "Five Years of Social Science Research," in Harold Guetzkow (ed.), *Groups, Leadership and Men* (Pittsburgh, 1951), 11; John B. Fox and Jerome F. Scott, *Absenteeism: Management's Problem* (Boston, Harvard Business School, Business Research Studies, No. 29, Dec., 1943); Alexander H. Leighton, *Human Relations in a Changing World* (New York, 1949), 43; Mayo and Lombard, *Teamwork and Labor Turnover;* A. T. Poffenberger, "Psychology: Academic and Professional," *JCP,* IX, *1* (Jan.-Feb., 1945), 1; Walter Dill Scott *et al., Personnel Management* (5th ed., New York, 1954), 251; *The Training Within Industry Report, 1940–1945* (Washington, 1945), x, 126.

6. R. S. Livingstone to Personnel Supervisors, May 13, 1941, Thompson Products Co. MSS; "Beating the Wartime Personnel Shortage," *American Business,* XX, *11* (Nov., 1950), 20; Daniel Bell, "Adjusting Men to Machines," *Commentary,* III, *1* (Jan., 1947), 79; Milton L. Blum, *Industrial Psychology and its Social Foundations* (New York, 1949), 5; Wayne Dennis, "The Background of Industrial Psychology," in *Current Trends in Industrial Psychology* (Pittsburgh, 1949), 12; International Harvester Co., *Practical Psychology* (Chicago, [1946 (?)]), 3; Arthur W. Kornhauser and Richard S. Schultz, "Research on Selection of Salesmen," *JAP,* XXV, *1* (Feb., 1941), 2; Norman R. F. Maier, "A Human Relations Program for Supervision," *Industrial and Labor Relations Review,* I, *3* (April, 1948), 460–464.

7. George B. Holderer to Elton Mayo, March 12, 1943, Mayo MSS; Fox and Scott, *Absenteeism,* iii–iv, 27.

8. Mayo and Lombard, *Teamwork and Labor Turnover,* 1.

9. Life Insurance Sales Research Bureau, *Morale and Agency Management*, Vol. I, *Morale: The Mainspring of Management* (Hartford, 1940), 11, 46–47; F. J. Roethlisberger, *Management and Morale* (Cambridge, 1942), 194; William F. Whyte (ed.), *Industry and Society* (New York, 1946), 184–185; J. L. Wolff, "Employe Morale," *Advanced Management*, VI, 3 (July-Sept., 1941), 107. Cf. "Best Workers Gripe the Most," *Business Week*, Feb. 10, 1951, 69; Eliot D. Chapple, "The Analysis of Industrial Morale," *Journal of Industrial Hygiene and Toxicology*, XXIV, 7 (Sept., 1942), 165.

10. Robert Dubin, "Constructive Aspects of Industrial Conflict," in Arthur Kornhauser *et al.* (eds.), *Industrial Conflict* (New York, 1954), 42–43; Daniel Katz, "Satisfactions and Deprivations in Industrial Life," *ibid.*, 98; Katz, "Survey Research Center," in Guetzkow, *Groups, Leadership and Men*, 77–78; Morris S. Viteles, *Motivation and Morale in Industry* (New York, 1953), 9–10; Charles R. Walker and Robert H. Guest, *The Man on the Assembly Line* (Cambridge, 1952), 38–39, 143.

11. James C. Worthy, "Factors Influencing Employee Morale," *HBR*, XXVIII, 1 (Jan., 1950), 67, 73. Cf. Arthur N. Turner, "Foremen—Key to Worker Morale," *ibid.*, XXXII, 1 (Jan.-Feb., 1954), 76–86.

12. Richard Centers, "Motivational Aspects of Occupational Stratification," *Journal of Social Psychology*, XXVIII (Aug., 1948), 190; "The Fortune Survey: A Self-Portrait of the American People—1947," *Fortune*, XXXV (Jan., 1947), 10; Elmo Roper, "The Fortune Survey: The American Factory Worker," *ibid.* (May, 1947), 5; Viteles, *Motivation and Morale*, 4.

13. See, e.g., R. E. Roberts, "Human Relations in Industry," (N.P., [1948 (?)]), 4, mimeographed, Ford Motor Co. MSS; American Telephone & Telegraph Co., Personnel Relations Dept., "Introduction," *Human Relations in Management* (New York, 1949), 3–4; William J. Giese and H. W. Ruter, "An Objective Analysis of Morale," *JAP*, XXXIII, 5 (Oct., 1949), 421; Katz, "Satisfactions and Deprivations," in Kornhauser, *Industrial Conflict*, 106; C. H. Lawshe *et al.*,

Psychology of Industrial Relations (New York, 1953), 4; Survey Research Center, *Factors Related to Differences in Group Productivity* (Ann Arbor, Dec., 1949), iii, 49.

14. "Opinion Poll for Labor," *Business Week*, Aug. 8, 1953, 114; "Workers Air Gripes, Discuss Production in Questionnaire," *Printers' Ink*, CCIV (July 30, 1943), 68.

15. NICB, *Experience with Employee Attitude Surveys* (CBR, SPP No. 115, New York, 1951), 45.

16. Arthur Kornhauser, "Are Public Opinion Polls Fair to Organized Labor?" *Public Opinion Quarterly*, X (Winter, 1946), 484–500.

17. "Deep Therapy on the Assembly Line," *Ammunition*, April, 1949, 48. For an accessible account of the conflict between General Motors and the UAW over an attitude study related to the guaranteed annual wage, see "The Workers Poll that Kicked Up a Fuss," *Business Week*, Feb. 19, 1955, 30–31.

18. Solomon Barkin, "Discussion," *Proceedings of the Fourth Annual Meeting, Industrial Relations Research Association, Boston, Mass., Dec. 28–29, 1951* (N.P., 1952), 81–82.

19. Otis Brubacker, research director, United Steelworkers of America, to L. Baritz, Dec. 15, 1955.

20. Ralph L. Mason, "Experience with Employee Opinion Surveys," *Advanced Management*, XIV, 3 (Sept., 1949), 98–100.

21. NICB, *Experience with Employee Attitude Surveys*, 7; NICB, *Personnel Activities in American Business* (rev., CBR, SPP No. 86, New York, 1947), 13.

22. Bill Crowell to R. S. Livingstone, Sept. 29, 1943, Thompson Products, Inc., "Bulletin to Office Employees," Nov. 17, 1943, T.P. Co. MSS.

23. "A Message from Fred Crawford," Nov. 20, 1943, T.P. Co. MSS.

24. International Association of Machinists, District 54, "T.P. Shop News," I, *12* (Dec. 1, 1943), 2, T.P. Co. MSS.

25. John M. Kerwin to all Foremen and Supervisors, Dec. 1, 1943, T.P. Co. MSS; Thompson Products, Inc., *Friendly Forum*, XI, 2 (Feb. 4, 1944), 1, 13; Thompson Products, Inc., *We Led with Our Chin! A Report on a Survey of*

Employee Opinion Conducted in Cleveland Plants of Thompson Products, Inc. and Thompson Aircraft Products Co. (Cleveland, Aug., 1944), 4, 8.

26. See, e.g., Tom N. Boggs and Louis L. Maness, "How to Conduct Employee Opinion Surveys," *FMM*, CIV (March, 1946), 91.

27. Gordon L. Walker, "Employee Opinion Surveys at Ford," speech before American Marketing Association, March 16, 1948, mimeographed, 3–4, Ford Motor Co., "Results of Employee Questionnaire No. 1," March 28, 1947, F.M. Co. MSS; *The Rouge News*, II, 8 (April 15, 1947), 7; "Employes Polled," *ibid.*, II, *19* (Sept. 13, 1947), 1; "Poll Critical of Company but Notes Improvement," *ibid.*, III, *3* (Jan. 24, 1948), 1. Cf. "Employee Opinion Survey Aids Ford in Policy Making," *FMM*, CV, *6* (June, 1947), 132; " 'Human Engineering' Program Pays Off for Ford," *Business Week*, Oct. 30, 1948, 94.

28. C. T. Lile, "Inter-Office Correspondence, to all [Koppers Co., Inc.] Employees," Pittsburgh, July 1, 1947, mimeographed, K. Co. MSS; Eugene J. Benge, "Measuring Employe Morale," *Petroleum Refiner*, XXXII, *2* (Feb., 1953), 128–130; L. R. Boulware, "How G.E. is Trying to Sell Employees on Giving Full Skill, Care and Effort at Work," *Printers' Ink*, CCXXV (Dec. 10, 1948), 76; Caterpillar Tractor Co., *You Said It—Here It Is: Michigan Survey Results* (N.P., [1951 (?)]), 1–4; Detroit Edison Co., "Employe Surveys Help Us," *Synchroscope*, Dec., 1951, 16–17; Chester E. Evans and LaVerne N. Laseau, *My Job Contest* (Washington, 1950), *passim*; Peter F. Hurst, "This Small Plant Made a Morale Survey," *FMM*, CVI, *5* (May, 1948), 78–79; A. V. Larson, "Worker Opinion Survey Did a Good Job for Us," *ibid.*, CIV (Sept., 1946), 156–157; Opinion Research Corp., *A Report on the Employee Opinion Survey Conducted for Continental Oil Company and Continental Pipe Line Company* (N.P., [1952 (?)]), *passim*; Pitney-Bowes Co., *What You Think about Your Company* (N.P., 1949), 2–3; James W. Redfield, "Appraising Employee Attitudes," *Advanced Management*, XIII, *4* (Dec., 1948), 165–166; Scott *et al.*, *Personnel Management*, 456; "Sears Polls

Employee Morale," *Business Week*, May 20, 1950, 31–32; Worthy, "Factors Influencing Employee Morale," *HBR* (1950), 61–65.

29. Louis A. Allen, "Attitude Surveys: How to Plan and Conduct Them," *FMM*, CX, 8 (Aug., 1952), 101–105; Joseph C. Bevis, "Finding Out What Your Workers Think," *Gas Age*, CI, 3 (Feb. 5, 1948), 17; Victor I. Bumagin, "Unlocking Workers' Minds through Attitude Research," *Mill and Factory*, XLIV (March, 1949), 111; Herbert Moore, "Employee Attitude Surveys," *Personnel Journal*, XIX, 10 (April, 1941), 363; Stanley L. Payne, "Is Economic Fact the Answer?" *Public Opinion Quarterly*, XV (Spring, 1951), 145; Edward C. Stodel, "Custom Made Men," *Diesel Power and Diesel Transportation*, XXV (June, 1947), 44, 103.

30. Blum, *Industrial Psychology*, 49; Robert N. McMurry, "Management's Reaction to Employee Opinion Polls," *JAP*, XXX, 3 (June, 1946), 212, 215–216.

31. A. H. Brayfield and W. H. Crockett, "Employee Attitudes and Employee Performance," *Psychological Bulletin*, LII, 5 (Sept., 1955), 421; C. A. Myers and J. G. Turnbull, *Research on Labor-Management Relations* (New York, 1949), 18–20.

32. NICB, *Experience with Psychological Tests* (CBR, SPP No. 92, New York, 1948), 1; Scott *et al.*, *Personnel Management*, 250–251, 623; "Testing Wins Wider Acceptance, Surveys Show," *Personnel*, XXX, 3 (Nov., 1953), 167.

33. E.g., "Getting the Right Man for a Job," *Business Week*, Sept. 13, 1952, 159.

34. "Aptitude Tests Aid in Placing Beginners on the Right Job," *Textile World*, XCIV (April, 1944), 93; "Employment Tests," *Business Week*, Sept. 10, 1949, 112–114.

35. "Aptitude Tests by the Bundle," *ibid.*, Sept. 15, 1951, 72, 74; "Psychologists Spot Square Pegs for Industry," *ibid.*, June 14, 1952, 106.

36. Michael J. Balma, "Take Another Look at Personnel Testing," *FMM*, CXII, 11 (Nov., 1954), 250; "Is Industry Buying a Fad?" *Business Week*, July 19, 1952, 84–85; Forrest H. Kirkpatrick, "Psychological Racketeers," *Personnel Journal*, XX, 8 (Feb., 1942), 283–286; NICB, *Experience with Psy-*

chological Tests, 3; "The Tests of Management," *Fortune*, XLII (July, 1950), 92; "What Can Industrial Psychology Do?" *Business Week*, Nov. 1, 1952, 120; Frederic R. Wickert, "Current Use (and Misuse) of Psychological Tests in Business and Industry," *Personnel*, XXVII, *1* (July, 1950), 47–52.

37. Leonard Cohen, "To Test or Not to Test," *Personnel Journal*, XXV, *2* (June, 1946), 73; Edward N. Hay, "The Use of Psychological Tests in Selection and Promotion," *Personnel*, XVI, *3* (Feb., 1940), 121; "A Removal of Baloney," *Fortune*, XXXVI (Sept., 1947), 124; "Testing for Talent," *ibid.*, XXIII (Jan., 1941), 95.

38. Paul S. Achilles, "Trends in Employment Procedures," *Personnel*, XIX, *4* (Jan., 1943), 612; W. S. Allen, "Psychologists Answer Moot Questions about Aptitude Testing," *Sales Management*, LIV, 7 (April 1, 1945), 73; Marion A. Bills, "Psychology Applied to Problems of Office Personnel," *JCP*, VIII, *3* (May-June, 1944), 161; Charles A. Drake, "Aptitude Testing," *Personnel Journal*, XVIII, *9* (March, 1940), 340–345; Charles D. Flory and J. Elliott Janney, "Psychological Services to Business Leaders," *JCP*, X, *3* (May-June, 1946), 116–117; Mason Haire, "Use of Tests in Employee Selection," *HBR*, XXVIII, *1* (Jan., 1950), 51; Whyte, *Industry and Society*, 184–185.

39. National Association of Manufacturers, Employee Relations Division, *Employee Testing* (Information Bulletin No. 21, New York, July 29, 1954), 2.

40. Solomon Barkin, "A Trade Unionist Appraises Management Personnel Philosophy," *HBR*, XXVIII, *5* (Sept., 1950), 62.

41. The quotation is from a personal letter whose author prefers to remain unidentified.

42. *In re Stauffer Chemical Company, Inc.* [Monongahela, Pa.] and *United Mine Workers of America, District 50, Local 12233 (AFL), Aug. 20, 1947,* 8 LA 278.

43. Otis Brubacker to L. Baritz, Dec. 15, 1955.

44. NAM, *Employee Testing*, 3.

45. "Union Agrees to Psychological Tests Instead of Seniority as Basis for Promotion to Key Jobs," *Industrial Relations News*, VI, *6* (Feb. 6, 1956), 1.

46. See, e.g., American Telephone & Telegraph Co., *Human Relations*, Appendix C, 3; Blum, *Industrial Psychology*, 413–414; "Costly Collegians," *Business Week*, Nov. 27, 1948, 30; William H. Knowles, *Personnel Management* (New York, 1955), 59.

47. "New Psych Quiz," *Business Week*, Nov. 2, 1940, 18; "Testing for Talent," *Fortune* (1941), 96.

48. Knowles, *Personnel Management*, 59.

49. Chrysler Corp., "Functions and Activities of Supervisory Training in Chrysler Corporation" [1949 (?)], 22, mimeographed, C.C. MSS.

50. NICB, *Personnel Activities* (1947), 12–13.

51. Thompson Products, Inc., *Foremen's Bulletin*, I, 2 (Feb. 24, 1939), 1, T.P. Co. MSS.

52. *Matter of Interlake Iron Corporation, a corporation* and *Local Union No. 1657, Steel Workers Organizing Committee, C.I.O.*, 33 N.L.R.B. 613, decided July 21, 1941; "Strictly Personnel," *Personnel*, XIX, 6 (May, 1943), 702.

53. *In re Western Automatic Machine Screw Company* [Elyria, Ohio] and *United Automobile, Aircraft and Agricultural Implement Workers of America, Local 101 (CIO)*, *Jan. 26, 1948*, 9 LA 606; *In re Jefferson Standard Broadcasting Co.* [Charlotte, N.C.] and *International Brotherhood of Electrical Workers, Local 1229 (AFL)*, *June 26, 1951*, 28 LRRM, 1215–1224; *In re Merrill Stevens Dry Dock & Repair Co.* [Jacksonville, Fla.] and *Industrial Union of Marine & Shipbuilding Workers of America, Local 32 (CIO)*, *Oct. 19, 1951*, 17 LA 517.

54. Otis Brubacker to L. Baritz, Dec. 15, 1955.

55. Harold F. North, Swift & Co., to Elton Mayo, June 4, 1941, Mayo MSS; Western Electric Co., "Impact of Hawthorne Studies and Counseling," New York, 1955, V, 1–2, W.E. Co. MSS; Helen Baker, *Employee Counseling* (Princeton, 1944), 8; Nathaniel Cantor, *Employee Counseling* (New York, 1945), 24; "Employee Counsellors," *Business Week*, May 20, 1944, 119; S. E. Fuller, "Goodyear Aircraft Employee Counseling," *Personnel Journal*, XXIII, 4 (Oct., 1944), 145–153; "Here Is Industry's Verdict on Women Counselors," *FMM*, CII, 3 (March, 1944), 125–126.

56. Baker, *Employee Counseling*, 51–52; Cantor, *Employee Counseling*, 25, 135, 139; "Here is Industry's Verdict," *FMM* (1944), 129; D. C. Miller and W. H. Form, *Industrial Sociology* (New York, 1951), 472; H. W. Wedaa, "Tomorrow's Counselor," *Personnel Journal*, XXIII, *10* (April, 1945), 395.

57. "Employes Gripe, They Listen," *World Oil*, CXXXV, 5 (Oct., 1952), 82, 86; Al Reese, "I Need Help!" *Petroleum Refiner*, XXXI (Aug., 1952), 117–118; Standard Oil Co. (N.J.), Employee Relations Dept., *Employee Relations Research in Standard Oil Company (New Jersey) and Affiliates* (New York, 1955), I, 117; S.O., *Notes: Conference on the Use of Employee Tests and Measurements* (N.P., [1948]), 39.

58. Baker, *Employee Counseling*, 39; Cantor, *Employee Counseling*, 155.

59. E.g., Cantor, *Employee Counseling*, 96; Everett Van Every, review of A. Garett, *Counseling Methods for Personnel Workers* (New York, 1945), in *Personnel Journal*, XXIV, *8* (Feb., 1946), 318; C. Wright Mills, "Contribution of Sociology to Studies of Industrial Relations," *Proceedings of the First Annual Meeting, Industrial Relations Research Association, Cleveland, Dec. 29–30, 1948* (N.P., 1949), 214–216.

60. "Deep Therapy on the Assembly Line," *Ammunition* (1949), 47.

CHAPTER 9:

Human Relations and Power

1. *Boston Globe*, Jan. 22, 1956, 26; R. L. Demmerle, "Boxing the Compass of Chemical Personnel," *Chemical and Engineering News*, XXV, *48* (Dec. 1, 1947), 3562; *New York Times*, Sept. 4, 1955, 36; Sylvia F. Porter, "Era of Research," *New York Post*, Jan. 7, 1957, 28.

2. Wilbert E. Moore, *Industrial Relations and the Social Order* (New York, 1946), 203; NICB, *Personnel Activities in American Business* (rev. ed., CBR, SPP No. 86, New York, 1947), 6; Walter D. Scott *et al.*, *Personnel Management* (5th ed., New York, 1954), 615, 631.

3. "Executive Poll Shows Human Relations to be Prime Responsibility," *Iron Age*, CLVIII, *12* (Sept. 19, 1946), 153; "Human Relations: Key Coal Factor," *Coal Age*, LII, *3* (March, 1947), 56; H. G. Simpson, " 'Humanized' Industry a Management 'Must,' " *Forbes*, LXII, 5 (Sept. 1, 1948), 15.
4. "Psychologists at Work," *Business Week*, Sept. 19, 1953, 52.
5. A. W. Brown, manager of Esso Employee Relations, "Comments at Sept. 14, 1954, Management Conference of Standard Oil Co.," *Human Relations in Esso Standard Oil* (N.P. [1954 (?)]), 6. Cf. Earl G. Planty, "Managing the Modern Man," *Petroleum Engineer*, XXVI (Feb., 1954), E–16.
6. Personal interview with Douglas McGregor, Jan. 26, 1956; Standard Oil Co. (N.J.), Employee Relations Dept., *Employee Relations Research in Standard Oil Company (New Jersey) and Affiliates* (New York, 1955), I, 5, 6–7, 164; S.O., *Made to Measure* (N.P., 1951), 78; S.O., *Notes: Conference on the Use of Employee Tests and Measurements* (N.P., [1948 (?)]), 38.
7. Nathan Kelne, "College Professors Go to Business!" *Printers' Ink*, CCXXXVI (July 20, 1951), 31–32; Fred Massarik and Paula Brown, "Social Research Faces Industry," *Personnel*, XXX, *6* (May, 1954), 454; U.S. Bureau of Labor Statistics, *Employment Outlook in the Social Sciences* (Bull. No. 1167; Washington, 1954), 2.
8. Elton Mayo to George Lombard, April 3, 1943, Mayo MSS; Willard Beecher to L. Baritz, Oct. 13, 1955; Beecher, "Industrial Relations in the Light of Individual Psychology," *American Journal of Individual Psychology*, XI, 2 (1955), 123; "Business and Sociology," *Business Week*, Oct. 10, 1953, 126; Demmerle, "Boxing the Compass," *Chemical and Engineering News* (1947), 3562; J. P. Fleming, "Motivation of Employees' Behavior," *Edison Electric Institute Bulletin*, XXIII, *1* (Jan., 1955), 11; S.O., *Employee Relations Research*, I, 5; Eugene Staley *et al.* (eds.), *Creating an Industrial Civilization* (New York, 1952), 49, 211.
9. Quoted in Massarik and Brown, "Social Research," *Personnel* (1954), 456.
10. Lawrence E. Davies, "Jargon Held Bane of Psychologists," *New York Times*, Sept. 4, 1955, 36; Alexander R. Heron,

Why Men Work (Stanford, 1948), 8; Ordway Tead, *Human Nature and Management* (2nd ed., New York, 1933), 2–3; William H. Whyte, Jr., and the editors of *Fortune, Is Anybody Listening?* (New York, 1952), 207–208, 222.

11. See, e.g., John S. Ellsworth, Jr., *Factory Folkways* (New Haven, 1952), 73, 75; Albert Lauterbach, *Man, Motives, and Money* (Ithaca, 1954), xii; Rensis Likert and Stanley E. Seashore, "Employee Attitudes and Output," *Monthly Labor Review*, LXXVII, 6 (June, 1954), 643; U.S. Bureau of Labor Statistics, *Supplementary Wage Practices in American Industry* (Bull. No. 939; Washington, 1948), 7.

12. Arthur Kornhauser *et al.* (eds.), *Industrial Conflict* (New York, 1954), 511.

13. Daniel Katz, "Satisfactions and Deprivations in Industrial Life," in *ibid.*, 96–97; L. O. Stockford and K. R. Kunze, "Psychology and the Pay Check," *Personnel*, XXVII, 2 (Sept., 1950), 141.

14. One recent example of such popularization is Vance Packard, *The Hidden Persuaders* (New York, 1957).

15 American Telephone & Telegraph Co., Personnel Relations Dept., *Human Relations in Management* (New York, 1949), 1; Baxter Brent, "Employee-Management Relations," in *Current Trends in Industrial Psychology* (Pittsburgh, 1949), 136–137; Fleming, "Motivation," *Edison Electric Institute Bulletin* (1955), 11; Heron, *Why Men Work*, 8; Donald A. Laird, "Motivation for Morale," *Personnel Journal*, XXVIII, 6 (Nov., 1949), 205; "The Management Shortage," *Business Week*, Oct. 16, 1948, 20.

16. Lewis Corey, "Human Relations Minus Unionism," *Labor and Nation*, VI, 2 (Spring, 1950), 50.

17. "Deep Therapy on the Assembly Line," *Ammunition*, April, 1949, 48.

18. See, e.g., Keith Davis, "Learning to Live with the Informal Groups," *Advanced Management*, XVI, 10 (Oct., 1951), 18; Donald A. Laird, "We Long to Belong," *Banking*, XLIII (Aug., 1950), 94; Leonard R. Sayles, *Behavior of Industrial Work Groups* (New York, 1958), *passim*; Stanley E. Seashore, *Group Cohesiveness in the Industrial Work Group* (Ann Arbor, 1954), 98–100; J. Watson Wilson, "Criteria for

Organization Unity," *Advanced Management,* XIV, *1* (March, 1949), 23–25; A. Zaleznik, *Worker Satisfaction and Development* (Boston, 1956), 130–131.

19. See, e.g., "By All Means Discourage Cliques," *Textile World,* XCII (Aug., 1942), 78–79; Jerome F. Scott, "Teamwork," *Modern Management,* VI, *4* (May, 1946), 15–16. Cf., however, L. R. Boulware, "How G.E. is Trying to Sell Employees on Giving Full Skill, Care and Effort at Work," *Printers' Ink,* CCXXV (Dec. 10, 1948), 76; R. W. Ells, "How to Help People Work Better," *American Business,* XV, *8* (Aug., 1945), 8ff.

20. Carey O. Pickard, "Small Group Plan," *Personnel Journal,* XXIII, *6* (Dec., 1944), 236.

21. Katz, "Satisfactions and Deprivations," in Kornhauser, *Industrial Conflict,* 104.

22. See, e.g., A. J. Hayes quoted in Staley, *Creating an Industrial Civilization,* 28.

23. Yvonne Beaudry, "The Sociogram," *Mill and Factory,* XLI, *5* (Nov., 1951), 107; J. J. Gillespie and A. K. Rice, "A Study of Relationships in Industry," *Engineer,* CLXXXIII (June 20, 1947), 544–546; Mason Haire, "Group Dynamics in the Industrial Situation," in Kornhauser, *Industrial Conflict,* 377; Forrest H. Kirkpatrick, "Interpersonal Relations," *Personnel Journal,* XXIII, *2* (June, 1944), 73; Jacob L. Moreno, *Who Shall Survive?* (New York, 1934), *passim;* Raymond H. Van Zelst, "Sociometrically Selected Work Teams Increase Production," *Personnel Psychology,* V, *3* (Autumn, 1952), 175–185.

24. Marion A. Bills, "Predicting Managerial Success," *JPR,* IV, *2* (1925), 51; David R. Craig and W. W. Charters, *Personal Leadership in Industry* (New York, 1925), 5; "What Makes the Boss Tick?" *Business Week,* Oct. 18, 1952, 186.

25. See, e.g., Glen U. Cleeton and Charles W. Mason, "What is Executive Ability?" *Personnel,* XI, *4* (May, 1935), 127; Harry W. Hepner, *Psychology in Modern Business* (New York, 1931), 336–337; T. S. Knowlson, *Business Psychology* (Libertyville, Ill., 1912), 37; Robert N. McMurry, "Can Aptitude Tests Guide Us in Picking Men for Promotion?" *Sales Management,* XLVI, *11* (May 15, 1940), 48.

26. Donald A. Laird, *How to Use Psychology in Business* (New York, 1936), 359–360. Cf. "Characteristic Traits that Mark the Leader," *Management Review*, XXII, 2 (Feb., 1933), 50.

27. Burleigh B. Gardner, "What Makes Successful and Unsuccessful Executives?" *Advanced Management*, XIII, 3 (Sept., 1948), 116–125; Orlo L. Crissey, "Personnel Selection," in *Current Trends*, 75–76; "The Tests of Management," *Fortune*, XLII (July, 1950), 92.

28. Jerome G. Kunnath and Willard A. Kerr, "Function Analysis of Thirty-Two American Corporate Boards," *JAP*, XXXVII, 2 (April, 1953), 66.

29. Leslie N. Perrin, "A Businessman's View of Training for Business," in *The Challenge of Business Education* (Chicago, 1949), 49.

30. See, e.g., "Managerial Rule by Dictation Gone," *Iron Age*, CXLIII, 8 (Feb. 23, 1939), 63; "On Getting Along with People," *American Dyestuff Reporter*, XXIV (Aug. 26, 1935), 491–492.

31. "The Fortune Forum of Executive Opinion on U.S. Executives Themselves," *Fortune*, XXXIV (Oct., 1946), 16.

32. American Telephone & Telegraph Co., "Introduction," *Human Relations in Management*, 5, 7; General Foods Corp., Dept. for Personnel Administration, *Solving Problems by Practicing Consultative Supervision* (N. P., [1949]), 4; *New Yorker*, Oct. 12, 1957, 39.

33. Delbert C. Miller and William H. Form, *Industrial Sociology* (New York, 1951), 195.

34. Detroit Edison Co., Personnel Planning Dept., *Human Relations in Supervision* (N.P., 1951), mimeographed, 1–16; Robert N. McMurry, *Handling Personality Adjustment in Industry* (New York, 1944), 64; Whyte, *Is Anybody Listening?* 129; Auren Uris, "How Good a Leader Are You?" *FMM*, CIX, 7 (July, 1951), 69–70; Uris, "How Good a Leader Are You at Shaping Attitudes?" *ibid.*, CIX, 8 (Aug., 1951), 105.

35. Solomon Barkin, "Discussion," *Proceedings of the Fourth Annual Meeting, Industrial Relations Research Association, Boston, Mass., Dec. 28–29, 1951* (N.P., 1952), 80; Arthur Kornhauser, "The Contribution of Psychology to Industrial

Relations Research," *Proceedings of the First Annual Meeting, Industrial Relations Research Association, Cleveland, Ohio, Dec. 29–30, 1948* (N.P., 1949), 183.

36. Morris S. Viteles, *Motivation and Morale in Industry* (New York, 1953), 443–444.

37. Cessna Aircraft Co., Personnel Dept., *How to Win Workers (Or—Hosswhippin' Won't Work)*, (Wichita, Kansas, [1942(?)]), 2; Fleming, "Motivation," *Edison Electric Institute Bulletin* (1955), 13; Ford Motor Co. of Canada, Ltd., Personnel Dept., *Human Engineering* (N.P., [1947(?)]), 4, 29–35; Rexford Hersey, "The Foreman as a Practical Psychologist," *Mill and Factory*, XLVI, 6 (June, 1950), 121–124; "Knudsen Outlines His Ideas of Good Foreman," *Automotive Daily News*, Oct. 6, 1934, 5; Cleve Rumble, "Employee Cooperation Can be Wooed, Won," *Editor and Publisher*, LXXXVI (April 18, 1953), 56; Survey Research Center, *Factors Related to Differences in Group Productivity* (Ann Arbor, Dec., 1949), ii.

38. C. Wright Mills, *White Collar* (New York, 1953), 90.

39. Ford Motor Co., Ltd., *Human Engineering*, 4; "Ford Students," *Business Week*, April 13, 1946, 75.

40. "Deep Therapy," *Ammunition* (1949), 48.

41. K. R. Andrews, "Executive Training by the Case Method," *HBR*, XXIX, 5 (Sept., 1951), 58; Caterpillar Tractor Co., Training Dept., *Supervisor Conferences* (Peoria, Ill. 1946), 1, 10; Chrysler Corp., Dept. of Industrial Education, *Human Relations in Industry* (N.P., 1948), 33–72; Peter F. Drucker, *The New Society* (New York, 1949), 7; Norman R. F. Maier, "A Human Relations Program for Supervision," *Industrial and Labor Relations Review*, I, 3 (April, 1948), 446; Michigan Bell Telephone Co., *Human Relations in Supervision* (N.P., 1947), 1–2; NICB, *Personnel Activities* (1947), 6; Joseph M. Rich, "Measuring Supervisory Training," *Personnel*, XXIX, 1 (July, 1952), 79; F. J. Roethlisberger, "Training Supervisors in Human Relations," *HBR*, XXIX, 5 (Sept., 1951), 47, 57; Robert E. Schwab, "Putting Human Relations Research to Work," *Public Utilities Fortnightly*, LIII, 5 (March 4, 1954), 286.

42. Mason Haire, "Some Problems of Industrial Training,"

Journal of Social Issues, IV, *3* (Summer, 1948), 41–47; Walter R. Mahler and Willys H. Monroe, *How Industry Determines the Need for and Effectiveness of Training* (Psychological Corp., Personnel Research Section Report No. 929, New York, March 15, 1952), 137; Carroll L. Shartle, "Studies in Naval Leadership," in Harold Guetzkow (ed.), *Groups, Leadership and Men* (Pittsburgh, 1951), 132.

43. Mason Haire, "Group Dynamics in the Industrial Situation," in Kornhauser, *Industrial Conflict,* 377; Walter G. O'Donnell, "Role-Playing as a Practical Training Technique," *Personnel,* XXIX, *3* (Nov., 1952), 276.

44. O'Donnell, "Role-Playing," *Personnel* (1952), 285.

45. American Steel and Wire Co., "Memo to Management," *Supervision,* XI, *12* (Dec., 1949), 16B; Chrysler Corp., *Functions and Activities of Supervisory Training in Chrysler Corporation* (N.P., [1949(?)]), 20–21; "Group Meetings Pay Off," *Busineses Week,* May 20, 1950, 86; C. B. Hedrick, "Feedback," *Personnel,* XXXII, (July, 1955), 3; Johnson and Johnson Co., "Executive Development Activities in Johnson and Johnson and Affiliated Companies," [1950(?)], mimeographed, 1, J&J Co. MSS; Maier, "Human Relations Program," *Industrial and Labor Relations Review* (1948), 447; K. A. Moody, "Role-Playing," mimeographed statement from American Steel and Wire Co., N.D., 2, AS&W Co. MSS; "Pajamas and the Ego," *Fortune,* XXXIV (Aug., 1946), 140; "Problem for the Front Office," *ibid.,* XLIII (May, 1951), 154; "Tests of Management," *ibid.* (1950), 107.

46. Whyte, *Is Anybody Listening?* 215.

47. Harold J. Leavitt, "Small Groups in Large Organizations," *Journal of Business,* XXVIII, *1* (Jan., 1955), 8; NICB, *Techniques of Conference Leadership* (CBR SPP No. 77; New York, 1946), 3.

48. General Foods, *Solving Problems,* 9; NICB, *Techniques of Conference Leadership,* 32.

49. See, e.g., Detroit Edison Co., *Making the Most of Your Meetings* (N.P., 1945), 1–15; General Foods, *Solving Problems,* 16; Johnson and Johnson, "Executive Development," 2; Minneapolis-Honeywell Regulator Co., Industrial Rela-

tions Dept., *Conference Leadership* (N.P., 1951), 5; NICB, *Techniques of Conference Leadership*, 5; Procter and Gamble Co., "Training Program: Factory Division," June 1, 1949, mimeographed, II, 3, P&G Co. MSS.

50. Alex Bavelas, "Some Problems of Organizational Change," *Journal of Social Issues*, IV, 3 (Summer, 1948), 51–52; Kurt Lewin, *Resolving Social Conflicts* (New York, 1948), 139.

51. D. G. Marquis *et al.*, "A Social Psychological Study of the Decision-Making Conference," in Guetzkow, *Groups, Leadership and Men*, 62–63, 66.

52. H. H. Carey, "Consultative Supervision," *Nation's Business*, XXV, 4 (April, 1937), 44.

53. American Telephone & Telegraph Co., *Human Relations in Management*, "Leadership," 7; Carnegie-Illinois Steel Corp., Industrial Relations, *Supervisory Problems in Employee Relations* (Pittsburgh, 1942), 1; Caterpillar Tractor Co., *Supervisor Conferences*, 1; C. W. Cook, "Consultative Supervision," *Advanced Management*, XVI, 10 (Oct., 1951), 21; General Foods Corp., *Solving Problems*, 2; Schwab, "Putting Human Relations Research to Work," *Public Utilities Fortnightly* (1954), 285; Standard Oil Co., *What is Employee Participation?* (N.P., 1954), 3–14; Western Electric Co., General Personnel Dept., *History of Supervisory Conference Training in the Western Electric Company* (mimeographed, N.P., 1932), 2, 14.

54. Atlantic Refining Co., *A Manual on Conference Leadership* (N.P., N.D.), 3–4, 6; Cessna Aircraft Co., *How to Win Workers*, 4; "Industrial Psychology Pays in this Plant," *Modern Industry*, (July, 1948), 70.

55. Corey, "Human Relations," *Labor and Nation* (1950), 50.

56. Whyte, *Is Anybody Listening?*, x–xi.

57. Peter F. Drucker, "Communications," *Advanced Management*, XVI, 2 (Feb., 1951), 7–9; R. S. Edwards, "Words are Dynamite," *JAP*, XXXII, 4 (Aug., 1948), 370n, 372; Robert Newcomb, "Here is How—and Where—Management Should Talk to Workers," *Printers' Ink*, CCXIV (Feb. 22, 1946), 39, 42; Paul Pigors, "Communication in Industry," *Industrial and Labor Relations Review*, VI, 4 (July, 1953), 508-509; Carl R. Rogers and F. J. Roethlisberger, "Barriers and Gate-

ways to Communication," *HBR*, XXX, *4* (July-Aug., 1952),
49; E. J. Tangerman, "Needed: Human Engineering," *American Machinist*, XCI, *12* (June 5, 1947), 85.

58. Henry Ford II, "Human Engineering Necessary for Further
Mass Production Progress," *Automotive and Aviation Industries*, XCIV, *2* (Jan. 15, 1946), 76.

59. "Exit the Attitude: 'I Just Work Here,'" *Chemical Week*,
LXXIV, *12* (March 20, 1954), 20; NICB, *Industrial Relations* (New York, 1931), 74; Whyte, *Is Anybody Listening?*,
ix–x, 3.

60. Alex Bavelas and Dermot Barrett, *An Experimental Approach to Organizational Communication* (New York,
1951), 2.

61. Thompson Products, Inc., "Foremen's Bulletin," I, *11* (Nov.
3, 1939), 1, T.P. Co. MSS.

62. Burleigh B. Gardner, *Human Relations in Industry* (Chicago, 1945), 288–289; Gardner, "The Factory as a Social
System," in W. F. Whyte (ed.), *Industry and Society* (New
York, 1946), 13; "What the Factory Worker Really Thinks
about his Company, his Foreman, and his Union," *FMM*,
CVI, *12* (Dec., 1948), 82.

63. "Problem for the Front Office," *Fortune* (1951), 148; Whyte,
Is Anybody Listening? 24–25.

CHAPTER 10:

The Servants of Power

1. Henry Ford, II, "Human Engineering Necessary for Further Mass Production Progress," *Automotive and Aviation
Industries*, XCIV, *2* (Jan. 15, 1946), 39.

2. George R. Eastman, *Psychology for Business Efficiency*
(Dayton, 1916), 9, 12; G. Stanley Hall, address to Vocational Educational Association of the Middle West, Jan.
17, 1919, in Lionel D. Edie (ed.), *Practical Psychology for
Business Executives* (New York, 1922), 36; T. Sharper
Knowlson, *Business Psychology* (Libertyville, Ill., 1912),
11, 12; Hugo Münsterberg, *Psychology and Industrial Efficiency* (New York, 1913), 244, 306–309; W. D. Scott, *In-*

creasing Human Efficiency in Business (New York, 1911), 6–7.

3. Floyd H. Allport *et al.*, "Psychology in Relation to Social and Political Problems," in Paul S. Achilles (ed.), *Psychology at Work* (New York, 1932), 252; Walter V. Bingham, "The Future of Industrial Psychology," *JCP*, I, *1* (Jan.-Feb., 1937), 9–11; George C. Brandenburg, "Personality and Vocational Achievement," *JAP*, IX, *3* (1925), 282; Harold E. Burtt, *Principles of Employment Psychology* (Boston, 1926), 508; J. McKeen Cattell, "Retrospect: Psychology as a Profession," *JCP*, I, *1* (Jan.-Feb., 1937), 1; Edgar A. Doll, "Preparation for Clinical Psychology," *ibid.*, III, *5* (Sept.-Oct., 1939), 139–140; Eliott Frost, "What Industry Wants and Does Not Want from the Psychologist," *JAP*, IV, *1* (March, 1920), 23–24; George W. Hartmann, "Summary for Psychologists," in Hartmann and Theodore Newcomb (eds.), *Industrial Conflict* (New York, 1939), 544; Edward N. Hay, "Sizing Up Job Applicants," *Personnel Journal*, XVIII, 7 (Jan., 1940), 261; Harry W. Hepner, *Psychology in Modern Business* (New York, 1931), 436; Forrest A. Kingsbury, "Applying Psychology to Business," *Annals*, CX (Nov., 1923), 11; Morris Viteles, "The Clinical Viewpoint in Vocational Selection," *JAP*, IX, *2* (1925), 135; Viteles, *Industrial Psychology* (New York, 1932), 4; Robert M. Yerkes, "What is Personnel Research?" *Monthly Labor Review*, XIV, *1* (Jan., 1922), 11.

4. W. V. Bingham, "Industrial Psychology and Government," *JAP*, XXIV, *1* (Feb., 1940), 3; Milton L. Blum, *Industrial Psychology and its Social Foundations* (New York, 1949), 1; Orlo L. Crissey, "Personnel Selection," in *Current Trends in Industrial Psychology* (Pittsburgh, 1949), 81; George Katona, *Psychological Analysis of Economic Behavior* (New York, 1951), 282–283; C. H. Lawshe *et al.*, *Psychology of Industrial Relations* (New York, 1953), v; Douglas McGregor, "Foreword," *Journal of Social Issues*, IV, *3* (Summer, 1948), 4; Willard E. Parker and Robert W. Kleemeier, *Human Relations in Supervision* (New York, 1951), v, 11–12; May Smith, *An Introduction to Industrial Psychology*

(London, 1943), 5–6; Harold C. Taylor, "Industrial Psychology and the Community," in *Current Trends*, 197; Robert M. Yerkes, "Psychology in World Reconstruction," *JCP*, X, *1* (Jan.-Feb., 1946), 2.

5. William F. Whyte to Elton Mayo, April 27, 1943, Mayo MSS; John S. Ellsworth, Jr., *Factory Folkways* (New Haven, 1952), 1; Delbert C. Miller and William H. Form, *Industrial Sociology* (New York, 1951), 100; Eugene Staley *et al.* (eds.), *Creating an Industrial Civilization* (New York, 1952), 180; W. F. Whyte, "Social Science and Industrial Relations," *Personnel*, XXVII, *4* (Jan., 1951), 266; William H. Whyte, Jr., *Is Anybody Listening?* (New York, 1952), 219–220.

6. Warren W. Coxe, "Professional Problems of Applied Psychology," *JCP*, IV, *3* (May-June, 1940), 103; V. E. Fisher and Joseph V. Hanna, *The Dissatisfied Worker* (New York, 1931), 246; C. Wright Mills, *White Collar* (New York, 1953), 157.

7. Arthur W. Kornhauser and Forrest A. Kingsbury, *Psychological Tests in Business* (Chicago, 1924), 174–175.

8. Quoted from a personal letter whose author prefers to remain unidentified.

9. Frank W. Braden to L. Baritz, Sept. 13, 1955; John G. Darley, "An Overview of the Conference and its Controversies," in Harold Guetzkow (ed.), *Groups, Leadership and Men* (Pittsburgh, 1951), 263–264; Arthur Kornhauser, "The Contribution of Psychology to Industrial Relations Research," *Proceedings of the First Annual Meeting, Industrial Relations Research Association, Cleveland, Dec. 29–30, 1948* (N.P., 1949), 174; Fred Massarik and Paula Brown, "Social Research Faces Industry," *Personnel*, XXX, *6* (May, 1954), 455; C. Wright Mills, "The Contribution of Sociology to Studies of Industrial Relations," *Proceedings of IRRA*, 204.

10. Elton Mayo in F. J. Roethlisberger and William J. Dickson, *Management and the Worker* (Cambridge, 1939), xiii–xiv.

11. See, e.g., Howard Bowen, *Social Responsibilities of the Businessman* (New York, 1953), *passim*.

12. Quoted in U.S. Congress, *Automation and Technological*

Change, Hearings before Subcommittee on Economic Stabilization of the Joint Committee on the Economic Report, 84th Cong., 1st Sess., Oct. 14–28, 1955 (Washington, 1955), 105.

13. "Industry Appraises the Psychologist," *Personnel Psychology,* IV, *1* (Spring, 1951), 63–92.

14. See, e.g., Murray Kempton, "Pre-Tested Miracles," *New York Post,* Jan. 3, 1957, 26.

15. H. L. Hollingworth and A. T. Poffenberger, *Applied Psychology* (New York, 1917), 20; Hugo Münsterberg, *Business Psychology* (Chicago, 1915), 181–182.

16. Harold E. Burtt, *Psychology and Industrial Efficiency* (New York, 1929), 273; C. F. Hansen, "Psychology in the Service of the Life Insurance Business," *Annals,* CX (Nov., 1923), 190.

17. Elton Mayo, "The Fifth Columnists of Business," *Harvard Business School Alumni Bulletin,* XVIII, *1* (Autumn, 1941), 33.

18. William H. Knowles, *Personnel Management* (New York, 1955), 156.

19. See, e.g., Lewis Corey, "Human Relations Minus Unionism," *Labor and Nation,* VI, *2* (Spring, 1950), 48; W. A. Koivisto, "Value, Theory, and Fact in Industrial Sociology," *AJS,* LVIII, *6* (May, 1953), 564–567; Mills, "Contribution of Sociology," *Proceedings of IRRA,* 209n.

20. Robert N. McMurry, *Handling Personality Adjustment in Industry* (New York, 1944), 13–14.

21. John H. Gorsuch, "Industrial Psychology's Growing Pains," *Personnel,* XXIX, *2* (Sept., 1952), 154.

22. See, e.g., Hepner, *Psychology in Modern Business,* 578–583; Morris S. Viteles, "The Role of Industrial Psychology in Defending the Future of America," *Annals,* CCXVI (July, 1941), 157; C. R. Walker and R. H. Guest, *The Man on the Assembly Line* (Cambridge, 1952), 134; William F. Whyte, "Who Goes Union and Why," *Personnel Journal,* XXIII, *6* (Dec., 1944), 216–217.

23. McMurry, *Handling Personality Adjustment,* 15, 17.

24. E.g., Arthur W. Ayers, "Personality Considerations in Collective Bargaining," *JCP,* VIII, *3* (May-June, 1944), 144;

George C. Homans, "Industrial Harmony as a Goal," in Arthur Kornhauser *et al.* (eds.), *Industrial Conflict* (New York, 1954), 49; Elton Mayo, "The Great Stupidity," *Harper's*, CLI (July, 1925), 231; Ross Stagner, "Psychological Aspects of Industrial Conflict: II—Motivation," *Personnel Psychology*, III, *1* (Spring, 1950), 1; U.S. Bureau of Labor Statistics, *Strikes in 1941 and Strikes Affecting Defense Production* (B.L.S., Bull. No. 711; Washington, 1942), 17; B.L.S., *Strikes in 1942* (B.L.S. Bull. No. 741; Washington, 1943), 14; B.L.S., *Strikes in 1943* (B.L.S. Bull. No. 782; Washington, 1944), 18; B.L.S., *Strikes and Lockouts in 1944* (B.L.S. Bull. No. 833; Washington, 1945), 1; T. N. Whitehead, "Human Relations within Industrial Groups," *HBR*, XIV, *1* (Autumn, 1935), 2.

25. Elton Mayo, "The Irrational Factor in Human Behavior," *Annals*, CX (Nov., 1923), 122; Mayo, "Mental Hygiene in Industry," in Henry C. Metcalf (ed.), *The Psychological Foundations of Management* (New York, 1927), 276; Mayo, "Orientation and Attention," *ibid.*, 270–271.

26. Reinhard Bendix, "Bureaucracy," *ASR*, XII, 5 (Oct., 1947), 502; Bendix and Lloyd H. Fisher, "The Perspectives of Elton Mayo," *Review of Economics and Statistics*, XXXI, *4* (Nov., 1949), 314; Elton Mayo, "Research in Human Relations," *Personnel*, XVII, *4* (May, 1941), 265; Miller and Form, *Industrial Sociology*, 79.

27. Hadley Cantril and Daniel Katz, "Objectivity in the Social Sciences," in Hartmann and Newcomb, *Industrial Conflict*, 12; Robert S. Lynd, *Knowledge for What?* (Princeton, 1939), 116, 119–120, 128, 185–186.

28. E.g., Herbert Blumer, "Sociological Theory in Industrial Relations," *ASR*, XII, *3* (June, 1947), 272; Douglas McGregor, "Industrial Relations," *Advanced Management*, XIV, *4* (Dec., 1949), 2–6.

29. Wilbert E. Moore, "Current Issues in Industrial Sociology," *ASR*, XII, *6* (Dec., 1947), 651.

30. George W. Hartmann, "Summary for Psychologists," in Hartmann and Newcomb, *Industrial Conflict*, 541–542.

31. Arthur Kornhauser, "Industrial Psychology as Management

Technique and as Social Science," *American Psychologist,* II, 7 (July, 1947), 224.

32. Mills, "Contribution of Sociology," *Proceedings of IRRA,* 206; Mills, *White Collar,* 82; Lynd, *Knowledge for What?* 178.

33. Walter V. Bingham, "Psychology as a Science, as a Technology, and as a Profession," in John Elmgren and Sigvard Rubenowitz (eds.), *Applied Psychology in Industrial and Social Life* (Göteborg, 1952), 24.

34. Whyte, *Is Anybody Listening?* 209.

35. Kornhauser, "Industrial Psychology," *American Psychologist* (1947), 225; Moore, "Current Issues," *ASR* (1947), 654.

36. Solomon Barkin to L. Baritz, Dec. 6, 1955; Otis Brubacker to L. B., Dec. 15, 1955; Sylvia B. Gottlieb to L. B., Dec. 2, 1955; Carl Huhndorff to L. B., Nov. 29, 1955; Solomon Barkin, "A Pattern for the Study of Human Relations in Industry," *Industrial and Labor Relations Review,* IX, 1 (Oct., 1955), 95–99; Barkin, "Technology and Labor," *Personnel Journal,* XVIII, 7 (Jan., 1940), 239.

37. Quoted from a personal letter whose author prefers to remain unidentified.

38. F. H. Allport, *Social Psychology* (Boston, 1924), 408; American Telephone & Telegraph Co., Personnel Relations Dept., "Motivation and the Job," *Human Relations in Management* (New York, 1949), 2; Atlantic Refining Co., *A Manual on Conference Leadership* (N.P., N.D.), 3–4, 6; Willard Beecher, "Industrial Relations in the Light of Individual Psychology," *American Journal of Individual Psychology,* XI, 2 (1955), 124; Cessna Aircraft Co., Personnel Dept., *How to Win Workers (Or—Hosswhippin' Won't Work)* (Wichita, [1942 (?)]), 4; General Foods Corp., Dept. for Personnel Administration, *Solving Problems by Practicing Consultative Supervision* (N.P. [1949]), 4; Knowles, *Personnel Management,* 59; Life Insurance Sales Research Bureau, *Morale and Agency Management,* Vol. I: *Morale: The Mainspring of Management* (Hartford, 1940), 22; U. S. Congress, Senate, *Violations of Free Speech and Rights of Labor,* Hearings before a Subcommittee of the Committee on Education and Labor, U.S. Senate, 75 Cong.,

1st Sess., on S. Res. 266, Part 6, "Labor Espionage, General Motors Corp.," Feb. 15–19, 1937 (Washington, 1937), 2037.

39. Mason Haire, "Group Dynamics," in Kornhauser, *Industrial Conflict*, 384–385.

40. "People: What's Behind Their Choices—in Buying, in Working," *Business Week*, Aug. 14, 1954, 50–60.

41. S. E. Asch, "Effects of Group Pressure upon the Modification and Distortion of Judgments," in Guetzkow, *Groups, Leadership and Men*, 189–190.

42. Richard Crow, "Group Training in Higher Management Development," *Personnel*, XXIX, 6 (May, 1953), 458; "Group Meetings Pay Off," *Business Week*, May 20, 1950, 82, 84; Alfred Marrow, "Group Dynamics in Industry," *Occupations*, XXVI, 8 (May, 1948), 476; "People," *Business Week*, Aug. 14, 1954, 50–60; "Psychologists at Work," *ibid.*, Sept. 19, 1953, 52–53.

43. Mills, *White Collar*, 110.

44. Harold L. Wilensky, "Human Relations in the Workplace," Industrial Relations Research Association, *Research in Industrial Human Relations* (New York, 1957), 40–41.

Index